Introducing the Orthodox Church: Its Faith and Life

by

Anthony M. Coniaris

A handbook for use by those who wish to become acquainted with the ancient and apostolic Orthodox Church. Excellent for use with converts in adult membership classes.

Z
F O S
E

Light and Life Publishing Company
P.O. Box 26421
Minneapolis, Minnesota 55426-0421

Copyright © 1982
Anthony M. Coniaris
Library of Congress Card No. 81-81309

ISBN 0-937032-25-5

TABLE OF CONTENTS

Page

TABLE OF CONTENTS

Page

DEDICATED TO

Mr. and Mrs. Michael Coniaris
and
Mr. and Mrs. Theodore H. Pappas

Foreword

Here is a genuinely different and practical book for the inquirer and potential convert to Orthodox Christianity. It is different in a number of ways, all of which commend this volume to wide use by pastors whose task it is to introduce the members of their inquirers classes to an Orthodox way of life which will touch their lives in a full and complete way.

Anyone familiar with Fr. Coniaris' previous writings knows that whatever the subject he writes about, he does it in a lively and interesting way. He has the knack of taking even the most difficult topic and presenting it in varying ways so that even the reader who is familiar with the topic is fascinated by the many different approaches to it. This book is interesting.

It would fail in its purpose, however, if the information that it contained was not a reliable introduction to the Orthodox Church. Yet, in spite of the fact that it avoids the pitfall of being ponderous and heavy—so characteristic of other introductions to the Orthodox faith—it is not shallow. This book is a full and authentic introductory guide to the Orthodox Church.

One of the unique features of this introduction is the way in which the witness of Scripture and the holy Fathers of the Church, especially the Greek Fathers is presented in conjunction with the contributions of modern and contemporary figures, thus serving to relate the inquirer to ancient truths which are witnessed to as well by more familiar contemporary voices. This book speaks the ancient truths in a modern voice.

So often, Orthodoxy has been presented as an exotic faith, strange and unrelated to the daily lives of contemporary people. Yet, if Orthodoxy is what it claims to be, this cannot represent the correct approach. If Orthodoxy is held to be "the true faith" of necessity it has its application to the lives of all people of every status, class, education and culture. This book presents Orthodox Christianity as a contemporary and livable faith.

Unlike other introductions for the potential convert, this volume is written so that it appeals to the whole person, not just the intellect. It is written to inspire as well as to inform, a special *charisma* of the author, Fr. Anthony Coniaris. It speaks concretely about what people are to *do,* how they are to *share* in the concrete and practical aspects of the Orthodox Christian way of life. This book is a practical guide for learning to share practically in the life of the Orthodox Church.

In all, the reader will find this volume a refreshing, interesting, authentic, contemporary, down to earth and practical introduction to the Orthodox Christian faith. It has been written primarily to introduce Orthodoxy to the potential convert. It has fulfilled its purpose.

Rev. Stanley S. Harakas,
Professor
Holy Cross Greek Orthodox School of Theology
Brookline, Mass.

The One, Holy, Catholic And Apostolic Church

What do we mean when we use the word "church"? Look at the tremendous variety of groups that call themselves "churches". In fact, anyone can establish a "church" for himself. There are many cults and other groups today that use the name "Jesus" and "church" very freely. You'll hear them calling themselves "Jesus People" or "Jesus Church," etc. But are they truly churches? Were they founded by Jesus and the Apostles? What kind of historical connection do they have with the apostles and the early church? If the Devil appears as an angel and quotes Scripture, then he can use even "churches" to lead people away from the one true God and His plan of salvation.

We need to define our terms carefully. Exactly what do we mean when we say "church"? We Orthodox Christians mean by Church the Body through which Jesus is present and active in the world today. It was founded by Christ through the apostles and has maintained a living, historical connection with the apostles through the ordination of its clergy. The fact that the bishop who ordains an Orthodox priest today can trace his ordination historically all the way back to the apostles and through them to Christ is a guarantee that the Orthodox Church was not founded by someone called Joe Smith a few centuries ago but by Christ Himself and traces its existence historically back to Jesus. We call this "apostolic succession". It means that our Church is the authentic and genuine Church or Body of Christ in the world today. It continues to teach not one man's interpretation of the faith but the complete deposit of faith as it was handed down to the Apostles by Jesus.

So there are some very important questions to ask when one hears the word "church". Was this "church" founded by God or by man? Does it have an unbroken historical connection with the early apostolic church? How else can we be certain that what it teaches is truly apostolic, truly Christian, truly the word of God and not one man's interpretation, or misinterpretation of that faith?

A group of evangelicals banded together recently to seek to find what they feel is lacking in their tradition: a living connection with the early church. They call themselves "The Orthodox Evangelicals" and they are in conversation with leaders of the Orthodox Church. Let me share with you what they are saying, "We are, for the most part, a people without roots. Some of us can only trace the beginnings of our denomination or church to some time in this century—arising over a split in this or that doctrine, or maybe even a personality clash between two strong leaders. Most of us have no sense of the past, no understanding of where we came from. . ." [1] They are seeking their roots in the early apostolic Church of which the Orthodox Church is an historical continuation.

AN UNBROKEN HISTORICAL CONNECTION

In order to be used as evidence in court, the bullet used in the attempted assasination of President Reagan some time ago had to have an unbroken connec-

---

[1] *"The Orthodox Evangelicals"* Edited by Webber and Bloesch. pp 35-36. Thomas Nelson Co.

tion with the bullet that was removed from the president's body. Accordingly, a secret service agent was present during surgery. He witnessed the removal of the bullet. The surgeon signed a statement upon giving the bullet to the agent. The agent signed another statement when he delivered the bullet to the laboratory, etc. Such evidence of an unbroken connection between a bullet and a body is required in a court of law. Equal evidence is required to show that a church is indeed the genuine church founded by Jesus: the evidence of an unbroken historical connection with the apostolic church.

A church is the true Church of Christ if it can show historically that it was founded by Christ and has maintained a living connection over the centuries with that early Church. We need this historical connection in order to be assured that the deposit of the faith has not been tampered with but has been handed down to us in its entirety.

Fr. Theodore Stylianopoulos, Professor of New Testament at Holy Cross Greek Orthodox Theological Seminary, writes:

> ". . . the Orthodox Church is the true Church of God on earth and maintains the fulness of Christ's truth in continuity with the Church of the apostles. This awesome claim does not necessarily mean that Orthodox Christians have achieved perfection: for we have many personal shortcomings. Nor does it necessarily mean that the other Christian Churches do not serve God's purposes positively: for it is not up to us to judge others but to live and proclaim the fulness of the truth. But it does mean that if a person carefully examines the history of Christianity he or she will soon discover that the Orthodox Church alone is in complete sacramental, doctrinal and canonical continuity with the ancient undivided Church as it authoritatively expressed itself through the great Ecumenical Councils." [2]

CHANGELESSNESS

One of the distinguishing features of the Orthodox Church is her changelessness. The Orthodox Church baptizes by a three-fold immersion as was done in the early Church. It still confirms infants at baptism bestowing upon them the "seal of the gift of the Holy Spirit." It still brings babies and small children to receive Holy Communion. In the liturgy the deacon still cries out, "The doors, the doors," recalling early days when none but baptized members of the Christian family could participate in the liturgy. The Nicene Creed is still recited without the later additions. The Orthodox Church has two distinctive features: (1) her changelessness; (2) her sense of living continuity with the church of the early apostles.

THE NICENE CREED

In the Nicene Creed we confess: "I believe in one, holy, catholic and apostolic church." What do these words mean?

---

[2] *"Christ in Our Midst"* Dept. of Rel. Education. Greek Orthodox Archdiocese. Brookline, Mass.

ONE means that the Church is one because God is one. ''There is one body, and one Spirit . . . one hope . . . One Lord, one faith, one baptism, One God and Father of all'' (Eph. 4:4-6). In His great Priestly Prayer, Jesus prayed that the Church may be ''one'' even as He and the Father are one (John 17:22).

HOLY. The Church is holy because our Lord made her so. ''Christ also loved the Church, and gave Himself for it; that He might sanctify and cleanse it with the washing of water by the word, that He might present it to Himself a glorious Church, not having spot or wrinkle, or any such thing but that it should by holy and without blemish'' (Eph. 5:25-27). Not only is the Church holy but it is also her purpose to make us holy, i.e., different from the world, conformed to God's will.

CATHOLIC. The Orthodox Church is Catholic, meaning whole, because she has preserved the *wholeness* of the faith of Christ through the centuries without adding or subtracting to that divinely revealed faith. For this reason she has come to be known as the ''Orthodox'' Church, i.e., the Church that has preserved the full and true faith of Christ. Orthodox Christians believe that the Church, which has Christ Himself as Head and which is the temple of the Holy Spirit, cannot err. Her voice is the voice of Christ in the world today. The word ''Orthodox'' is applied to the Orthodox Church to designate that it has kept the true ''Faith which was once delivered to the Saints'' (Jude 1:3).

Catholic means also that the Church is universal. It embraces all peoples, the entire earth. ''God so loved the *world* that He gave His only Son. . .'' Just as there are no distinctions within the love of God, so the Church stretches out her arms to the world. ''Here there cannot be Greek or Jew, circumcised and uncircumcised, barbarian, Scythian, slave, free man . . .'' (Col. 3:11). God's love is all-inclusive; so the Church is Catholic.

APOSTOLIC. The Church is apostolic because she teaches what the apostles taught and can trace her existence historically directly back to the apostles.

It was the Apostle Paul, for example, who established the Christian Church in Greece through his early missionary journeys. His letters to the Corinthians, the Thessalonians, the Philippians were written to the churches he had established in those Greek cities. The Church he founded there has never ceased to exist. It is known today as the Greek Orthodox Church. The Apostle Peter founded the church in Antioch which exists to this day as the Antiochian Orthodox Church. Other apostles established the church in Jerusalem, Alexandria and Cyprus. The Eastern Orthodox Church has existed in these places since the days of the apostles. From these cities and countries, missionaries brought the Gospel (Good News) of Jesus to other countries: Russia, the Ukraine, Serbia, Romania, Bulgaria, etc. This self-governing family of churches is known today as the Eastern Orthodox Church.

Thus, the Orthodox Church is the legitimate and historical continuation of the early Church. She has the same faith, the same spirit, the same ethos. ''This is the Apostolic faith, this is the faith of the Fathers, this is the Orthodox faith, this faith has established the universe'' (From the Sunday of Orthodoxy vespers).

The Church is both visible and invisible. The visible Church is the Church Militant on earth. The invisible Church is the Church Triumphant in heaven, ''the heavenly Jerusalem . . . innumerable angels in festal gathering . . . the assembly of the first-born who are enrolled in heaven'' (Hebrews 12:22-23).

Christ has promised that the gates of hell will not prevail against the Church (Matthew 16:18) and that He would be with it until the end of the world (Matthew 28:20). St. Paul calls the Church ''the pillar and ground of truth'' (I Tim. 3:15).

SOURCE OF AUTHORITY

The highest authority of the Eastern Church is the Ecumenical Council, involving the whole church. When the bishops of the church define a matter of faith in an Ecumenical Council, a requisite for its recognition is the acceptance and consent of the whole Church. Only then can it be considered infallible, or inspired of the Holy Spirit, who resides in the whole church, consisting of clergy and laity, to guide it to all truth. This makes every person within the church responsible for Christian truth. There have been instances where decisions of the bishops in an Ecumenical Council have not been accepted because they were rejected by the church as a whole.

THE ORTHODOX CHURCH TODAY

Originally the early Church consisted of the five ancient Patriarchates: Rome, Constantinople, Alexandria, Antioch, and Jerusalem. These cities constituted the chief centers of Christianity in the early days. Between the eleventh and thirteenth centuries Rome became separated from the other Patriarchates due to the latter's insistence on its supremacy. The other ancient patriarchates considered the bishop of Rome ''first among equals,'' granting him a primacy of honor but not of jurisdiction. Constantinople then rose to primacy among the other Patriarchates since it was the capital of the Eastern Roman Empire. The primacy of Constantinople, however, has always been a primacy of honor—not of jurisdiction.

Through the years new Orthodox churches were established in many lands through missionary work so that the present family of Orthodox Churches covers the globe as shown in the outline listed below:

A. Ancient Patriarchates
   1. Constantinople which includes Turkey, Crete, the Dodecanese Islands and the Diaspora.
   2. Alexandria which includes Egypt and the rest of Africa.
   3. Antioch which includes Syria, Lebanon, Iran and Iraq.
   4. Jerusalem which includes Israel and Jordan.
B. National Churches (some of which are newer Patrichates)
   1. The Church of Russia—the Soviet Union excluding Georgia
   2. The Church of Cyprus
   3. The Church of Greece
   4. The Church of Bulgaria

5. The Church of **Romania**
6. The Church of Serbia
7. The Church of Albania
8. The Church of Georgia
9. The Church of Czechoslovakia
10. The Church of Poland
11. The Church of Sinai

C. Missionary Churches
1. Korea
2. Uganda and **Kenya**
3. China
4. Australia
5. South America
6. Western Europe
7. North America

D. Churches in the Diaspora
1. The Greek Orthodox Archdiocese of North and South America
2. The Orthodox Churches in the U.S.A., including the OCA whose autocephalous status is to be clarified at the forthcoming Ecumenical Council.
3. Japan
4. Finland
5. China
6. Macedonia

Fr. Kallistos Ware writes,

"In the East there were many Churches whose foundation went back to the Apostles; there was a strong sense of the equality of all bishops, of the collegial and conciliar nature of the Church. The east acknowledged the Pope as the first bishop in the Church, but saw him as the first among equals. In the west, on the other hand, there was only one great see claiming apostolic foundation— Rome—so that Rome came to be regarded as *the* Apostolic see . . . the Church was seen less as a college and more as a monarchy—the monarchy of the Pope." [3]

The insistence on the monarchy of the Pope aggravated by the atrocities the Crusaders inflicted on the population of Constantinople in 1204 led to a lamentable estrangement and separation of the Eastern Churches and Rome which we pray will be healed in time since the two Churches are apostolic and have so much in common.

WHAT IS THE CHURCH

The early Jews believed that God dwelled in a box which they called the tabernacle. They carried the box with them always. The box, of course, contained the stone tablets on which God had written the ten commandments. No one was ever to touch this sacred box. Once, a man did touch it by accident and was

[3] *"The Orthodox Churchs,"* Timothy Ware. Viking-Penquin Press. New York, NY.

immediately struck dead. At another time when the box was captured by the Philistines, the Jews felt it was the end for them because they had lost their God. Later, they built a tent to house this box. Still later when Solomon built his famous temple in Jerusalem, the box or tabernacle was placed in the holy of holies.

R. L. Bruckberger writes, "In the deserts, God lived beneath a tent, in His tabernacle, and often during the night a column of fire stood above that tent among all the others, revealing to every eye that glory of His reassuring and terrible Presence. When His people were settled in the Promised Land, God continued for a long time to be satisfied with a tent, close to the palace of the king and the houses of man. It was only with regret, as it seemed, that He left His tent for the magnificent Temple that Solomon built." [4]

Ever since Solomon built the Temple to house the tabernacle people have had the impression that the Church is a building. Yet when Solomon dedicated his Temple he said in his prayer of dedication: "But will God dwell indeed with man on the earth? Behold, heaven and the highest heaven cannot contain Thee; how much less this house which I have built" (2 Chron. 6:18). How can God live in a building when even the whole universe is not big enough to contain Him? Solomon knew that God cannot be boxed in a house, no matter how magnificent it is. God is everywhere, in the streets, in factories, in schools, on lonely roads, in rooming houses. He cannot be contained or limited to a temple or a church. The whole universe is His Church.

God does not need this building we call a church, but we do. We need places that are specially dedicated to God, where people meet together with the one purpose of praising God and seeking to know His will. Of course, we can worship God on the golf course but we don't. We need a house of worship where everything: architecture, icons, music, vestments, chalices, sermon, incense, candles conspire to help us worship by bringing God into focus. A woman called a church one day and asked, "Will the President be in your church tomorrow?" The answer she received was, "I don't know if the President will be here, but God will." Truly, God is always present in His Church. He speaks through the Scripture readings. He offers Himself to us through Holy Communion. It is indeed His house. The ever-present danger, however, is that we will confine God to this house, imprison Him there and feel that the building is the only place where God is present, that it is His *only* house. It is not.

THE PEOPLE OF GOD

The God who lived in a tent with His people in the Old Testament, pitched His tent in a Person in the New Testament. This is the literal meaning of the word "eskinose" or "dwelt among us" in John 1:14, "And the word became flesh and pitched his tent among us, full of grace and truth; we have beheld his glory, glory as from the only Son from the Father." The Son of God, the second person of the Trinity, took on a human nature. "God has moved from the Temple of Jerusalem into the human nature of Jesus, as formerly He had moved form the Tabernacle

---

[4] *"The History of Jesus Christ"* by R. L. Bruckburger. The Viking Press.

into the Temple of Solomon."[5] God now lives not in a Temple but in a human person. The Lord Jesus becomes the living Temple of God.

This same Jesus in turn comes to pitch his tent in us through the great Sacrament of Holy Communion. "He who eats my flesh and drinks my Blood abides in me, and I in him" (John 5:56). Through the Sacrament of Chrismation (Confirmation) we receive within us God the Holy Spirit which prompts St. Paul to say, "Do you not know that you are God's temple, and that God's Spirit dwells in you?" Now God abides in His people. Each one of us becomes a temple, a walking church.

So the church is not only a building; it is also the people in whom God dwells. The building is not merely the house of God; it is even more the house of God's people. The people are the Church. (By people we mean clergy and laity together constituting the fulness of the Church.) During the first three centuries of Christianity some Christians even worshipped underground in catacombs because of the persecutions. Yet the Church existed—and even flourished-despite the paucity of church buildings; for, you see, the Church is God's people. There was also a period when the early Christians worshipped in private homes. Again the Church was not identified with a specific building; the Church was God's people. If your church building is ever destroyed this will not mean that your church will cease to exist. The people are the Church. They will worship in homes, or in a hall. The Church is not primarily a building; it is a group of people who have responded to God's call and gather every Sunday to be with Him. The Greek word for church EKKLESIA means "those who have been called out." A Christian is one who has been called out of the world and belongs to Christ.

In the Old Testament God had chosen the Jews to be His people. They were to be a new community through which God would save the world. He revealed Himself to them that they in turn may reveal Him to the other nations. When the old Israel refused to believe in Jesus as the Promised Messiah, the Church was called by God to be the "new Israel," the new chosen people, the new saving community that is to spread the "good news" of what God has done in Christ to all people across the face of the earth. We the people became the Church, the tabernacle of God's saving presence in the world. "But you are a chosen race, a royal priesthood, a holy nation, God's own people, that you may declare the wonderful deeds of him who called you out of darkness into his marvelous light" (I Peter). Human beings, not stone and mortar, were to be the symbol of God's presence in the world. God has chosen man himself as His Temple.

YOU ARE CHRIST'S BODY

Desiring to work among us, God the Son took to Himself a human body like ours. We call this the Incarnation: With and through that body God acted in Christ during the 33 years that He lived in this world. He taught; He healed; He forgave; He offered Himself on the Cross for our salvation. Then on Ascension Day His body left the earth, and was no longer active among us.

If God intended, after the Ascension, to do any more work among us, He must either bring that body back again (as He will do when He comes at the Last

---

[5] *"The History of Jesus Christ"* by R. L. Bruckburger. The Viking Press.

Judgement), or else He must use some other body. He has chosen to do the latter. This time it is not a physical body like the one born of the Virgin Mary. It is instead an organism which St. Paul likens to a body when he says, "You are Christ's body." All those Christians who have been baptized, who have received the Holy Spirit, who share in the life of Christ through Holy Communion, make up the Body that is to be the instrument of Christ's work on earth. In other words, Christ lives and works today through all those who make up this new Body in the world, i.e., the Church. We are the Church.

"WHO DO YOU SAY THAT I AM?"

Jesus asked Peter one day, "Who do you say that I am?" Peter replied, "You are the Christ, the Son of the Living God." Then Jesus said to Peter, "Blessed are you Simon. . . You are Peter, and on this rock I will build my church." What did Jesus mean by "rock"? Did He mean that the Church was to built on Peter the man? Or did He mean Peter's confession of faith in Jesus? We believe it was both. The Church is founded on Peter's confession that Jesus is the Christ, the Son of the Living God. It is also founded on Peter and the other apostles as true believers, fully surrendered to Jesus. It is on such believing, surrendered people that God has done His building down through the ages. It is on them that He is building now.

THE CHIEF CORNERSTONE AND THE PILLARS

St. Paul compared the Church to a structure. The chief cornerstone is Jesus (Eph. 2:20-22). "Other foundation can no man lay than that which is laid" (I Cor. 3:10-11). The foundation consists of the apostles and prophets (Eph. 2:20). The "living stones" that make up the structure are the believers. The first of these living stones are Peter, Andrew and the other apostles who were first to confess Jesus as the Messiah.

The picture of the church as a structure whose cornerstone is Christ brings to mind the saying of a Spartan king. He had boasted that no nation in the world had walls like Sparta. But when a visitor came to visit Sparta he saw no walls at all, and asked the Spartan king where the walls were. The king pointed to a group of Spartan soldiers: "These are the walls of Sparta," he said, "and every man of them a brick." In exactly the same manner, every Christian is a living stone built into the structure of the Church.

Jesus says in Revelation, "He who conquers, I will make a pillar in the house of my God." In the old days it was customary when an eminent leader had finished his years of service that the highest honor to be paid him was to have a pillar erected in one of the pagan temples. Sometimes those pillars, such as the Porch of the Maidens on the Acropolis in Athens, were actually sculptures of the persons being honored. They were literally holding up the roof and walls of the temple. Each one of us is called to be such a living pillar in the Church of Christ doing our share to hold up the canopy of God's witness in the world.

BODY OF CHRIST

We have said that the Church is more than a building; it is the people of God. As the people of God we make up the Body of Christ that is active in the world today. Through Baptism we are grafted into the Body of Christ and made members of it. Through Holy Communion we receive the Body and Blood of Jesus within us. Thus the Body of Christ is constituted. "We, who are many, are one bread, one body; for we all partake of the one bread" (I Cor. 10-17). As Christ was present in the world in His physical body for thirty-three years, so today He continues to be present in us, the members of His mystical body, in whom He dwells. As God humbled Himself by taking the form of a human being and concealing His divinity under the figure of a suffering and crucified Servant, so now He humbles Himself by allowing this body of believers, this weak and imperfect body, which is the Church, to represent Him on earth, to speak, to judge, and to prophesy in His name.

All this means that Christ is dependent on the Church. As St. Chrysostom said, "So great is Christ's love for the Church that He, as it were, regards Himself as incomplete, unless He has the Church united to Him as a body." This means that we are the instruments through which Christ must work in the world today. As Annie Johnson Flint wrote,

"He has no hands but our hands
To do His work today,
He has no feet but our feet
To lead men on His way.
He has no voice but our voice
To tell men how He died,
He has no help but our help
To lead men to His side."

BE THE CHURCH

It is clear, then, that the Church is more than a building, it is people; believing people; baptized people, chrismated people, surrendered people, people in whom Christ dwells, people who listen to and obey the voice of God, people who have truly committed their lives to Him as Lord, people who have a personal praying relationship to Him, who listen to and obey His voice.

As Bishop Dmitri writes the Church is "the company of those who have put on Christ by being baptized in Him, sealed with the gift of the Holy Spirit in *Chrismation,* forgiven of their sins in *Confession,* and nutured by the Heavenly Food in the *Holy Mystery* of His *Body* and *Blood.* . . The Church is a divinely instituted unity of people, united by the Orthodox Faith, the law of God, the hierarchy, and the Holy Mysteries. It is the Mystical Body of Christ." [6]

Someone said, "The holiest moment of the church service is the moment when the Church—God's people—strengthened by preaching and sacrament—go out the church door into the world *to be the Church.* We don't merely go to church; we *are* the Church."

Recently a student was telling his pastor about a conversation he had with a fellow student in the dormitory. The fellow student did not believe in God. The

---

[6] *"Orthodox Christian Teaching"* Bishop Dmitri. Dept. of Christian Education. Orthodox Church in America. 1980. Syosset, NY.

student said to the pastor, "How can I get this fellow to church, so he can get some help?" The pastor replied, "Don't try to get him to come to church. He'll probably refuse anyway. *You must be the Church to him where you are* . . . in the wash room, in the locker room, in the class, in the dorm, on the playing field. You are the Church to that fellow student."

The reason we come to church every Sunday is to listen to Christ, to praise Him, to receive Him within us that we may go out into the world and be the Church the rest of the week.

> "O when will you start being the church;
> stop making the church a place to go to,
> and make it something to be." [7]

A LIFE-GIVING STREAM

The Prophet Ezekiel (Chapter 47:1-2 and 6-12) sees a vision of the river of life. It flows from the altar of the Temple into the world. As the stream flows on, it gets deeper and deeper. As a result, the stale waters of the dead sea are revived and the sea swarms with fishes. Wherever the stream flows there is life as it makes trees and plants grow. What is this but a picture of the streams of blessings that are to flow from the Church into the world? What is this but a picture of the refreshment, the renewal and the life that Christ wishes to bring to the world through His Church, i.e., through us His people, the members of His Body, His saving community.

CHRIST WITH US

A person who visited West Germany following the Second World War said that in visiting the bombed-out cities he noticed that people were coming out of the basements of wrecked buildings, gathering bricks and building first not factories to restore the economy, but churches. When asked why, the reply he received was, "We build churches first because it is here that our people will get the spirit to rebuild."

The Church is a source of strength because it is none other than Christ prolonging Himself through space and time; Christ continuing to be present with us; Christ continuing to save us; Christ continuing to fill us with the fullness of God's life.

There is a legend about Zacchaeus the dishonest tax collector whom Jesus called down from a sycamore tree one day to have dinner with him. Zacchaeus, as you recall, was converted as a result of this personal encounter with the Master. In later years, the legend says, Zacchaeus used to rise early every morning, carry a bucket of water to this tree and carefully water its roots. On one occasion his wife followed him and when asked the reason for this strange concern over an old sycamore tree, Zacchaeus replied, "This is where I found Christ." The Church is where we find Christ. There we are baptized. There we hear His word. There He comes to dwell in our hearts when we receive Him in the Holy Eucharist. This is

---

[7] *"The Prophets on Main Street"* J. Elliott Corbett. John Knox Press.

why we love the Church. This is why we support it. This is why we work for it. This is why we go out into the world every Sunday to be the Church wherever we are.

SUMMARY

1. The Church is the Body of Christ in the world today. Through this Body, Christ continues to be present and active in the world.

2. In order to be genuine, the Church must have an unbroken historical connection with the early apostolic church that was founded by Jesus.

3. The Orthodox Church, one, holy, catholic and apostolic, is the true Church of God on earth. It has kept the fulness of Christ's truth, the complete deposit of faith, in continuity with the Church of the apostles.

4. The decisions of an Ecumenical Council, formulated by the bishops under the guidance of the Holy Spirit and accepted by the clergy and the laity, constitute the highest authority of the Orthodox Church.

5. The Church is not to be identified with a building but with God's people in whom God dwells and through whom He is active in the world.

6. The Body of Christ is constituted through Baptism, Chrismation, and the Eucharist. Through Baptism we are grafted into the Body as members; through Chrismation we are sealed with the gift of the Holy Spirit; through the Eucharist Christ comes to dwell in us making us truly members of His Body, the Church. In the words of St. John Chrysostom: "Christ is the Head of the Body, but of what use is the Head without hands, without eyes, without legs, without ears?"

7. As members of Christ's Body, as God's people, we are called to be the Church wherever we are. We leave the liturgy and go out into the world to be the Church.

Fr. Lev Gillet, a French Orthodox monk, who wrote many books on Orthodoxy, described the Orthodox Church as follows:

"Equally far removed both from authoritarianism and individualism, the Orthodox Church is a Church both of tradition and freedom. She is above all a Church of love . . . a strange Church so poor and so weak . . . a Church of contrasts at the same time so traditional and so free, so archaic and so alive, so ritualistic and so personally mystical, a Church where the pearl of great price is so preciously preserved, sometimes under a layer of dust, a Church which has often been unable to act but which can sing out the joy of Easter like no other. . ." [8]

---

[8] Sermon given by Fr. Lev Gillet at the anniversary service for the death of Mgr. Irenee Winnaert (March 1938) in Vincent Bourne "La Quete de Verite & Irenee Winnaert" (Geneva 1970).

What We Believe
About the Nicene Creed

The word "creed" is derived from the Latin word credo meaning, "I believe." What you believe and base your life on is your creed. And everyone—even the atheist—has a creed, because everyone bases his life on something. Sartre, for example, an atheist and an existentialist had his creed. He expressed it this way: "Life is absurd. Love is impossible."

The Old Testament creed was the Shema: "Hear, O Israel: The Lord our God is one . . ." (Deut. 6:4).

Orthodox Christians also have a creed. Some of the earliest Christian creeds are found in the Bible. For example, John 3:16: "For God so loved the world that He gave His only begotten Son that whoever believes in Him should not perish, but have life everlasting." This is a creed. Another very early Christian creed that we find several times in the Scriptures is the simple declaration: "Jesus Christ is Lord" (I Cor. 12:3; Phil. 2:11).

A SYMBOL OR PASSWORD

The Christian creed is also called a symbol. The term "symbol" comes from a word that meant a watchword or a password in a military camp. Thus for the early Christian the creed or symbol was a password which identified him as a true Christian.

The creed has also been defined in terms of a map. A. Leonard Griffith writes, "Creeds are to religion what maps are to geography. The early explorers who landed on the shores of North America drew maps of the regions through which they traveled. . . So through the centuries men have experienced something of God . . . and of what they have experienced they have formulated creeds, religious maps for the guidance of future generations." [1]

Others have compared the Christian creed to the Pledge of Allegiance. It's sort of a summary of what we believe, and when we recite it, it's like making our pledge of allegiance to God.

A password, a map, a summary of our faith, a pledge of allegiance—all of these tell us something of what the creed is. Now we come to the question:

HOW DID THE CHRISTIAN CREEDS ORIGINATE?

First, there was a need for a short summary of the faith to which those who were being baptized could subscribe. Some of the earliest Christian creeds were written to be confessions of faith for those about to be baptized.

Secondly, the early creeds, as St. Athanasius said, were written to be "Signposts against heresy." They were written to combat false teachings. As a matter of fact, it was the great heretics who prompted the writing of the great creeds. The creeds were written as replies to the false teachings of those in the early church who tried to distort the truths of Christ.

---

[1] "What is a Christian?" A. Leonard Griffith. Abingdon Press. 1962 Used by permission.

Many creeds existed in the early Church: the Apostles' Creed and the Athanasian Creed among them. The Apostles' Creed dates from the middle of the second century. According to tradition, each one of the Twelve Apostles contributed a clause to its composition—hence its name. Although it is not apostolic in origin, the Apostles' Creed is apostolic in its teaching. The Athanasian Creed dates from the fifth century. This creed was influenced by the writings of St. Athanasius. Both these Creeds were written by local churches to be recited at Baptism as confessions of faith.

In the 4th Century the Church decided to compose one uniform, official creed for the whole Church. The result was the Nicene Creed written by the First and Second Ecumenical Councils. The fact that the Creed was written by the Church assembled in Ecumenical Council demonstrates that the Creed is not one man's opinion. ("I'm entitled to my belief and you to yours.") The Nicene Creed is the whole Church articulating and expressing its faith under the guidance of the Holy Spirit. This is why in reciting the Nicene Creed the early Christians said not "I believe . . ." but "We believe . . ." They were saying, in other words, "This is not only my own personal faith; it is also the expression of faith of the entire Christian community."

It goes without saying that no finite creed can ever say everything there is to say about the infinite God. The Creed is merely a divinely inspired human statement to help us in our understanding of God. St. Paul called Christ, God's "inexpressible gift" which underlines the fact that no creed can ever capture or exhaust the full meaning of Christ.

Nevertheless, acknowledging our finitude, we cannot remain silent about what God has done for us. We must communicate our faith however inadequately. This is what the Church has attempted to do through the Creed. We need to know what we believe and in Whom we believe if we are to live as Christians.

This is why we have the Nicene Creed which has been described as ". . . a spellbinding summary of the Christian faith accepted today by most of the major Christian bodies as a superlative expression of our faith. Through it we hear echoing the voices of the Scriptures and of the early martyrs and saints. It is indeed a faith to live by." [2]

CREEDS AND DEEDS

Of course, Christianity is much more than a creed; it is a deed, a life to be lived. Those who look down on creeds and say, "It is not creeds but deeds that are important"—these people forget that every deed proceeds from a creed. So a creed is important because what we really believe will ultimately find expression in our lives.

Sometimes we hear people say, "It doesn't matter what one believes as long as he is sincere in his belief." This is quite naive because Hitler was sincere— very sincere in what he believed but unfortunately he had the wrong creed.

Most of the trouble caused in the world today is caused by people who have the wrong creed whether it be Communism, materialism, play-boyism, secularism

---

[2] *"Meditations on the Nicene Creed,"* Princess Ileana. Morehouse-Gorham Co., N.Y. Used by permission.

or atheism. If we Christians believe that we have the right creed then we have an obligation to become better acquainted with it that we may translate it into deeds—deeds that will bring glory to God. This is what creeds are made for: to be translated into life.

"WHO PROCEEDS FROM THE FATHER"

Originally, the Holy Fathers who composed the Nicene Creed stated that the Holy Spirit "proceeds from the Father." Later the Western Church arbitrarily inserted the words "and from the Son," meaning that the Holy Spirit proceeds from the Father and the Son. This is the famous "filioque" clause which was a cause of much friction between the Eastern and Western Churches. The Orthodox Church preserved the Nicene Creed in its original form without the filioque for the following reasons:

First, the Ecumenical Councils forbade any changes to be introduced into the Creed except by another Ecumenical Council. The Creed belongs to the whole Church and one small part of the Church has no right to alter it. Secondly, the Orthodox believe the "filioque" to be theologically untrue. The Orthodox Church logically thinks that God knows best about Himself. It was Jesus Himself who said, "When the Paraclete has come, *whom I will send to you from the Father*—he will bear witness to me" (John 25:26). "But when the Counselor comes, whom I shall send to you from the Father, even the Spirit of truth *who proceeds from the Father,* he will bear witness to me" (John 15:26). Orthodoxy has always taught what the Bible teaches: Christ sends the Spirit but the Spirit proceeds from the Father. This preserves the unity in the Godhead according to which the Father is the unique origin and source of the Trinity.

Thus, the Nicene Creed has been preserved by the Orthodox Church in its original entirety and completeness.

A CORRECT CREED FOR CORRECT PRAYING

In addressing the catechumens in the early Church, Augustine said:

"What you have just recited, by the grace of God, is the Orthodox statement of the Christian faith, on which the Holy Church is firmly established. You have received the Creed and rendered it back. Be sure that you keep it for ever in your minds and hearts. Say it over to yourselves when you get up in the morning, think of it as you walk down the street, remember it during meals. Let your heart meditate upon these precious words even while you are asleep.

"Now according to the Church's tradition, after giving you the Creed we next go on to teach you the prayer our Savior gave us (the Lord's Prayer). This, too, must be learned by heart and recited next week; and this too must be repeated continually by all who embrace the Christian faith.

"There is a text of scripture that says that all who call on the name of the Lord shall be saved (Joel 2:32). But, as St. Paul says, how can people call on the name of the Lord unless they believe in Him? (Rom. 10:13-15). This passage of scripture explains why we do not teach you the Lord's Prayer until you have learned the Creed. We give you the Creed first so that you will know what to believe, and then the prayers so that you will know who it is that you are praying to and what to ask Him for. Then you will be praying in faith, and your prayer will be heard.''

SUMMARY

1. The creed is a short summary of faith required of those who were baptized.

2. The Nicene Creed, written by the First and Second Ecumenical Councils represents the official creed of the Orthodox Church. It is a statement of faith written by the entire Christian Church under the guidance of the Holy Spirit.

3. One's creed matters since what we believe ultimately finds expression in our lives.

4. The Orthodox Church has preserved the Nicene Creed in its original form without the filioque clause.

5. A correct creed is necessary for correct praying.

6. Recited in every liturgy, the Nicene Creed is a constant renewal of our baptismal confession of faith.

THE NICENE CREED

We share with you the words of the Nicene Creed:

I believe in one God, the Father Almighty, Maker of
heaven and earth, and of all things visible and invisible.
And in one Lord, Jesus Christ, the only-begotten Son of God,
begotten of the Father before all ages.
Light of light, true God of true God, begotten not made, of one
essence with the Father, through Whom all things were made.
Who for us men and our salvation came down from heaven, and
was incarnate of the Holy Spirit and of the Virgin Mary, and became man.
Crucified for our salvation under Pontius Pilate, He suffered and
was buried.
And on the third day He rose again according to the Scriptures.
And ascended into heaven, and sat at the right hand of the Father.
And He shall come again in glory to judge the living and the
dead; Whose kingdom shall have no end.
And I believe in the Holy Spirit, the Lord, the Giver of Life,
Who proceeds from the Father, Who, together with the Father
and the Son, is worshipped and glorified; Who spoke through the
Prophets.
I believe in One, Holy, Catholic and Apostolic Church.
I acknowledge One Baptism for the remission of sins.
I await the resurrection of the dead.
And the life of the Ages to come. Amen.

What We Believe About Jesus

A group of English writers were discussing what they would do if certain heroes of history were suddenly to enter the room. What would they do if Shakespeare or Dante were to appear before them? Finally someone asked, "What would we do if Jesus were to appear before us?" One member of the group, Charles Lamb, replied, "If Shakespeare were to enter this room, I should rise up to do him honor; but if Jesus Christ were to enter, I should fall down and give Him worship."

Charles Lamb expressed the difference between Jesus and the great men of history. The greatness of men would make us rise in respect; the greatness of Jesus would compel us to kneel in worship.

The Nicene Creed states correctly what Orthodox Christians believe about Jesus when it says we believe: ". . . in one Lord Jesus Christ, the only begotten Son of God, begotten of the Father before all ages. Light of Light, True God of True God, begotten not made, consubstantial with the Father, through Whom all things were made."

It has been said that the Nicene Creed contains 101 Greek words of which 84 are concerned with the Son. The most dominant emphasis of the Creed is Christ.

St. John repeatedly refers to Christ as the Word. The term is most appropriate. Unless a man speaks a word, we cannot know him. Words communicate meaning. They enable others to know what is on our mind. As words express our inner thoughts, so Christ—the Word of God—communicates to us the thoughts of God. He came to earth to be God's "language" in speaking to man. In Christ dialogue with God is re-established.

LORD

The Creed proceeds to tell who Jesus is. It describes Him as Lord—a word which was used throughout the Old Testament for God. It is a title the early Church deliberately gave to the glorified Jesus to express that He is the absolute and undisputed creator and possessor of the entire universe, that He is the Master, we the servants. One of the earliest Creeds of the Church was "Jesus is Lord" (Romans 10:9; I Cor. 12:3; Col. 2:6).

JESUS

After the word "Lord" in the Nicene Creed, we come to the word "Jesus." This was the name indicated from heaven for the Child born in the manger in Bethlehem. "And the angel said to her, 'Do not be afraid, Mary, for you have found favor with God. And behold you will conceive in your womb and bear a son, and you shall call his name Jesus' "(Luke 1:30-31). Jesus is the Greek for the Jewish name "Joshua" which means "God is salvation." A further explanation of the name Jesus is found in Matthew 1:21, "You shall call His name Jesus, for He will save His people from their sins.' "

The nature of Christ's mission was announced from heaven before He was born. He was to be named JESUS (God's salvation) because His primary purpose was to save His people from their sins. There is no mention at all of His teaching, for His teaching would be ineffective unless there was first salvation.

Is there any name more precious than Jesus? "Jesus"—the name at whose mention all things bow, those in heaven, those on earth and those under the earth. "Jesus"—the name that brings comfort to the afflicted, strength to the weak, hope to the hopeless, forgiveness to the sinner, courage to the faltering, life to the dying. "Jesus"—the name that is above all other names; the name that becomes a prayer expressing and fulfilling the needs of our souls; the name at whose prayerful mention impossible things begin to become possible.

Jesus is the human name of God's Son. It denotes His human nature since He was fully man and fully God in one and the same person.

CHRIST

The next name the Creed applies to Jesus is "Christ." Christ is a Greek word which means "the anointed one." It recalls the ancient Hebrew custom of anointing a person who was set apart for a high office, as David was anointed by Samuel in the name of the Lord before he became King. The Greek word "Christ" is the equivalent of the Hebrew word for "Messiah". Thus the title "Christ" means the Messiah or the anointed one. It is important to remember this, because it means that when we speak the words "Jesus Christ" we are confessing the essence of what we believe as Orthodox Christians. Since "Jesus" is a name, and "Christ" is a title, when we put the two words together and say "Jesus Christ" we are confessing our faith that Jesus is the Messiah, or the One anointed by God to save His people. As Peter proclaimed, "Thou art the Christ, the Son of the Living God" (Matt. 16:16).

A Jewish soldier who had attended Christian services during World War II went to a rabbi and asked him the difference between the Messiah of the Jews and the Jesus of the Christians. The rabbi explained, "The difference is that we Jews believe the Messiah is still to come, whereas Christians believe he has already come in Jesus." To this, the soldier asked what was an unanswerable question, "But, rabbi, when our Messiah does come, what will he have that Jesus does not have? Will he have more love? more positive goodness? more miraculous power? more purity of life? more divine forgiveness? more perfect righteousness?"

The ancient Jews had such great fear of God that they would not even pronounce His name. God Himself dispelled this fear by giving us His name in two of the most beautiful words mankind has ever known: "Jesus Christ"—words that make real the presence of God and bring Him into our hearts.

TRUTH UNVEILED

The whole truth of who God is and who man is has been disclosed to the world in and by Jesus. That is why Jesus could say, "I am the Truth." It is as if truth were wearing a veil before and now in Jesus the veil is removed. Jesus is the Son of God, the second person of the Trinity, with the veil removed. As we read in Hebrews 1:1-2,

> "In many and various ways God spoke of old to our fathers by
> the prophets; but in these last days He has spoken to us by a

Son, whom He appointed heir of all things, through whom also He created the world.''

The Apostle John writes about Jesus,
"No one has ever seen God; the only Son who is in the bosom of the Father, He has made Him known" (John 1:18).

St. Paul summarizes our faith as to who Jesus is:
"He (Jesus) is the image of the invisible God, the firstborn of all creation; for in him all things were created, in heaven and on earth, visible and invisible, whether thrones or dominions or principalities or authorities—all things were created through Him and for Him. He is before all things, and in Him all things hold together. He is the head of the body, the Church; He is the beginning, the first-born from the dead, that in everything He might be pre-eminent. For in Him all the fullness of God was pleased to dwell, and through Him to reconcile to Himself all things, whether on earth or in heaven, making peace by the blood of His cross" (Col. 1:15-20).

Augustine's response to Jesus should be our response:
"I listen, He is the one who speaks.
I am enlightened; He is true Light.
I am the ear; He is the Word.''

NOT THE WINDOW BUT THE LIGHT

An American lady of the Bahai religion was once lecturing in India. According to the Bahai faith all religions are equally true. They believe, for example, that Jesus was just another great teacher like Buddha. He was not *the* way but one of the many ways to God. Since the Bahai lady spoke only English, an Indian was translating for her. In her lecture she said, "The sun rises in the morning, and as it ascends in the heavens it shines through the various windows in the house, one after another. Each religion represents a window through which the light shines. Jesus is one such window." The Indian translator interpreted faithfully what she said, but at the end of the sentence he added in his own language, "I beg to differ with the lady, Jesus Christ is not the window. He is the Light itself.''

Pascal summarized what Jesus means to us with these beautiful words:
"Not only do we understand God only through Jesus Christ, but we understand ourselves only through Jesus Christ. We understand life and death only through Jesus Christ. Apart from Jesus Christ, what we know is neither our life nor our death, neither God nor ourselves.''

TRANSFORMED HUMANITY

Jesus took on our humanity, cleansed it and transformed it into a holy and glorious humanity. He made man the tabernacle of God's presence, the temple of the Holy Spirit. Through His ascension Jesus even took our human nature into

Heaven with Him. How can anyone now say, "I'm only human" in a derogatory and cheap way?

Sometimes we are tempted to think that the closer we come to God, the more we must give up our human nature; the more like God we would be, the less human we can be. But that is not true. The only time we deny our humanity is when we fall into sin. The farther away we travel from God, the less human we are. Then it is that we lose our humanity and need to come back to God to recover it.

TO DEHUMANIZE JESUS

To dehumanize Jesus is to make Him an ideal impossible of fulfillment. Jesus was fully God but also fully man. Sometimes we find it difficult to keep the two natures together. Most often we feel that His divine nature was so overpowering that it swallowed up His human nature so that He came out in the end more divine than human. But this is not so. He was *complete* God and *complete* man in one and the same Person.

To be truly human is to be like Christ Who was *truly* God but also *truly* human, like us in everything except sin. If we are going to say, "I'm only human," let's say it not as an excuse for sinning; let's say it as we look at the perfect example of what a human can truly be: Jesus! Jesus came to show us what it means to be truly human and to give us the power to become like Him.

JESUS PRESENT THROUGH THE AGES IN THE LITURGY

This same Jesus is made present to us today through the Divine Liturgy. This is expressed so beautifully and so simply in the epiclesis prayer that is addressed to the Holy Spirit for the consecration of the bread and wine:

"And make this Bread the Precious Body of Thy Christ. Amen. And that which is in this cup, the Precious Blood of Thy Christ. Amen. Changing them by Thy Holy Spirit. Amen. Amen. Amen."

The continuing presence of Jesus in our midst is the main theme of the liturgy as expressed in the words the celebrant priest addresses to the priest co-celebrating with him during the liturgy: "Christ is in our midst," to which the response is given: "He is and ever will be." The liturgy is thus the sacrament of Christ's permanent saving presence among us today.

SUMMARY

1. As words express our inner thoughts, so Christ—the Word of God—communicates to us the thoughts of God. He is God's self-communication.

2. Jesus is Lord—absolute and undisputed creator and possessor of the entire universe. He is the Master, we the servants.

3. The human name JESUS (meaning God is salvation) expresses Christ's mission. He came to save His people from their sins.

4. When the title "Christ" (meaning the Anointed One or the Messiah) is applied to Jesus it becomes a confession of faith indicating our faith that Jesus, the Son of God, the Second Person of the Trinity, is the Messiah.

5. Jesus is God with the veil removed.

6. To be truly human is to be like Jesus.

7. Jesus is fully human and fully God.

8. The liturgy is the sacrament of Christ's permanent saving presence among us today.

What We Believe
About the Holy Trinity

Epiphany, or more specifically *Theophany,* is the manifestation, the showing forth of God in His fullness! Christ's baptism in the Jordan is a manifestation of God to the world for two reasons. First, it is the beginning of our Lord's public ministry. Jesus went down into the water of the Jordan known to most people only as the son of Mary and Joseph. He came out ready to reveal Himself in word and deed as what He had been from all eternity, the Son of God. Secondly, Epiphany is the manifestation of God, because it was there at the baptism of Jesus that all three Persons of the Holy Trinity appeared together for the first time. The Father's voice testified from on high to the divine Sonship of Jesus. The Son accepted His Father's testimony, and the Holy Spirit was seen descending from the Father in the form of a dove and resting upon the Son.

> "So Jesus was baptized, and as He came straight up out of the water, suddenly heaven was opened, and he saw the Spirit of God coming down like a dove and resting upon Him. And with that, a voice came from heaven, which said, This is my beloved Son, in Whom I am well pleased" (Matt. 3:16).

The threefold disclosure of God is also the subject of the troparion of the feast:

> "When Thou, O Lord, was baptized in the Jordan,
>   The worship of the Trinity was made manifest.
> For the voice of the Father bore witness unto Thee,
>   Calling Thee the beloved Son,
> And the Spirit in the form of a dove
>   Confirmed His word as sure and steadfast.
> O Christ our God, Who hast appeared and enlightened
>   the world,
>   Glory to Thee."

THE TRINITY IN DAILY WORSHIP

God—Father, Son and Holy Spirit—plays an important role in the life and worship of the Orthodox Christian. We make the sign of the cross with the thumb and first two fingers representing the Father, the Son, and the Holy Spirit. We bring these three fingers together to signify that we believe not in three Gods but in One. We are baptized in the name of the Trinity; we are forgiven in the name of the Trinity; we are married in the name of the Trinity; every liturgy begins with the name of the Trinity; we bless the name of the Trinity: "Glory be to the Father and to the Son and to the Holy Spirit"; we are blessed in the name of the Trinity: "The grace of our Lord Jesus Christ, and the love of God the Father and the fellowship of the Holy Spirit be with you all"; every Sunday we confess our faith in the Holy Trinity when we say in the Nicene Creed: "I believe in one God, the Father Almighty . . . and in one Lord Jesus Christ . . . and in the Holy Spirit."

All prayer in the Orthodox Church is addressed to the Triune God. We pray to God the Father through our Lord Jesus Christ in the Holy Spirit.

DO WE BELIEVE IN THREE GODS

Does this mean that we believe in three Gods? A Jewish girl testifying for those who sought to outlaw religious practices in public schools said, "Talk about God in school was about a God who was not my God. These other people don't believe in one God . . . they believe in a Trinity—a Father, a Son, and a Holy Spirit."

The Moslems emphasize the oneness of God. Their basic creed is, "There is no God but God, and Muhammed is the apostle of God." Again and again they stress that "God is one" and "God has no partners". They accuse Christians of worshipping *three* Gods—Father, Son, and Holy Spirit. There is even a joke which says that Christians offer three Gods and one wife whereas Moslems offer three wives and one God!

WHY BOTHER?

A story is told of a little boy who, singing in the choir of a church which used the Athanasian Creed in its liturgy, added under his breath whenever he came to the eighth verse "The Father incomprehensible, the Son incomprehensible, the Holy Ghost incomprehensible—the whole thing incomprehensible."

Dorothy Sayers has said, "Of all the Christian dogmas, the doctrine of the Trinity enjoys the greatest reputation for obscurity and remoteness from common experience."

If the whole thing is so incomprehensible, obscure and remote, why bother about it? When there are so many urgent, down-to-earth problems that we have to face every day, why waste time talking about Father, Son, and Holy Spirit? It reminds me of Cardinal Cushing's story about the time he was called on to give last rites to the victim of a fatal accident. He asked the victim, "Do you believe in God the Father, God the Son, and God the Holy Ghost?" The man opened one eye and said to those around him, "Here I am dying, and he's asking me riddles."

The doctrine of the Trinity may seem obscure and remote; yet it is one of the basic teachings of the Orthodox Church. It is basic because it tells us so much about God, about how Christians have experienced His presence in the past and about how we may experience the fulness of His presence today.

WHAT THE TRINITY IS NOT

To understand what we mean by the Trinity, let us first state what it is not. The Trinity is not the name of a phase that God went through. First, He was the Father Who in the beginning set everything in motion; then God was the Son Who came to earth in the form of Jesus; and, now, God is the Spirit Who is trying to get us to believe about the Father and the Son. The Bible doesn't say that. At the baptism of Jesus, all three persons were involved simultaneously in one event.

Other wrong doctrines are: (1) the Father alone is God; the Son and the Holy Spirit are creatures as we are; (2) God is one; the Son and the Spirit are merely names for relations which God has with Himself, i.e., the Thought and Speech of

God is called Son, while the Life and Action of God is called the Spirit; (3) the Father is one God, the Son another God, and the Holy Spirit still another God. In other words, there are three Gods. All these doctrines have been rejected by the Church. How then does the Church defend its doctrine that God is both One and yet Three?

THREE PERSONS—ONE SUBSTANCE

As Orthodox Christians we do not believe that God is only one person, and also three persons; and we do not believe that God has only one nature, and also three natures. This would be absurd. But we believe that what is in certain respects one is in other respects three. God is one if we consider His nature, but three if in this one nature we consider His person.

For example, in *what* they are, three men are one: they are all human beings. But in *who* they are, they are three persons, each absolutely unique and different from the others. Now in *who* God is, there are three persons, who are each unique and distinct, but in *what* they are, these three persons are one: one God, one substance. We do not say that there are three Gods, and yet these three are one. That would be ridiculous. But there are three divine persons in the *one* Godhead. The divine substance or nature is not three but one. One in *what* they are, three in *who* they are: Father, Son, and the Holy Spirit. In the words of the Athanasian Creed:

> And the Catholic faith in this, that we worship one God in
> Trinity, and Trinity in Unity;
> Neither confounding the Persons, not dividing the
> Substance
> For there is one Person of the Father, another of the Son,
> and another of the Holy Ghost.
> But the Godhead of the Father, of the Son, and of the Holy
> Ghost is all one: the glory equal, the
> majesty coeternal . . . .

ONE GOD

All this talk about one-in-three and three-in-one is not a lot of mumbo-jumbo. The Gospel is very positive. If the church believes in and teaches the doctrine of the Trinity, it is for very good reason. We believe that the whole Christian Gospel is summed up in this mysterious doctrine of three Persons, Father Son, and Holy Spirit in one God.

Let us begin with the basic Christian teaching that God is one. We cannot imagine what good news this was to the pagan world which believed not in one God but in many gods. We can read in missionary books today of the tremendous relief pagans feel when they learn from Christian missionaries that, instead of a whole host of gods and spirits to be satisfied, there is only one great God Who rules over all.

It is a terrible thing to believe in many gods. If one believes in blind fate, in astrology, in lucky numbers and charms and mascots as well as in the Almighty

Dollar, then one's heart is torn apart. There are too many gods to satisfy. "No man can serve two masters," said Jesus. Anything more than one God is too many. For there is only one true God. This was one of the most precious truths that God revealed in the Old Testament: "Hear, O Israel: the Lord our God is one God."

Wasn't this great truth enough? Why did Christianity have to go on from the One God to the Three-in-One? Why did it have to say something so complicated about God as the Trinity? Some say that all of this was the product of the Greek mind. Philosophy—they tell us—somehow got mixed up with the Bible somewhere in the second, third and fourth centuries and that ruined the simple God of the Old Testament. Admittedly, the early Christian Fathers used certain words and ideas like *consubstantial* that were floating around during those centuries, but they used them in order to stammer out their reaction to an astonishing fact they had experienced through the coming of Christ. Something happened to those early disciples that gave them a more complete picture of God. Let us see what it was.

THE EXPERIENCE OF THE EARLY CHRISTIANS

The Trinity is based primarily on the *experience* of the early Christians. When they met Christ, they met God. "My Lord and my God!" said Thomas. "You are the Christ, the Son of the living God," said Peter. "He who sees me, sees the Father," said Jesus. "I and the Father are one." "God was in Christ reconciling the world unto Himself," said Paul. Then at Pentecost they experienced the overwhelming sense of the divine Presence in their lives and they remembered that this was the Spirit of God promised by the prophet Joel in the Old Testament.

The doctrine of the Trinity was not dropped from heaven by God. In fact, the word Trinity is never even mentioned in the Scriptures. It came from the way the early Christians experienced God. It was an experience before it ever became a doctrine. The doctrine was an intellectual expression of what the early Christians found to be compellingly real in their own lives.

Peter, for example, knew God in three ways. He knew God as "Father". He knew God as "Son" in the person of Jesus Christ. On Pentecost he experienced God as "Holy Spirit", as a Presence and Power within his own heart and within the Church.

How clearly we see the Trinity in God's plan of salvation. "God (the Father) so loved the world that He gave His only Son (Jesus) that whoever believes in Him may not perish but have life everlasting" (John 3:16). Then Jesus sent the Holy Spirit to abide with us forever. The Holy Spirit is as necessary for salvation as is Jesus. It was the Holy Spirit Who originally brought Jesus to us. " Joseph, Son of David, do not fear to take Mary your wife, for that which is conceived in her *is of the Holy Spirit . . ."* (Matt. 1:20). It is the Holy Spirit Who continues to bring Jesus to us today. In every liturgy we kneel as the priest prays the EPICLESIS asking that the Holy Spirit may come upon us and upon our gifts of bread and wine to transform them into the Precious Body and Blood of Jesus.

St. Paul speaks of the "grace of our Lord Jesus Christ, the love of God the Father and the communion of the Holy Spirit." These were blessings of the Trinity that He had experienced personally. David H. C. Read says, "That there is one God, and that we know Him as Father, Son and Holy Spirit, is the witness of the New Testament, the continuous faith of the Church, and the experience of every one of us who believes."

When Elizabeth Barrett poured out her love for Robert Browning she wrote, "How do I love thee? Let me count the ways." That is what the early Christians said of God: "How do I love Thee? Let me count the ways. I love You, Lord, as Creator, I love You as Savior, I love you as the Holy Spirit, comforter, the power of God's presence within me."

The doctrine of the Trinity then, is an expression of the three aspects of our experience of God. We think of Him as God the Creator or Father. We think of Him as revealed historically in the Person of Jesus as the Son of God. We experience Him as a pervading, continuing presence and power in our lives—as God the Holy Spirit.

There are people who will say, "The Trinity . . . that's a little too complicated for me. I want a simple God, a God I can understand." Well, we shall never be able to understand God completely. This is the reason we cannot understand the Trinity. This is not to say, however, that we cannot express the Trinity in a way that is easy to understand. The Trinity means that I believe in God the Father Who made me, God the Son Who saves me, God the Holy Spirit Who lives in me. God the Father: *for* us in love eternally! God the son: *with* us in grace, historically, but also eternally! God the Holy Spirit: *in* us in power, experientially, historically, and eternally! God the Father: God *above* me. God the Son: God *beside* me. God the Holy Spirit: God *within* me and within the Church.

We learned a few moments ago that it is good news to learn that God is One. But, as we have seen, there is still better news in the message that the One God is a Father in heaven Who loves us, a Brother Savior Who died for us, a Holy Spirit Who dwells with us today as powerfully as He dwelt among the apostles 2,000 years ago. The doctrine of the Trinity, then, in summing up the entire New Testament experience of God, also sums up the whole Christian Gospel.

THE TRINITY IN SCRIPTURE

The doctrine of the Trinity, which is based on man's experience of God in the New Testament, is anchored in Scripture. The Lord Jesus said in His great commission, "Go therefore and make disciples of all nations, baptizing them in the name of the Father and of the Son and of the Holy Spirit . . ." (Matt. 28:19). The Three Persons are mentioned specifically in the great commission yet the unity of the three is stated in the use of the word "name" not "names". No one can be a Christian without being baptized said Jesus. And no one can be baptized except in the name of the Father, Son, and Holy Spirit, which is to say that no one can be a Christian unless he believes in the Trinity. This is the great gate, the only entrance to Christianity.

We saw previously that the Trinity was present at the baptism of Jesus in the Jordan River. Jesus stood there as the Holy Spirit descended upon Him in the form of a dove and the voice of the Father was heard saying, "This is my beloved Son." The Three Persons appeared together.

St. Paul speaks of "the grace of our Lord Jesus Christ and the love of God and the fellowship of the Holy Spirit" in II Corinthians 13:14.

St. Peter mentions the Trinity in his first letter, "Peter, an apostle of Jesus Christ . . . chosen and destined by God the Father and sanctified by the Spirit for obedience to Jesus Christ . . ." (I Peter 1:2).

There are also glimpses of the Trinity in the Old Testament. When God is about to create man He says, "Let *us* make man in *our* image and likeness" (Genesis 1:26). In the next verse we read, "And God made man in *his* image and likeness." The plural words, "us" and "our", seem to suggest several persons. The singular word "his", however, suggests that the several persons were somehow one.

The Hebrew word for God in the Old Testament "Elohim" is plural yet it takes a verb in the singular, and if an adjective goes with it, that too is in the singular. Three Persons yet one God.

A MYSTERY

Our belief in the Trinity, firmly anchored as it is in Scripture, remains a mystery. It reveals the fulness of God to us and yet at the same time it hides Him from us. For no one can really understand how God can be three distinct Persons yet one God.

When we say that the Trinity is a mystery, we should define what we mean by mystery. An excellent definition of mystery is found in the book "What is Faith" by Eugene Joly:

> "A mystery is not a wall against which you run your head, but
> an ocean into which you plunge. A mystery is not night; it is
> the sun, so brilliant that we cannot gaze at it, but so luminous
> that everything is illuminated by it."

This is what the mystery of the Trinity is to us, like "the sun, so brilliant that we cannot gaze at it; but so luminous that everything is illuminated by it."

There are those who refuse to believe in a God they cannot understand. They seem to forget that a God fully explained would cease to be a God. God is so great that He will remain beyond our comprehension. St. Paul expresses this truth when he writes, "O the depth of the riches both of the wisdom and knowledge of God. How unsearchable are his judgements, and his ways past finding out . . . For who hath known the mind of the Lord? . . . For of him and through him and for him are all things: to whom be glory forever."

Dorothy Sayers has written, "Why do you complain that the proposition that God is three-in-one is obscure and mystical and yet acquiesce meekly in the physicist's fundamental formula, '2P-PQ equals IH over 2Pi where I equals the square of minus 1', when you know quite well that the square root of minus 1 is paradoxical and Pi is incalculable." We readily accept this paradoxical formula that we do not understand and yet we balk at accepting the mystery of the Infinite as expressed by the Trinity.

We cannot explain how the seed draws from the soil the exact chemicals it needs to produce its own particular color, fragrance and fruit. This is but one of many mysteries in life that we do not understand. If we cannot understand these how can we expect to understand God fully and completely? If we are bewildered and baffled by the many, ordinary, natural mysteries here on earth, such as the nature of electricity, how can we expect to understand completely the nature of God?

St. Augustine was walking along the seashore one day. His thoughts were centered on the doctrine of the Holy Trinity. How could God be Three—and yet be One? He passed a little girl filling a hole in the sand with water. He asked what she was doing. The reply was, "I'm emptying the sea into this little hole I've dug." The wise theologian smiled and said to himself, "I am trying to do exactly what that little girl is doing. I'm trying to crowd the infinite God into this finite mind of mine."

It is not that we cannot understand God at all. The very purpose of the Trinity is to help reveal God to us. The water in the sand hole is *part* of the ocean, yet not the *whole* of it. Out there, there is more—infinitely more. So it is with our knowledge of God.

ANALOGIES

Throughout history many analogies have been used to try to help us understand how God can be three Persons yet one God. None of these analogies is perfect, yet each helps cast some light on the mystery.

For example, a soul has three capacities: will, understanding and memory; yet it is but one soul. Water has three forms: solid (ice), liquid (water), and vapor (steam), yet its chemical composition does not change; it remains one. The sun is composed of heat, gas and a gigantic mass of matter; yet it is one. The author of "Jesus—A Dialogue With the Savior" writes, "The Father has a thought and His thought is expressed and pronounced by the Word (Jesus). And what is the Spirit? The Spirit is the breath which bears the words. He is the voice which conveys the Word. He is the tongue of fire." The work of salvation *begins* with the Father who "so loved the world," is *realized* by the Son, and is *completed* by the Spirit.

All these analogies are but weak human efforts to try to understand the infinite God. Immanuel Kant said once that there are limitations to our finite minds and that with these limitations we can *contemplate* but not *engulf* things that are infinite. When we come into the presence of God, we do not understand; rather, we bow in awe and cover our eyes, for His brilliance is so great as to be blinding.

THE REAL MEANING OF MYSTERY

It is good that God is so great, so high above our understanding. That is the kind of God we need, a God who cannot be captured with words, a God who stretches our thoughts so that we have to use symbols and sacraments to express Him.

But mystery is not enough. We can't live on mere mystery. Moreover, this word *mystery* never means sheer mystery in the New Testament. It means a divine secret which it has pleased God to reveal to us; a secret so mysterious that we could never even begin to discover it for ourselves by human search, if God had not taken the initiative and given us the clue. But He has done this in Jesus Christ and through the Holy Spirit.

And that brings us to the meaning of the Holy Trinity. What does it say to us?

HOW ACCESSIBLE GOD IS

It says, first, not only how mysterious God is but how *accessible*. God becomes one of us in Christ. He becomes our Brother sharing our sorrows, our weaknesses, our temptations, our suffering, our death. The ancient pagan gods dwelt high on Mt. Olympus. Jesus comes to stand beside us as Immanuel: God with us. How near, how approachable, how available, how inescapable, every day, everywhere, with ordinary people in this ordinary world—this is the God who became man in Jesus; the God Who at Pentecost came as the Holy Spirit to abide within each of us filling us with the Presence and Power of God. God above us. God beside us. God within us. This is what the doctrine of the Trinity tells us. Without the Trinity God would be unknowable as well as inaccessible.

When the early fathers said that there were three *"Persons"* in the Godhead, they did not use the term in exactly the same way we use it when speaking of people. They used it only for the lack of another word to express what they meant. Augustine wrote, "They are certainly three, but if we ask' three what?' human speech is overcome by its great poverty. Then we say, 'three persons'; not to express the reality, but to save ourselves from silence" (De Trinitatae VII, 8). They used the word "Person" not to limit God to our level; they used it because personality was the highest they knew and God could not be less than that. He had to be more—far more! Jesus expressed this often with His words: *"how much more."* "If you who are evil know how to give good things to your children, *how much more* will your Father in heaven give good things to those who ask Him".

The word "Person" was chosen to help us understand that each Person of the Trinity is Someone to Whom we can speak, of Whom we can make a request, Whom we can love and with Whom we can have a personal relationship. The Trinity, then, is like the brilliant sun, impossible to gaze into, yet illuminating our knowledge of God as One Who is approachable and accessible in Christ and through the Holy Spirit.

GOD IN HIS FULLNESS

The doctrine of the Trinity preserves God in His fullness. To the Christian the word "God" by itself is too vague. The Trinity amplifies and describes God more fully. To us "God" means the Father Who loves us, the Son who saves us, the Holy Spirit Who abides within us. God the Creator. God the Redeemer. God the Inspirer. Anything less than this would not be the God of the New Testament. In the words of St. Paul, the fullness of God consists of "the grace of our Lord Jesus Christ, the love of God the Father, and the communion of the Holy Spirit." The only way we Christians can express everything we mean by that overwhelming word "God" is to say "Father, Son and Holy Spirit." We cannot in any way speak adequately about God without speaking of Christ and the Holy Spirit in the same breath. The doctrine of the Trinity, then, preserves God in His fullness.

Bishop Theophan the Recluse has said, "We are saved by the good will of the Father through the merits of the Son by the grace of the Holy Spirit."

We need the Holy Trinity. Who is it who does not need the grace of our Lord Jesus Christ? "You know the grace of our Lord Jesus Christ," writes St. Paul, "that, though he was rich, yet for your sake he became poor, so that by his poverty, you might become rich" (2 Corinthians 8:9). Who is it who does not need the love of God? "God so loved the world that he gave his only Son that whoever believes in him might not perish but have life everlasting" (John 3:16). Who is it who does not need the communion of the Holy Spirit? "You shall receive power when the Holy Spirit has come upon you" (Acts 1:8). Yours can be the grace of Christ, yours the love of God, yours the communion of the Holy Spirit. This is the meaning of the Trinity which sums up the whole Gospel, presenting us with the fullness of God's presence, power and love. God above me. God beside me. God inside me. The French author, Francois Mauriac, said once that no one who is created by the Father, redeemed by the Son, and indwelt by the Holy Spirit can ever count himself unimportant. This is why the Church never tires of singing in gratitude: "Glory be to the Father, and to the Son, and to the Holy Spirit, now and ever and unto ages of ages. Amen."

St Irenaeus pictures the Trinity as God the Father stretching His two arms out to us in love, one arm is Jesus and the other arm is the Holy Spirit. Surely such love demands a response!

PRAYER

My hope is the Father,
My refuge is the Son,
My protection is the Holy Spirit,
Holy Trinity,
Glory to Thee.

— An Orthodox Prayer

SUMMARY

1. God is one. There are not a whole host of gods to be satisfied. Though He is one in substance, God has been experienced in the history of God's people as the Father Who created us, Son Who saves us, the Holy Spirit Who empowers us. He is three Persons yet one God, one substance.

2. Although the doctrine of the Trinity reveals God to us, i.e., God above us, God beside us, God within us, it also serves to hide God from us by reminding us that we shall never be able to understand God completely with our finite intelligence. No one can understand how God can be three Persons yet one God. It is a mystery.

3. The doctrine of the Trinity is anchored in Scripture (Matt. 28:19, 2Cor. 13:14).

4. The Trinity expresses the essence of our Orthodox Christian faith: the work of salvation *begins* with the Father who "loved the world," is *realized* by the Son through His death and resurrection, and is *completed* by the Holy Spirit on Pentecost.

5. The Trinity makes God *knowable* as Father, Son and Holy Spirit and *accessible* as One Who comes to us through Jesus ("God with us") and the Holy Spirit (Pentecost).

6. The word "God" is amplified and described more fully through the Trinity. The fullness of God is "the grace of our Lord Jesus Christ, the love of God the Father, and the communion of the Holy Spirit" (2 Cor.13:14).

What We Believe
About the Divine Liturgy

THE BREAD OFFERING OR PROSFORA

Jesus said, ''I am the living bread which came down from heaven; if any one eats of this bread he will live forever; and the bread which I shall give for the life of the world is my flesh'' (John 6:51).

St. Paul writes, ''The Lord Jesus on the night when he was betrayed took bread, and when he had given thanks, he broke it and said, ''This is my body which is for you. Do this in remembrance of me' '' (I Cor. 11:24).

Jesus is the bread of life Who offers Himself for our salvation. ''Unless you eat the flesh of the Son of man and drink his blood you have no life in you; he who eats my flesh and drinks my blood has eternal life, and I will raise him up at the last day'' (John 6:53-54).

A very meaningful project for the Orthodox Christian family is to bake a loaf of altar bread (prosfora) and bring it to church for the liturgy.

The significance of the bread may be explained as follows.

The offering bread represents Jesus Who is the Bread of Life. It is baked by someone in the congregation and brought to the priest for each liturgy. In many Slavic churches, instead of one loaf, five small loaves are used to commemorate the five loaves which Jesus blessed and multiplied.

Bread is used not only to represent Jesus Who is the Bread of Life, of which if any man eat he shall never hunger, but also to express the offering of our life to God. The Greek word for offering bread is *prosfora* which means an offering to God. Bread is used as an offering because it represents life. It is the staff of life. Once consumed it becomes part of us, i.e., our flesh and bones. Thus in bringing the loaf of bread to God, we are, in effect, offering our life to Him. It is the gift of our love.

The priest accepts the gift and places it on the holy altar. This act represents God accepting our gift. It now passes into His possession. God is so pleased with the gift of our life that He transforms it through the Holy Spirit and gives it back to us as His Precious Body. Thus it is that communion with God results. We give ourselves to God and He, in turn, gives Himself to us. We come to the liturgy not just to *receive* Christ but also to *give* ourselves to Christ.

WHY BREAD?

Some may object: ''What meaning can a small loaf of bread have in the eyes of God? If you are going to give God a gift, don't give Him something that symbolizes life. Give Him your very life surrendered to His will.''

To understand this, let us use an illustration. Suppose there is a little girl— say four or five—who sees her father give to her mother a birthday present at breakfast. It's Mummie's birthday! Then she too will want to give her mother a birthday present. What can she do? She wanders out into the garden and there the bright yellow glow of a dandelion flower catches her eye. It is only a weed, really: but she does not know that. To her it is a pretty flower. So she plucks it, toddles into the house and gives it to her mother as a birthday present.

The mother, of course, is delighted. Why? Does she want a dandelion? Obviously not for herself—it has no value. But it is a gift from her daughter; and because it is a gift it has meaning. It means the love of that little girl, and that is why it is so precious to the mother. Clearly, then, a gift which is poor in value such as a dandelion can be rich in meaning because of what it expresses; what it means.

And so it is with us and God. We give Him a present. In itself this present consists of a round loaf of bread—a very small value! But because it is a gift, it bears the meaning we put into it. We should, then, make it mean all that we can in the way of praise and love; we should put ourselves into that bread just as the child put herself into the flower. Then it will be precious to God as the flower was to the mother.

WE POUR OURSELVES INTO THE GIFT

That is our part in the sacrifice of the liturgy. When the priest holds up the bread and the wine at the altar, he tells God what we intend them to mean. It is not just the priest but everybody in the congregation who is helping to offer the sacrifice, so it is our business at that time to tell God what those gifts—which are *our* gifts—are intended to mean as far as we are concerned.

They stand for us. We put ourselves onto that paten with the altar bread, offering to God our mind and heart, our soul and body, all that we have and are. We must, as it were, pour our heart out into that chalice with the wine, and put into it all our hopes and fears, our joys and sorrows, our love and adoration, our obedience and commitment—our whole self. For all this is to go to God in the shape of a gift.

That is our part at this point in the sacrifice: we are to put the meaning into the gifts by offering ourselves. If we do not offer ourselves to God under these symbols of bread and wine, then we are not really offering the liturgy as we should. We are not "in on it." The bread and the wine may mean somebody else. But they don't mean us because we haven't done anything to make them mean us.

A COMMON ACTION

The word liturgy means a common action, something that many people are doing together. That is why all the prayers in the liturgy are in the plural. The priest does not say "*I* offer this sacrifice to You, Lord . . . but *we* . . ."

This means only one thing: the liturgy is something that we do all together—priest and people. During the liturgy we are all offering a sacrifice to God. We are not just watching something being done by the priest at the altar. Nor is it being offered for us, even at our request or with our approval, in our presence. We ourselves are offering it. We are sacrificing. We are bringing the bread and the wine to God. We are laying our lives on the altar in complete surrender to God. We are in effect saying to God, "Dear Lord, like the little girl who brought dandelions for her mother's birthday, so I bring you this bread and this wine. It is really of no value, Lord, except as a sign signifying that under the symbols of bread and wine I place my whole life on your holy altar because I love you."

STAMPED WITH A SEAL

A special seal is stamped on top of the loaf before it is baked. Your priest will know where you can borrow or purchase such a seal. The middle part of the seal contains a square piece of bread with the words IC, XC, NIKA. This is a Greek abbreviation for JESUS CHRIST CONQUERS. Since this is the piece that will be changed into the Body of Christ, it is called the Lamb of God. A large triangular piece is removed from the left of the Lamb of God and placed on the paten. This represents the Virgin Mary, our Lord's mother. Then nine smaller triangular pieces are removed from the seal to commemorate the angels, prophets, apostles and saints of the Church. These are placed on the paten to the right of the Lamb of God. Following this, the priest prays for the living members of the congregation especially for those whose names have been submitted to him. As he prays for each name he cuts a small piece of bread, representing the person prayed for, and places it immediately below Jesus, the Lamb of God. Finally, he removes a piece of bread for each deceased person for whom we have requested prayers. Thus, around the Lamb of God on the paten is gathered the entire Church consisting of the angels, saints, and loved ones in heaven together with members of the local congregation. ALL are alive in God's presence and all constitute the one living Body of Christ.

Since the loaf represents us, it is recommended that the family submit a list of names to the priest when presenting the loaf. One column should be entitled *Living,* containing the names of members of the immediate family who have baked the bread plus any others they wish to have remembered in prayer. A second column should be entitled *Departed* under which may be listed the names of loved ones now with God in heaven.

RECIPE

We offer below a recipe for baking of altar bread:

5 cups flour (sifted)	1 teaspoon salt
1½ cups warm water	2 cakes yeast
1 religious seal	

Dissolve the yeast in warm water. Add salt and flour and knead until smooth. Place in bowl, cover, and let rise. When it doubles in size, knead again. Then divide dough in half and put in cake pans that have been floured only (no grease). This will make two loaves. Dip seal in flour and stamp bread, leaving stamp on bread until it is ready to bake. Let rise, remove seal and bake for about 30 minutes at 375 degrees.

A PRAYER

After the bread has been baked, the following prayer may be said in unison by the family:

"Dear Lord, this bread that we have baked represents each one of us in this family and in our congregation. We are offering ourselves to You, our very life, in humble obedience and total commitment to You. We place ourselves on Your holy altar through this bread to be used by You in any way that You feel will help enlarge Your kingdom. Accept our gift and make us worthy to receive the greater gift that You will give us when You consecrate this bread and give it back to us as Your Precious Body. Amen."

WE ARE ON THE ALTAR

By baking the altar bread and bringing it to church, we come to realize that we are not only *at* the altar but *on* the altar in every liturgy. The bread and wine which the priest places on the altar represent us. When the priest elevates the bread and wine (chalice and paten) at the altar, we kneel. We remember that these are our gifts the priest is offering to God: our love, our thanksgiving, our obedience, our life. We remember that we are on the altar offering ourselves to God.

Once the bread is baked it may be taken to the church and presented to the priest by the entire family. This act involves everyone in the offering of the gift. Each family may decide how often they would like to prepare the altar bread in consultation with the priest.

A MULTI-FACETED PRESENCE

Although Jesus is truly present in the consecrated bread and wine at the liturgy, to focus exclusively on the presence there is to miss some vital aspects of the mystery of the Eucharist. At the liturgy Christ is also truly present in the readings of the Word of God as well as in the sermon. Listening to these, we are truly listening to Jesus. Christ is also present in the celebrant priest who symbolizes in a special way Christ's presence in our midst. Christ is present as well in all those taking part in the Eucharist, i.e., God's people. The same Christ dwells in all of us. As we minister and serve each other, we serve Christ. Seeing the Eucharist in this way we can see that Holy Communion is more than the consecrated bread and wine; it is truly a sacred event, a moment of encounter with the living Christ.

THE GOSPEL BOOK — GOD TALKS TO US

When a young man offers a box of candy to the girl he loves, he begins by saying, "Hello, dear! I've brought you a present and I hope you'll like it." And she replies, "What is it? Oh! How marvelous! You are a perfect dear to have thought of it"—or something like that. They begin by talking to one another; they *exchange* words. After they talk, they exchange gifts. When the young girl tastes the candy, she offers some to the young man so that he, too, may eat. He gives to her—so she gives to him. They exchange gifts.

The same thing happens in the liturgy. We come to give God a gift. We can't just do it in silence—we begin by talking to God. We say, "Kyrie eleison" "Dear God, have mercy on us." We say, "God, how wonderful You are! How great and strong! How blessed is Your kingdom!" We say, "God , forgive us!" We pray for peace, good weather, the sick, etc. We say, "Please, God, give us all things that will be good for our souls." Thus we begin by sending our words up to God.

And then God replies. He sends His words down to us. He speaks to us through one of His apostles in the reading of the Epistle (Apostolos). Then He speaks to us through His only-begotten Son, our Lord, in the reading of the Gospel. After this He speaks to us through His minister, the priest, in the sermon. Thus we hear the epistle, the gospel and the sermon—each called "The Word of God." What is all this but an exchange of words? We talk to God and He talks to us. We have a friendly talk with God.

"WISDOM, LET US ATTEND"

Thus, the first part of the liturgy is talking with God. We begin by praying for the world and its needs. Then Jesus comes to talk to us. To remind us that Jesus is coming to talk to us the priest does something to make us pay attention. He takes the Gospel book and carries it out to the people. He holds it high so that everyone can see it and says WISDOM. LET US PAY ATTENTION. He is telling us that Jesus is now about to come to speak His wise words to us. We are to pay complete attention to Him as He speaks to us.

Jesus comes in every liturgy to speak to us and to show us the way. The priest holds high the Gospel book to show us that it is not the priest but CHRIST Who will speak to us.

So, in every liturgy *we are there* as Christ speaks to us. He continues to come to us. He continues to speak to us. As He spoke to His disciples long ago, so He speaks to us today to give us light and guidance. The small entrance with the Gospel book held up high should always remind us that Christ comes to speak to us personally in every liturgy.

A THEOPHANY

The small entrance announces the coming of a *theophany,* a Greek word which means *God shows Himself* to us. God is about to show Himself to us by revealing His will to us in the Scripture readings and sermon. He will allow us to see how much He loves us, how precious we are to Him. The small entrance is like a window through which we look to see God as He reveals Himself to us.

The small entrance with the Gospel book also reminds us of the time in Jesus' life when He began to teach people in public shortly after His baptism. It tells us of the beginning of His teaching ministry at the age of 30. And it tells us that He continues to come to teach us today in the liturgy. He is the Greatest Teacher Who ever lived because He is God. And as God He never stops speaking to us and teaching us if we go to be where He is every Sunday, i.e., in the liturgy.

HOW THE SMALL ENTRANCE ORIGINATED

The small entrance began in the old days when the Gospel book was written by hand because the printing press had not been invented. It was a very expensive and precious book. To protect it from being stolen or burned, it was kept locked in a big vault or safe. The priest had to go to the vault, unlock it, and carry the Gospel book to the altar for the liturgy. The small entrance was built around this act.

Today the Gospel book does not have to be kept in a vault. It is kept enthroned on the holy altar of every Orthodox Church. So it should be kept enthroned on our family altar at home. Everyone of us can have a Bible by our bedside with an icon. The same Jesus Who comes to speak to us in the liturgy can also speak to us at home every day if we will open the Bible and read a chapter. And when we love someone, we love to speak to him and listen to him not just once a week but every day.

EXAMINE THE GOSPEL BOOK

The Gospel Book on the holy table is not the complete New Testament because it does not contain the epistles—only the four Gospels. The epistles are contained in another book called the ''Apostolos'' or Apostle which is used by the chanter.

On the four corners of the Gospel Book are engravings of the four persons who wrote the Gospels: Matthew, Mark, Luke, and John. On the the one side of the book there is an engraving of the *crucifixion*. This side faces up on the altar during the liturgical processions of the week, since during the week days we remember the life, passion and death of Jesus. The *resurrection* side of the Gospel Book faces up on the altar on Saturday and Sunday of every week since on these two days we remember and celebrate the resurrection of Jesus.

Through the Gospel Book, Christ speaks to us in every liturgy. He speaks to us the very same words He spoke to His disciples. He enters into conversation with us. It is as if He were here now. In fact, He really is here when we hear His word read to us.

TRY READING DIRECTIONS

How much we need to listen to Christ today! I remember once a man stopping his car to park in a strange city. He looked and looked for the coin slot in the parking meter but could not find it. Finally, he asked someone about it. The answer he received was, "Try reading the directions on the meter." He did, and he immediately found the coin slot.

We, too, have many questions about life. We fumble about not knowing who we are or where we are going or why we are here. All the while the Lord Jesus is trying to tell us, "Why don't you try reading my directions for life in this Book. Here is where I tell you what life is all about."

Whenever we buy a gadget or appliance the manufacturer gives us a set of directions to explain how it works and how to maintain it. Do you think God would give us the gift of life without at the same time giving us directions on how to live life? Of course not. His directions are to be found in this wonderful book that sits enthroned on the Holy Table of every Orthodox Church.

YOU ARE THERE

I heard someone tell the other day how dinner is served down on the farm. All the children and the hired help come in from the fields at noon. They wash their hands and sit at the table. Before the food is served, the mail is read. Then the instructions are given as to which chores must be completed that afternoon and evening. After this is finished, the food is served to give everyone the strength to carry out the job assignments just received.

Something similar takes place in every liturgy. In the first part of the liturgy—called the Liturgy of the Word—we receive the Word of God. God gives us His instructions as to what He wants us to do, how He wants us to live. We receive these instructions in the Epistle lesson, the Gospel lesson, and the sermon. But we are too weak to carry out the Word of God. We lack strength. That is why in the second part of the liturgy—called the Liturgy of the Faithful—God gives us the power we need. He gives us Himself—the Bread of Life—through the Sacrament of Holy Communion.

What is Holy Communion?

HE COMES IN DISGUISE

Dr. Panayiotis Trembelas, professor of theology at the University of Athens, wrote that when Christ was born in Bethlehem of Judea, He chose to be born not of a mother who was listed in "Who's Who," but of a poor, humble, pure peasant girl. He chose as His place of entry into this world not a palace but a cold, damp cave that served as a stable for animals. Who would have thought at the time that this child born of this humble mother in such a desolate place was God Himself? Yet doesn't this very same thing happen again in the Sacrament of Holy Communion? Doesn't the all-powerful Christ, Lord of heaven and earth, who holds the whole world in His hands, who is worshipped by all creation, doesn't He, even in this Sacrament, shed His divine glory and majesty for us under the humble forms of bread and wine?

What happened in Bethlehem long ago happens again today whenever the liturgy is celebrated. Christ comes to us again quietly, humbly, disguised under the forms of bread and wine. Have you ever imagined what would happen if

Christ were to descend on the altar with the same glorified body with which the disciples saw Him ascending into heaven? Who of us would dare approach Him? Or if He should offer us His body as it was when it was taken down from the cross on Good Friday, who of us would dare touch it? Through the great Sacrament of Holy Communion the Lord makes Himself utterly approachable, disguising Himself, even as He did in the manger, and coming to us ever so humbly under the forms of bread and wine. The Sacrament of Communion is the perpetuation of Christmas. In celebrating Christmas we observe not only God's coming into the world thousands of years ago; we celebrate also His coming into the world today to be born in the manger of our soul through this great Sacrament in every liturgy.

MEMORIALS

When something important happens we do not want to forget it. We make a memorial plaque to help us remember. For example, there is a memorial plaque below our church property in Minneapolis stating that the first house, school and church in our area was built on our church site in 1830. We do not want to forget this important happening. So we use a memorial plaque to help us remember.

In addition to memorial plaques which are lifeless, we can remember an important happening by making it into a play or a movie. For example, when you see a movie on the life of Abraham Lincoln, it is as if you are there. The life of Lincoln comes alive. It is lived before your very eyes.

The liturgy is not like a memorial plaque but more like a play or movie on the life of Jesus. What Jesus said and did two thousand years ago happens again before our very eyes in the liturgy.

A REMEMBRANCE

Thus, the liturgy is a remembrance. We remember again a real historical event that has great meaning for us: the life of Jesus. We do this in obedience to Jesus Who said, "Do this in remembrance of Me." St. Paul wrote, "As often as you shall drink this cup and eat this bread you shall show forth the death of Jesus till He comes again."

MAKING PRESENT AGAIN

But the liturgy is not just a remembrance. It is also a *making present again* today of the life of Jesus so that we are there just as the disciples were there when these great things happened.

The liturgy bridges the gap between what Jesus did two thousand years ago and us today. It is like the old TV program YOU ARE THERE which enacted great historical happenings and made us feel that we were actually there when they were happening. The sacrifice on Calvary, for example, is not repeated since the Lamb of God was sacrificed "once only, for all time." It is *made present again* mystically in the liturgy through the Holy Spirit so that *we are there* today:

1. *WE ARE THERE* when Jesus teaches even as His disciples were there. We sit at His feet on the Mount of Beatitudes and He speaks as He spoke then. What is the Epistle, the Gospel reading, and the sermon but Jesus speaking to us today? We are there!

2. *WE ARE THERE* as Jesus goes forth to die for us and we repeat the prayer of the dying thief, "Lord, remember me when You come into your kingdom." This happens in the Great Entrance when the priest carries the covered chalice and paten out to the people and prays, "Remember, O Lord, each one of us when You come into Your kingdom." We are at Calvary at this moment. The same Jesus is present. Only this time we are the dying thief who asks to be remembered. And we pray his prayer. With the ears of faith we hear the same response from Jesus, "Today you will be with me in paradise."

3. *WE ARE THERE* at the Last Supper and Jesus directs His invitation personally to each one of us: "Take, eat, this is my body which is broken for you for the forgiveness of sins," and "Drink ye all of it. This is my blood. . ." He is the Host. We are the guests. Through the liturgy the Last Supper is not a banquet that took place 2,000 years ago for twelve special people. It is your banquet and my banquet today. We are all invited. The same Jesus is there. We are there. He gives us the same Bread of Life He gave His disciples. Paul Evdokimov writes, "All the holy suppers of the Church are nothing else than one eternal and unique Supper, that of Christ in the upper room. The same Divine act both takes place at a specific moment in history, and is offered always in the sacrament."

4. *WE ARE THERE* as Jesus ascends into heaven and we ascend with Him. When the priest carries our gifts into the altar at the Great Entrance and places them on the holy table, we are carried into the very presence of God. Every liturgy is an ascension into the presence of God. Jesus takes us there. This is why we sing the very same hymn the angels sing in His presence, "Holy, holy, holy, Lord God of Sabaoth. . ."

5. *WE ARE THERE* as Jesus sends the Holy Spirit to His apostles on Pentecost. When we kneel during the liturgy for the epiclesis prayer, we experience Pentecost. We pray with the priest that God may send the Holy Spirit upon us and upon our gifts of bread and wine to change them into the Body and Blood of Jesus. This is a real Pentecost and we are there! We receive the wisdom and power of the Holy Spirit and we leave filled with God's wisdom, life, power and presence.

So it is that in every liturgy the life, the teaching, the suffering, the death, the resurrection, the ascension, and Pentecost are not just remembered but also made present again so that we are there to actually participate in them!

This is why Fr. Schmemann says, "The liturgy is, first of all, the Paschal (Easter) gathering of those who are to meet the Risen Lord and enter with Him into His kingdom."

And Nicholas Gogol says, "The liturgy is the eternal repetition of the great act of love for us."

The central event of the liturgy is the descent, the appearance, and the divine presence of the resurrected Christ. A person is frequently reminded of this presence. For example, at one point in the liturgy the priest says, "Christ is with us." And the co-celebrant priest responds, after receiving the kiss of peace, "He is with us and will be."

There are those who object, saying, "Christianity is not a creed. Christianity is not liturgy. Christianity is power." We agree but we also ask: "Where does this power come from if not from our creed and from our liturgy?"

P. Evdokimov sums it all up when he writes, "During the liturgy, through its divine power, we are projected to the point where eternity cuts across time, and at this point we become true contemporaries with the events we commemorate."

THE PROCESSIONS

The liturgy is full of processions or movements. These processions show what is happening in the liturgy. God is moving toward man, and man is moving toward God. We are all moving closer to the Second Coming of Jesus. For the Orthodox Christian, life is not going around in circles. It is movement toward a goal. The goal is the kingdom of God.

At the very outset the goal of the liturgy is announced. The first words of the liturgy are: "Blessed be the kingdom of the Father and of the Son and of the Holy Spirit. . ." As a bus driver announces at the beginning where the bus is going, so the priest announces at the very beginning that the goal of the liturgy is to take us to the Kingdom of Heaven. We hear this and we reply by saying, "Amen." This means, "O.K. That is where we want to go."

THE FIRST PROCESSION

The first procession of the liturgy begins even before we come to church. When we wake up on Sunday morning and decide to come to church we are making our first movement to God. Getting up out of bed, going to the bathroom to wash, climbing into the family car, driving to church is part of the first procession we are making to come to God. These processions at home are just as religious as any that take place in the liturgy. We are moving toward God.

SECOND PROCESSION

Another important procession or movement of the liturgy is the bringing of the bread and the wine to the altar for the liturgy. We are moving to come to God with a sacrifice: a gift that expresses our life. We are making a procession to God to lay our life on His altar in complete obedience and commitment to Him. We come to give first. Only after we have given do we receive.

THE PROCESSIONS OF THE SMALL ENTRANCE AND THE GOSPEL

Another procession is the small entrance. The priest brings the Gospel book out to us, holds it high and says, WISDOM. LET US PAY ATTENTION. He comes to announce the coming of Christ to speak to us and calls on us to pay attention to His wise words of life and peace.

Three other processions follow: the coming of a lay person to the front of the altar area to read the *Apostolos,* a reading from the Epistles. The coming of the priest to read God's word from the Gospel book, and thirdly, the coming of the priest to the pulpit to bring us God's word in sermon. All these movements show God coming to us time and again as He did in the history of salvation to speak to His people. He sent Moses, the prophets, the patriarchs and finally His own Son to speak to us. This is expressed today in the many processions God makes in the liturgy to come out from the altar to speak and to be with us.

THE PROCESSION OF THE GREAT ENTRANCE

The Great Entrance is one of the more impressive processions of the liturgy. As candle and standard bearers go before him, the priest carries our gifts of bread and wine in a solemn procession and places them on the holy table. This procession reminds us of Jesus on His way to suffer on the cross for our salvation. As He proceeds by us we pray the prayer of the thief who repented, "Remember me, Lord, when You come into Your kingdom."

The second meaning of the Great Entrance is that it is a procession that leads us into the very presence of God. It is a movement forward and upward, an ascension toward God, a procession of the Church to where it belongs, i.e., the Throne of God. Christ takes us with Him in His glorious Ascension to His Father. He enters the heavenly sanctuary and we enter with Him to stand before the Throne of God. In carrying our gifts to God's altar, our bread which signifies our life, the priest is carrying all of us into the presence of God. Mystically the whole congregation enters God's presence with the priest and stands before God singing the hymn of the angels, "Holy, holy, holy, Lord God of Sabaoth. . ."

THE PROCESSION FOR HOLY COMMUNION

The next procession is the priest proceeding out to us from the holy table with the chalice. We are at the Last Supper. Christ is the Host. He invites us with the same invitation He used for His disciples, "Take, eat . . . Drink ye all of it. . ." The movement of the priest from the altar to the people with the holy cup shows Christ coming to each one of us today with the Bread of Life.

In our desire to be one with Him, we make a movement to go forward at this moment. It signifies our going to God. In His great love, God has chosen to take the first step to come to us. We respond by going to Him. No liturgy is complete unless we take part in the procession to the altar to be united with Jesus. "He who eats my flesh and drinks my blood lives in me and I in him," said Jesus.

We are never "worthy" to come to Jesus. We come because only He can make us worthy. We come in obedience to Jesus who invites us to come. We come praying, "I am not worthy, Master and Lord, that You should come to me . . . yet since You in Your love for all men, wish to dwell in me in boldness I come. . ."

THE PROCESSION TO COLLECT OUR GIFTS

Still another movement or procession of the liturgy is the offering that is taken to support God's work in the world through His Church. When the offering plate comes before us it is like the paten which contains the gift of our life to God. Only this time we place on the paten not bread but the fruit of our labor and sweat—an offering of money to be used to translate our faith into deeds of love for Christ. We truly give ourselves to God through this gift. It is part of our sacrifice of love to God. In fact, the more one loves, the more one gives.

THE MOVEMENT OF LOVE

Another movement or procession of the liturgy comes at the time the priest says, "Let us love one another that we may with one mind confess." At this moment the priests at the altar exchange the kiss of peace. In the early Church the entire congregation did the same. Each person reached out to the nearest person(s) to express by a handshake or kiss the love of Jesus, to show that there were no resentments. The greeting used was—and still is—"Christ is in our midst." The response is: "He is and ever will be." There can be no movement to receive the Body and Blood of Jesus unless there is first a movement of love and reconciliation toward our fellow humans. Before we bring our gift at the altar, said Jesus, we must first go and be reconciled to our neighbor.

THE PROCESSION BACK TO THE WORLD

The final movement or procession of the liturgy can best be described as a RETURN, our return from heaven to earth, from the Kingdom of God back to our kitchen, or school, or home. But as we return we are different from what we were when we began the movement toward God at the beginning of the liturgy. We are not the same. For, "We have seen the True Light. We have received the Heavenly Spirit. We have found the true faith." We come to the liturgy wounded, and we leave healed. We come hopeless, and we leave with hope. We come weak, and we leave strong. We come as sinners, and we leave as saints. We come in darkness, and we leave in light. We come hungry, and we leave filled with the Bread of Life. We come in sadness, and we leave in joy. Now Christ sends us back as witnesses of what we have seen and heard, to proclaim the good news of His Kingdom, and to continue His work. We are His people. He is in us and we are in Him. We return to the world as "other Christs" to transform and change it for Him. The true liturgy begins when we return to the world to work for Christ, to make real His love through our acts of mercy.

This is "the liturgy after the liturgy" that is described so beautifully by Bishop Anastasios Yannoulatos, professor at the University of Athens:

"The Liturgy has to be continued in personal, everyday situations. Each of the faithful is called upon to continue a personal liturgy on the secret altar of his own heart, to realize a living proclamation of the good news 'for the sake of the whole world'. Without this continuation the Liturgy remains incomplete. Since the eucharistic event we are incorporated in him who came to serve the world and to be sacrificed for it, we have to express in concrete diakonia, in community life, our new being in Christ, the Servant of all. The sacrifice of the Eucharist must be extended in personal sacrifices for the people in need, the brothers for whom Christ died. Since the Liturgy is the participation of the great event of liberation from the demonic powers, then the continuation of Liturgy in life means a continuous liberation from the powers of the evil that are working inside us, a continual reorientation and openness to insights and efforts aimed at liberating human persons from all demonic structures of injustice, exploitation, agony, loneliness, and at creating real communion of persons in love.''

FOUR LITURGIES

There are four different liturgies in the Orthodox Church:

1) The Liturgy of St. John Chrysostom which is the most common liturgy celebrated on Sundays and weekdays.

2) The Liturgy of St. Basil the Great which is celebrated only ten times a year, mainly during the Sundays of Lent. St. Basil's liturgy is very much like that of St. John Chrysostom with the exception of the prayers offered privately by the priest. These are much longer.

3) The Liturgy of St. James, the Brother of the Lord, which is celebrated only once a year on the Feast Day of St. James, October 23, and only in certain places such as Jerusalem.

4) The Liturgy of the Pre-Sanctified Gifts which is used only on Wednesdays and Fridays of Lent and on the first three days of Holy Week. It is called *pre-sanctified* because no consecration takes place. The communion elements distributed are reserved from the Eucharist of the previous Sunday. Thus, the *Pre-Sanctified* is not a eucharistic liturgy but rather an evening Vesper Service that includes the distribution of pre-consecrated elements of Holy Communion. Its purpose is to offer us more frequent opportunity during Lent to receive Holy Communion. It is used during Lent because the normal liturgy is an extremely joyful expression of the Resurrection and is considered to be inappropriate to the deeply penitential season of Lent.

SUMMARY

The liturgy is full of movements of God to man and man to God:
1. We wake up and get ready for church; first Procession.
2. We bring a gift of bread to express the giving of our life to God.
3. The processions of the Small Entrance, the reading of the Epistle, Gospel and sermon that show Christ as coming to speak to us today.
4. We go to the altar to receive the Body and Blood of Jesus.
5. We give our offering of money to God to help the poor and the needy; to continue the work of His Church in the world today.
6. The movement of love and reconciliation to our neighbor through a handshake or the kiss of peace.
7. The movement back to the world to serve as witnesses of the resurrection.

God has made and continues to make many movements to come to us, but He will not forcefully break down the door of our heart; He awaits our response: "Let us then with confidence draw near to the throne of grace, that we may receive mercy and find grace to help in time of need." (Hebr. 4:16).

What We Believe About Salvation

A question that is often addressed to us is: "Are you saved?" There are those who delight in using this question in their Christian witnessing. It is really not a bad question, for it directs our thinking to an all-important subject. But repeated too often it can become overbearing. There is a story of a man at a baseball game who was looking for an opportunity to share his Christian faith. Finally someone spoke to him. "Is this seat saved?" "No," said the man, "are you?"

THE THREE STAGES OF BEING SAVED

A very godly bishop was walking down the street one day when a little girl, a very zealous Christian, no doubt, asked him, "Bishop, are you saved?" The bishop, a very kind man, smiled and said, "My dear friend, might I just inquire a little more exactly as to what it is you are asking me. Are you asking me, have I been saved? Or are you asking me, am I now being saved? Or are you asking me, shall I yet someday be saved?" Well, that pretty well flustered the little girl. She didn't respond. "Honey," said the bishop, "all three are true. I have been saved. I am being saved; and I shall yet be saved." You see, salvation is comprehensive. It has to do with our past—we have been saved from sin and death through baptism. This we call justification. It has to do with the present—we are being saved. This has to do with our daily walk and growth in the life of Christ and the Spirit. This we call sanctification. And salvation has to do also with our final glory in Christ. As Paul said, "When Christ Who is our life appears, then you also will appear with Him in glory" (Col. 3:4). That we call glorification.

Another bishop when asked the question, "Have you been saved?" replied, "I have." "And when were you saved?" he was asked. The bishop replied immediately "On a Friday afternoon at three o'clock in the spring of the year 33 A.D. on a hill outside the City of Jerusalem."

That is when we were all saved, but God will not force this salvation upon us. We must—each of us—accept it personally as the great gift of God's love. We were saved in baptism which is our personal Golgotha. Baptism is the *tomb* where "we were baptized into His death" (Rom. 6:3); it is also the *womb* from which we were born anew receiving within us the life of Christ.

WORK OUT YOUR SALVATION

We were saved at baptism but we must continue to "work out" our salvation for the rest of our lives by daily serving, loving, obeying, and following Jesus.

When you stand before God's altar to be married, you are pronounced man and wife in the Lord. You are married right then and there. No one can argue that point. But it is equally true that you will work out your marriage from that moment on till the end of your life together. As two wills seek to become one, your marriage becomes what God ordained it to be.

In Jeremiah 3:14 the Lord said to His people, "I am married to you." Our relationship to God is like a marriage relationship. More than anything else God wants our love, our heart. He wants us! In the Christian life, as in marriage, two wills are involved; God's will and ours. Jesus constantly yielded His will to the Father. It was the last thing He did before He went to the cross. That kind of obedience is not easy. And it is not something we can do once and forget. It is a way of life—a constant yielding of our will to God's will daily. Each time we choose God's will we are working out our salvation. In the words of St. Paul, "Therefore, my beloved . . . work out your own salvation with fear and trembling" (Phil. 2:12).

DAILY CONVERSION

The great saints of the Church were humble men and women who radiated grace and love. They were not converted once. Nor did they repent just once. Their life was a daily conversion and a constant repentance. They were saved once on the cross at Golgotha, but they were also being saved daily in the yielding of their will to Jesus. Daily they sinned and daily they repented. Daily they fell and daily they rose.

We have been saved but we *are also being* saved. "For the word of the cross is folly to those who are perishing but *to us who are being saved* it is the power of God" (I Cor. 1:18).

In the parable of the Pharisee and the Tax Collector, the proud Pharisee thought he was saved. His prayer was, "Thank God, I have made it! I am where I am supposed to be. Everyone else is below me on the ladder somewhere. I am not like other men. Would that they were all as good as I am." It was that kind of spiritual pride that condemned the Pharisee. The poor tax collector, on the other hand, was on a much lower level of spirituality and virtue, and he knew it. He acknowledged his sinfulness and, realizing the unlimited possibilities for growth, he moved on.

A CONSTANT MOVING TOWARD GOD

In Orthodox theology salvation is not static but dynamic; it is not a completed state, a state of having arrived, a state of having made it, but a constant moving toward theosis, toward becoming like Christ, toward receiving the fullness of God's life. And it can never be achieved fully in this life.

The more the great saints of the Church grew in their knowledge of Jesus, the more they realized their imperfection and sinfulness. When a saint was told, "You are a thief," he would agree that he was. "You are a liar." He would agree that he was. "You are a fornicator." He would agree that he was. The saints realized that we can lie, steal and fornicate in thought as well as in deed. Like the sinful tax collector they prayed the Jesus Prayer constantly: "Lord Jesus, Son of God, be merciful to me a sinner." They were saved at Golgotha, having died and risen with Christ in baptism. And they were being saved daily through repentance and the yielding of their mind, heart and will to God. And they looked forward to their glorification with Jesus at the Second Coming.

A CRY FOR SALVATION

People today are not running to church with the question: "What must I do to be saved?" But when they run to psychiatrists, when they take large doses of drugs, when they drown themselves with alcohol, when they try to resign from the human race, when they complain that life is not worth living and try to commit suicide, what are they doing but confessing a need—a need to be saved from themselves, from the sin and death of their daily existence.

AN INNER SALVATION

The salvation we are looking for is not to be found in education, or politics, or economics but in Christ. It is a spiritual, an inner salvation, which in turn produces an outer salvation. Changed people produce a changed society. The peace and the fulfillment we are all searching for can be found in a relationship to God that only Jesus can bring. "Peace I leave with you," He said, "my peace I give to you; not as the world gives do I give to you (John 14:27).

Jesus did not come to condemn us because we had become enslaved to sin. He came to save us by breaking the bonds of sin and death.

Recall the words of St. Gregory of Nyssa:

"Our nature was sick and needed a doctor.
Man had fallen and needed someone to raise him up.
He who ceased to participate in the good needed
    someone to bring him back to it.
He who was shut in darkness needed the presence
    of life.
The prisoner was looking for someone to ransom him,
The captive for someone to take his part.
He who was under the yoke of slavery was
    looking for someone to set him free."

"WHO WILL SAVE ME . . . ?"

A great scientist asked once, "The wild universe may yet be tamed; but the inner world of man's life, with its ignorance, prejudice, bitterness, instability, passion and sin—who will tame that?"

Years before this scientist, a great saint asked the same question in a different way:

"I do not understand my own actions. For I do not do what I want, but I do the very thing I hate. . . So then it is no longer I that do it, but sin which dwells within me. . . Wretched man that I am! Who will deliver me from this body of death? Thanks be to God through Jesus Christ our Lord!" (Romans 7:15, 17, 24-25).

Who shall deliver me? Thank God for Jesus Who came not to judge me but to deliver me from this body of sin and death!

YESTERDAY SAVIOR—TOMORROW JUDGE!"

Years ago a young lawyer, at the risk of his own life, grabbed the reins of a runaway team of horses and saved a man's life. The wagon turned over but the man was not seriously hurt. He dusted himself off and thanked the lawyer.

The scene has changed. More than twenty years have passed. The lawyer is now a respected judge. The place is the judge's courtroom. A man has been tried for murder and convicted. Prior to formal sentencing the judge asks the accused if he has anything to say. He indicates that he does.

He comes close to the judge's bench and says, "Judge, don't you remember me?" The judge replies, "No, I don't remember having met you prior to this trial." "But, Judge," the man answers, "don't you remember saving a man's life by turning a team of runaway horses twenty years ago?" "Oh, yes," replies the judge, "I remember that as though it were yesterday."

"Judge, I am that man," the accused states, "you were my savior then, can't you be my savior now?" The Christian judge dropped his head and when he had regained his composure he said, *"Yesterday I was your savior, but today I must be your judge."*

Jesus did not come to judge the world but to save the world. But one day He must come to judge the world. Today He is our Saviour. Tomorrow he will be our judge. How shall we meet Him at the end, as Savior or Judge?

WHAT ARE WE SAVED FOR?

Jesus came to save us from sin. Once saved, sin becomes an incident in the life of the Christian—not a practice. Love becomes the practice, not just an occasional incident—the love of Jesus. We are saved from sin *for* love. The non-judgemental, accepting, forgiving love of Jesus must flow through us to others. "Above all, put on love which binds everything together in perfect harmony" (Col. 3:14).

Secondly, we are saved *for* fruit bearing. The purpose of the True Vine (Jesus) and the branches (the members of His Body, the Christians) is the same: to bear fruit for God, to carry God's saving love to the world. Every branch that bears not fruit, He takes away. This is what we are saved for. We are made branches on the True Vine, members of Christ's Body, that the head (Jesus) may have us to carry out His saving work in the world today, that through us Jesus may bring life to men. We are saved not in order to sit around this world as ornaments. We are saved to love, to serve, to bear witness, to confess Jesus among men, to bear the fruit of the Heavenly Vine for dying men and women to eat and live.

WHAT IS SALVATION

What does it mean to be saved? What is salvation in Christ?

Salvation is freedom—freedom from the tyranny of self centeredness, freedom from the bondage of fear and death.

Salvation in Christ is being freed from myself so that I can become the person God created me to be and intends me to become.

Salvation is God lifting us up in Christ Jesus. It is God giving us hope. It is God working an unrelenting work in our personalities, in our characters, in our lives. It is God not giving up on us.

Salvation according to Orthodox theology is not the state of "I have arrived. I have made it. I am saved." Rather, it is the state of "I am on the way. I am moving. I am growing in God, for God, with God, and through the power of God."

Salvation is Christ overcoming for us our greatest enemy which is at the root of all our insecurity, the fear of death. God does not remain aloof in the heavens while men suffer and die. He takes on a body and by His death destroys our death so that now death becomes a doorway through which we must all pass to enter the splendor of His glorious presence.

> Salvation is:
> liberation from evil,
> the defeat of the devil,
> the transfiguration of man,
> living authentically,
> putting on Christ,
> the restoration of the image of God in man,
> participating in the life of God,
> restoration of communion with God,
> incorruption,
> receiving the Holy Spirit,
> becoming temples of the Holy Spirit,
> forgiveness of sins,
> ascending to the throne of God,
> participating in the kingdom of God,
> being by grace what God is by nature,
> the destruction of death,
> seeing the light,
> being in a process of growth that never ends,
> living life the way God meant it to be.

This is the salvation the Lord Jesus offers us.

POSITIVE SALVATION

The Orthodox Church has always emphasized the more positive aspect of salvation. Salvation for the Orthodox Church has not meant only justification or forgiveness of sins: it means also the renewing and restoration of God's image in man, the lifting up of fallen humanity through Christ into the very life of God. Christ forgives man and frees him from sin that he may proceed to fulfill this destiny, which is to become like God.

Christ came to save us *from* sin *for* participation in the life of God. This exalted vision of the Christian life was expressed by St. Peter when he wrote that we are invited "to become partakers of the Divine Nature" (2 Peter 1:4). It was also affirmed by St. Basil the Great when he described man as "the creature who has received an order to become god." The whole emphasis of the Orthodox way of life is on "putting on Christ" and receiving the Holy Spirit through prayer and the Sacraments so that we may begin to live a new life in union with Christ and in communion with the Holy Spirit.

THREE CONVERSIONS

In his book "The Year of Grace of the Lord," a monk of the Eastern Church writes about the three conversions that should take place in the life of an Orthodox

Christian according to God's plan of salvation:

"... in spiritual life three stages can be discerned, which are comparable to three conversions. The first conversion is the meeting of the soul with our Lord, when He is followed as a Friend and as a Master. The second conversion is a personal experience of pardon and salvation, of the cross and . . . resurrection. The third conversion is the coming of the Holy Spirit into the soul like a flame and with power. It is by this conversion that man is established in a lasting union with God. Christmas or Epiphany, then Easter, and finally Pentecost correspond the these three conversions." [1]

SAVED BY GRACE

St. Paul assures us that we are saved *by* grace *through* faith. Let us examine first the word *grace:* What is it? Grace is a gift rather than a wage we earn. It cannot be deserved. Sin give wages. God gives grace. "For the wages of sin is death, but the free gift of God is eternal life in Christ Jesus our Lord" (Rom. 6:23). "For by grace you have been saved through faith; and this is not your own doing, it is the gift of God—not because of works, lest any man should boast" (Eph. 2:8).

There is a story about a man who went to heaven. He was met at the pearly gates by Peter, who said, "It will take 1000 points for you to be admitted. The good works you did during your lifetime will determine your points."

The man said, "Unless I was sick, I attended church every Sunday, and I sang in the choir."

"That will be 50 points," Peter said.

"And I gave to the church liberally," the man added.

"That is worth 25 more points," said Peter

The man, realizing that he had only 75 points, started getting desperate. "I taught a Sunday school class," he said. "That's a great work for God."

"Yes," said Peter. "That's worth 25 points."

The man was frantic. "You know," he said, "at this rate the only way I'm going to get into heaven is by the grace of God."

Peter smiled. "That's 900 points! Come on in!"

In this world we get what we pay for, people say. Do we? What can we ever pay for the grace of God? What can we ever pay for His love? What can we ever pay for His sacrifice on the cross?

Grace is the unlimited pouring out of God's mercy. It is God's unconditional forgiveness offered to the unworthy. It is God accepting us as His children in Baptism, filling us with His Holy Spirit in Confirmation, and then sending Jesus to live in our hearts through Holy Communion. It is God loving us when we are unlovable. "But God shows His love for us in that while we were yet sinners Christ died for us" (Rom. 5:8).

THROUGH FAITH

We are saved by grace *through* faith. What is the role of faith in God's plan of salvation? Faith is saying "yes" to God's gracious gift of salvation. It is the

---

[1] *"The Year of Grace of the Lord,"* by a Monk of the Eastern Church. SVS Press. Crestwood, NY.

humble acceptance of God's gracious gift. It is the hand that takes the blessing. It receives what God gives, not as something we deserve, but as a gift of His grace. It is the marriage of Christ—the Bridegroom—to the bride which is my soul. Faith is the handle by which I grasp God's power and apply it to my weakness. It is remembering when I feel utterly worthless that I am the one for whom God gave His Son. Faith is the eye by which we look to Jesus; the hand by which we lay hold of Jesus; the tongue by which we taste the sweetness of the Lord; the foot by which we go to Jesus. Faith is Forsaking All I Take Him. F-A-I-T-H. Faith is man's hand reaching up to grasp the already outstretched hand of God's grace. "By grace you have been saved *through* faith "(Eph. 2:8). When man's hand (faith) grasps God's hand (grace), there is reconciliation and salvation.

A WORD ABOUT GOOD WORKS AND OUR SALVATION

The person who has accepted Christ, been baptized and received the Holy Spirit begins a new life which is expressed in love through good deeds. A person is not saved by faith alone but by faith which expresses itself through love as St. Paul writes. St. James asks, "What does it profit, my brethren, if a man says he has faith but has no works? Can his faith save him? If a brother or sister is ill-clad and in lack of daily food, and one of you says to them 'Go in peace, be warmed and filled,' without giving them the things needed for the body, what does it profit? So faith by itself, if it has no works, is dead" (James 2:14-17).

NOT MERITORIOUS

The good works that we do, do not earn us any special merit points in heaven. We can never buy God's love with them since Jesus specifically tells us: "So you also, when you have done all that is commanded you, say, 'We are unworthy servants; we have only done what was our duty' " (Luke 17:10).

Our good deeds do not put God in our debt. It is God's love in Christ that puts us forever in His debt. Our good deeds are a grateful response, a feeble attempt on our part to show appreciation to God for what He has done for us. We can never fully accomplish all that we should do, but neither should we stop trying. Love will not let us. "The love of Christ controls us," says Paul (2 Cor. 5:14).

CREATED FOR GOOD WORKS

Paul writes in Ephesians 2:10, "For we are His workmanship, created in Christ Jesus for good works, which God prepared beforehand, that we should walk in them." This verse seems to contradict the one just before it: "For by grace you have been saved through faith; and this is not your own doing, it is the gift of God—not because of works lest any man should boast" (Ephesians 2:8-9). One verse says: "You have been saved . . . not because of works," and the next says: "Created in Christ Jesus for good works."

A NEW CREATION PRODUCES NEW WORKS

Far from contradicting each other, these verses give us the Orthodox Christian position concerning good works. Good works do not produce salvation, but salvation produces good works. We are not saved because of good works, but we are saved for good works. Christ makes each one of us a new creation, a new being. The new being, through the power of the indwelling Trinity, produces new works. Christ does not begin by changing our deeds. He begins by changing us. The good deeds flow by God's grace out of the new person.

COUNTERFEIT WORKS

Only those good works that are done in the name of Christ are the fruit of the Holy Spirit. Good deeds—even the best—are worthless in a person who does not believe in Christ. A work is good only insofar as it is done in Christ and by the power of the Holy Spirit. For the Christian there is no good work apart from this.

A story is told of a ten-dollar bill that got into circulation and did a lot of good. It helped buy coal for a needy old woman; it helped buy medicine for a very sick child; and even showed up in the collection plate in church one Sunday morning. Then it fell into the hands of a bank teller who spotted it immediately as a counterfeit. The test is not how many good deeds we claim to our credit, but rather, can they pass inspection in the sight of God? Were our good deeds done in Christ and for Christ? Or are they products of pride: trying to parade our goodness or to buy God's favor and place Him in our debt?

We are created for those good works that are done in Christ and for Christ. All others are counterfeit; they cannot pass inspection in God's sight.

A SHOWPLACE OF GOOD DEEDS

The early Church was a showplace of good works done for Christ. Having been made a new creation in Christ, those early Christians began to produce new deeds that astounded the pagan world.

In one of the earliest apologetic works preserved, Justin the Martyr (d. 165), writes:

> "We used to value above all else money and possessions; now we bring together all that we have and share it with those who are in need (cf. Acts 4:34-37). Formerly we hated and killed one another and, because of a difference in nationality or custom, we refused to admit strangers within our gates. Now since the coming of Christ, we all live in peace. We pray for our enemies and seek to convert those who hate us unjustly . . ." (I Apology XIV).

Tertullian (160-220) said: "It is our care for the helpless, our practice of lovingkindness, that brands us in the eyes of many of our opponents. 'Only look,' they say, 'look how they love one another' " (Apology XXXIX).

"And let our people learn to apply themselves to good deeds, so as to help cases of urgent need, and not to be unfruitful." These words of St. Paul found eager expression in the lives of the early Christians who as we see from the history of the early Church:

1. gave alms to help the destitute (even poor Christians were urged to give through fasting);
2. supported widows and orphans;
3. supported the sick, the infirm, the poor, and the disabled (even establishing hospitals in many cities);
4. cared for prisoners and slaves
5. found work for those who were unemployed;
6. cared for those who journeyed;
7. cared for the victims of great calamities.

SUMMARY

Summarizing what we have said on the subject of salvation:

1. We have been saved form sin and death through baptism which is our personal Golgotha (Justification).
2. We are being saved daily as we repent of our sins and continue our walk with Jesus yielding our will to Him in humble obedience (Sanctification).
3. We shall be saved at the end of time. When Jesus comes again we shall share in His glorification.
4. Salvation is constant growth in the life of Christ, a dynamic movement toward theosis (becoming like Christ, receiving the fullness of God's life).
5. He Who is our Savior today will be our Judge tomorrow.
6. We are saved *from* sin *for* putting on Christ, *for* love, *for* fruit-bearing, *for* serving, *for* confessing Christ among men, *for* becoming partakers of divine nature.
7. We are not saved *by* good works. A new person in Christ produces good works in and by the Holy Trinity for God's glory. We cannot earn salvation through good works. They are our grateful response to God's love.
8. We are saved *by* grace (Salvation is God's gift) *through* faith, which is man reaching out to accept God's gift.

We Are the Church
Of the Early Fathers

"This here town has been mighty good to me," boomed the guest of honor at a reception honoring his fifty years of service to the community. "When I first arrived here, I was an inexperienced tenderfoot with only one suit on my back and all my worldly possessions wrapped in a red bandana over my shoulder. Today I own the bank, the newspaper, the two hotels, nine oil wells and the TV station!"

Later an impressed visitor asked, "Would you tell us just what was in that red bandana when you arrived here fifty years ago?"

"Let's see now," mused the guest of honor. "If I recall rightly, I was carrying over $400,000 in cash and $750,000 in negotiable securities."

This describes the Orthodox immigrant arriving in America years ago. What was in his bandana was far more precious than cash and securities. It was the Pearl of Great Price: our Lord Jesus and the heritage of a living faith going all the way back to the apostles.

REMEMBER WHAT YOUR FATHERS DID

Some time ago a father wanted his 14-year-old son to see Omaha Beach. He wanted him to see where once he had stood between life and death. Then he had been a lieutenant colonel with the Rangers in the United States Army. As he and his boy stood on the naked beach of France, everything became vivid in his mind. He recalled the scaling of the walls; he experienced again the fierce combat; he remembered the horrors of war. Everything he touched—a rotting piece of rope, an iron hook, a rusty chain, a broken tree—came back to life. It stood for something. Like the warriors of Joshua's time, he wanted to say to his son, "Remember what your father did."

As the Lutheran Church says, "Remember Martin Luther." As the Methodist Church says, "Remember John Wesley." As the Presbyterian Church says, "Remember John Calvin," so the Orthodox Church has always said, "Remember the Church Fathers. Remember the ancient, undivided, apostolic Church and do not depart from its catholic faith."

A LIVING CONNECTION WITH THE
ENTIRE PAST EXPERIENCE OF THE CHURCH

The Orthodox Church is often called the Church of the Fathers because she maintains a living connection with the early Church Fathers. We are not a Church that was instituted a few years ago, or even a few centuries ago. The early Fathers are part of our church history. In fact, our Church came to be called Orthodox, meaning true faith, because of the great emphasis the early Fathers of the Greek Church placed upon preserving the true faith of Christ. As Orthodox Christians, we have inherited all the experience of 19 centuries of Christian living and thinking and believing and witnessing and dying. We have behind us millions of believing men and women of every tribe and tongue, witnessing to the truth of the Gospel, often dying for it in order to hand it down to us.

That is why when we Orthodox Christians pick up the Bible to read it, we do not act as if these 19 centuries of church history did not exist. We read the Bible and we gain a better understanding of it because we consider how the Holy Spirit has guided the Church Fathers in the past to interpret Scripture. This is what we mean by Sacred Tradition. We do not mean, as Fr. Florovsky emphasizes, the traditions of men or a slavish attachment to the past. By Sacred Tradition we mean A LIVING CONNECTION WITH THE ENTIRE PAST EXPERIENCE OF THE CHURCH, nineteen centuries of it during which the Holy Spirit has been protecting and defining and proclaiming the truth of Christ through the Church.

EMPHASIS ON COMMUNITY

There is a great sense of community in the Orthodox Church. Orthodox Christians never pray alone. We pray together with all the saints who have passed on. We pray not as individuals, but as members of the body of Christ, i.e., the Church. We pray with the Theotokos, the apostles, the angels, the martyrs and the saints of all ages. They are present at every liturgy as depicted in the iconography of our Church. Around the figure of Christ in the dome are gathered the angels, apostles, saints and martyrs on the walls. All these constitute the Church Triumphant in heaven. Then we, the congregation, on the ground-floor of the Church, represent the Church Militant on earth. Thus around the figure of Christ in the dome is gathered for every liturgy the entire Church, both that in heaven and that on earth.

Dr. Howard Rome, psychiatrist at the Mayo Clinic, said once that when he sits with a patient in a room, he considers that he is not alone with the patient. Behind the patient, he says, stand like a Greek chorus, all the people with whom the patient has ever lived. They are all in the room with him, for they have left their indelible mark on this patient's personality either for good or ill.

The Orthodox Church reminds us that we do not stand alone. Behind us stands a cloud of witnesses. Behind us, for example, stand the 318 Church Fathers who came to the First Ecumenical Council. They came, bearing the scars of martyrdom, some with one eye and some with one arm. Some without legs and some with disfigured faces. They came with twisted and paralyzed limbs. They came from all over the Empire to bear witness with their whole personality to the truth they believed: that Jesus Christ is Lord.

These martyrs stand behind us. And behind them stand others: Peter and James and Stephen and Ignatius and Polycarp and Paul and Athanasius and Chrysostom—a whole aremy of noble martyrs who rejoiced that they were counted worthy to suffer for the name of Christ.

ORTHODOXY IS NOT ONE MAN'S EXPERIENCE OF GOD

In criticizing Paul Tillich's view of Christology (the study of who Christ is) Fr. George Tavard writes, ``. . . I believe in the existence of objective criteria in Christological matters. The norm of Christology cannot be the new insights that theologians may reach; it must always be the consistent interpretation of Jesus the

Christ that has developed in the Church along the lines set by the orthodox Fathers in the theological controversies of the early centuries of Christianity. Should Tillich's Christology stray from this standard, it must be branded as a betrayal of Christ himself." [1] In other words, the truth of the Orthodox Christian faith can never be based on one person's experience or thought of God, but on that of the whole of redeemed humanity. An Orthodox Christian would never say, "This has to be the truth because I know I had a special revelation from Christ or the Holy Spirit." That "special revelation" must agree and not depart from the collective Christian experience of the Church as a whole from the apostles down to the present. The Church Fathers are not dead. They still speak to us of their vast experience. We benefit from that experience. We still drink from the wells of their inspiration and wisdom.

WE OWE A GREAT DEBT

We owe a great debt to the Church Fathers. Where would we be without the liturgies of St. John Chrysostom and St. Basil the Great? the beautiful Kontakia of Romanos the Melodist? the precise definitions of Orthodoxy by St. John of Damascus? the glorious Nicene Creed? the exquisitely magnificent hymns written by monks and fathers in the early monasteries where prayer was a way life? the inspiring Jesus Prayer? the definitions of Christ and the Trinity as formulated by the Ecumenical Councils? the sublime icons? How many others have labored in our behalf that we could come to this hour as Orthodox Christians? All that we have, all that we are, the great treasure of our faith has been bought with enormous price. We are not our own. We were bought with a price none can repay. We are debtors living on great gifts from the past.

Hopefully, what Edward R. Murrow once said of Britain's heroic stand against Nazi tyranny may be said of us: "Unconsciously they dug deep into their history and felt that Drake, Raleigh, Cromwell, and all the rest were looking down at them and they were obliged to look worthy in the eyes of their ancestors."

WITNESSES TO THE TRUE FAITH OF CHRIST

The Orthodox Church honors the Fathers not because they are witnesses of antiquity, or of a very ancient faith. She honors them because they are witnesses of the *true* faith, witnesses of the *truth* of Christ. This is the faith the apostles received from Christ and passed on to us (I Cor. 11:23). The Church Fathers are witnesses and guarantors of that complete and unaltered truth given to us by Christ and the Holy Spirit. Thus, behind Basil and Chrysostom, John the Baptist and John the Theologian, Gregory of Nyssa and Symeon the New Theologian—behind them all—stands Jesus the Christ and His saving truth. We are not saved by the Church Fathers, but we are indebted to them because they are the earthen vessels who bring to us the great treasure which is Christ.

THE DANGERS OF A RICH TRADITION

There is a great danger involved in possessing a rich tradition as we Orthodox Christians do. One of the dangers was pointed out by the historian Gibbon who

[1] *"Paul Tillich and the Christian Message,"* George H. Tavard,

describes some of the degeneration of Christianity under the Greek scholars of the 10th century, who handled the literature and spoke the language of the spiritual but knew not the life: "They held in their lifeless hands the riches of their fathers without inheriting the spirit which had created and imparted that sacred patrimony. They read; they praised; they compiled; but their languid souls seemed alike incapable of thought and action." Admittedly, Gibbon was for the most part ignorant of and prejudiced against the Eastern Church. Nonetheless he pointed out a real danger for those who have inherited a rich patrimony.

Another danger is that our theology become merely a theology of repetition. While referring to the fathers is a method of maintaining continuity with the faith of the early Church, the practice can undermine and restrict the theological vigor of Orthodox theology. We are not just pulled by the past; we are also pulled by the future. There has to be a balance between the two. The pull of the past can be so strong as to neutralize the pull to the future. We must be open to the old without being closed to the new. The future is more than just clinging to the past. Fr Florovsky wrote, "It is a dangerous habit just to handle 'quotations' from the Fathers . . . outside of the total structure of faith, in which only they are truly alive. 'To follow the Fathers' does not mean simply to quote their sentences. It means *to acquire their mind,* their *phenomena.*" [2]

Another danger of inheriting the rich tradition of the Fathers is pointed out by Professor von Campenhausen: "The Fathers had become so holy that in the end they could no longer beget any sons who were their equal in vitality. . . Imprisoned in their own territorial and cultural confines, their Church rested upon its own perfection. It trusted in an unchanging and indestructible continuity with the apostles and Fathers of the past whose achievements it admired so much that it failed to observe the changing nature of the problems which faced theology. It preserved their intellectual inheritance without doing anything to renew it." [3]

Another way of stating this would be to say that we live by clipping coupons. Our fathers and grandfathers amassed the capital. Boasting about how much they had on deposit, we live on the interest without adding to the capital. But when the capital is used up, the coupons are useless. We have to keep adding to the capital.

We have two kinds of possessions—the things we inherit and the things we achieve. A rich inheritance can often make us complacent and prevent us from achieving.

Preserving the treasures of the past is important. But Orthodox Christianity is not just a past greatness. The Church Fathers have established the foundations. It is up to us to keep building on those foundations.

A PROCESSION OF TORCH BEARERS

When the 1964 Olympic Games opened in Tokyo, the Olympic Flame was brought by plane from Olympia, Greece, the site of the first Olympics in 776 B.C. From the plane the burning torch was carried by relays of runners, who passed the flame from one to the next until it reached the site of the games. It linked the Olympic Games in Tokyo with their source in the past.

---

[2] *"Aspect of Church History"* G. Ftorovsky. Nordland Press.
[3] *"The Fathers of the Greek Church"* Von Campenhausen. Panthcon.

As Christians we are all "torch bearers." We have received the light of life from its source in God. The torch was handed to us by a great line of believers stretching back to Christ himself—apostles, martyrs, saints. It is our privilege and duty to pass it on to others.

Einstein said once, "A hundred times every day I remind myself that my inner and outer life depend on the labors of other men, living and dead. I must exert myself in order to give in the measure as I have received and am still receiving." Think of those 318 Church Fathers—many of them blinded and crippled for their faith—meeting in Nicea in 325 A.D. to pass on to us the lighted torch of Christ. Think of what they suffered to place the torch in our hands today.

Violinist Jascha Heifetz has virtually retired from the concert stage to devote his talents to teaching. Explaining why he did this, he said, "I should like to pass on what I know to my pupils. To be an artist is like being entrusted with something precious for a brief time. It is the duty of an artist to hand it on, like those Greek runners who passed on the lighted torch, one to another."

We are all entrusted for a brief time with something precious—the Lord Jesus Christ "in whom are hid all the treasures of wisdom and knowledge" and, as the Gospel says, "whom to know is life eternal." We are entrusted with the apostolic faith. This is the lighted torch we are to pass on to our children and to our friends who do not know Christ.

A spectator told of watching the 1948 Olympic Games in London. A relay race was on. The French team had started well. But as the torch was being passed to the third runner he dropped it. The accident put the team out of the running. The runner threw himself on the ground, flung his hands to his head in a gesture of despair and openly wept. His emotional outburst continued as he was led from the area.

To take defeat so tearfully might seem a bit unsportsmanlike. But one should remember how many persons were involved in that runner's failure. There were his watching compatriots, whose hopes were dashed. There were the teammates who had run before him and whose work was ruined by his blunder. And then there were the runners who were to come after but who never got the chance to run because of the accident.

The whole spectacle made that spectator realize how much life was like a relay race. In the race of life, no one starts from scratch. Others have run the race before us. Still others wait to run the race after us. If we fail to pass on the lighted torch they have given us, we fail not only them but we also deprive countless others in the future of the light of Christ.

CHURCH FATHERS: A PERMANENT DIMENSION OF THE CHURCH

St. Symeon the New Theologian regarded as the most dangerous heresy the notion that the Church no longer possesses the same fulness of the charismata as it did in ancient times. The same gifts are assured to those who today, as yesterday, seek them in humility and self-surrender. To have Church Fathers is a permanent dimension of the Church.

We Orthodox have a great past, a great tradition. We are proud of this. But we must not live in the past. Where are our John Chrysostoms today? our Basils?

our Gregories? our new Athanasius, John of Damascus? We have the apostolic doctrine. We have the apostolic succession. But we can have, too, the apostolic power of the Holy Spirit to produce new and powerful witnesses for the Lord today, new Church Fathers—not carbon copies of the old but originals as they were. For God is always more interested in producing originals than carbon copies.

The Orthodox Church is not a museum of the first thousand years of Christianity. We must not succumb to the temptation that the Fathers have said everything and that all we have to do is to repeat them verbatim. Father Florovsky has reminded us that the notion of "father" is not limited to the period called "Patristic." St. Gregory of Palamas, for example, was a "Church Father" in the fourteenth century. To repeat, to have Church Fathers is a permanent dimension of the Church. The Fathers beget us in the faith that we in turn might become fathers, that is, free creators under the inspiration of the same Holy Spirit who empowered and guided the early Fathers.

RE-OPENING CHOKED WELLS

The Old Testament describes the great watering places which the patriarch Abraham planned and provided at strategic places in Palestine. When the Philistines pillaged the land, these wells were despoiled and filled. Isaac, Abraham's son, made it his business to re-open the well-springs of his father.

We must re-open the wells dug by the Church Fathers not only to receive refreshment from them but also to examine and see what were the qualities that made them great. Let us examine some of these qualities.

WHAT MADE THE CHURCH FATHERS GREAT:
A. THE PRIORITY OF KNOWING GOD

St. Basil wrote, "As our body cannot live without breathing, so our soul cannot keep alive without knowing the Creator; for the ignorance of God is the death of the soul." What made the Church Fathers such great and fervent witnesses of Christ was that for them to know God was the supreme privilege and task of life.

The Apostle John writes, "And this is life eternal, that they may know thee, the only true God, and Jesus Christ, whom Thou hast sent" (John 17:3). The supreme blessing of the human soul is that it can know God. The supreme tragedy is that often it does not want to know Him, being distracted by the things of this world.

The Catechism tells us that we were born for nothing else. We live for no other purpose than to know, love, and serve God on earth, and to enjoy Him for all eternity.

We read in Jeremiah 9:23-24, "Let not the wise man glory in his wisdom, let not the mighty man glory in his might, let not the rich man glory in his riches; but let him who glories glory in this, that he understands and knows me, that I am the Lord who practices kindness, justice, and righteousness in the earth; for in these I delight, says the Lord."

The purpose of all Christian preaching and teaching is to get to know God. By this we mean not just to get to know *about* Him, but to get to *know* Him. There is a world of difference between knowing about someone and really knowing him.

When the Bible talks about knowing God, it does not mean knowing certain ideas *about* Him, but knowing Him *personally*. The word *know* in Hebrew means knowledge that comes from a close, intimate relationship. "This is eternal life that they may know Thee and Jesus Christ Whom Thou hast sent." *"Know Thee"*, not *"about Thee"*. Knowing about God or Christ does not save, does not give eternal life. Knowing Christ does.

The essence of Christianity is a direct personal encounter between two persons—ourselves and God. Man is called to establish an intimate, deeply personal I-Thou relationship with God.

Getting to know someone is difficult—very difficult—unless the other person chooses to open up and reveal himself to us. God has already done this in Christ. He has opened Himself up. This is why we Christians believe that it is impossible to know God apart from Christ. "No one has ever seen God; the only Son, who is in the bosom of the Father, he has made him known" (John 1:18). Only He who is in the bosom of the Father—in the closest possible relationship to Him—can make God known. This is why St. Paul said, "I decided to know nothing among you except Jesus Christ and Him crucified." It is only by Christ that we can come to know God not as a distant, remote, unapproachable deity, but as a Friend who loves and cares personally and intimately.

We come to know God by spending time with Him in prayer every day, in divine worship every Sunday, and by reading His personal letter to us—the Holy Bible. One cannot really know a person if one is not willing to spend time with him. The Church Fathers spent much time with Jesus. They knew Him personally.

B. THEY EXPERIENCED GOD

The Church Fathers not only knew God personally, they also experienced His presence and power in their lives.

"Of the three ways of acquiring knowledge," said Roger Bacon, "authority, reasoning, experience, only the last (experience) is effective."

Walt Whitman was listening one night to an astronomer lecturing on the stars. The hall was stuffy, the lecture dull, and the charts even more dull, until, says Whitman, "I could no longer bear it. I rose and wandered out into the night and looked up at the stars themselves. I was overcome with breathless wonder."

There are people today who do the same with their religion. They stay inside poring over the charts and diagrams, memorizing the number of sacraments, concentrating on the mere mechanism of faith. They will not walk outside to see the stars for themselves. They need to proceed from theory to experience, from knowledge *about* God, which is abstract, to knowledge *of* God in Christ, which is personal.

For example, every Easter churches are filled to overflowing. If the Easter crowds really believed in the resurrection of Jesus, *really believed it,* the church would not be half-empty on the Sunday following Easter. It would be bursting at the seams. The resurrection is real, but people need to experience it in their own lives. They need to experience the power of Christ to resurrect them from their own dead hopes, dead dreams, dead lives, from the deadness of sin, to a new life, a life of glory and peace and hope and joy in the Lord.

God cannot be fully expressed. In fact, a God fully defined is no God, but He can be experienced. He expressed Himself once in the Person of Jesus. The purpose of that expression was that He might be experienced in the lives of His people as Emmanuel—God with us.

St. Macarius states that Christians do, and even must, experience consciously the presence of the Spirit in their hearts. His definition of the Christian faith as a personal experience of God was adopted by St. Symeon the New Theologian and other great saints of our Church.

The great appeal of the so-called "charismatics" is that they satisfy the need for man to experience God. The appeal to the intellect is not enough. The heart, too, has needs of which the intellect is unaware. God can be known intellectually, but He becomes real when He is experienced personally.

No one can ever prove to you that Christ is the Son of God. You've got to find out for yourself. It's like love—you can only love by experience, not by reading about it in a book.

That is why the call of God in the Bible is: "Come and see!" When Andrew found Christ, he said to his brother Simon, "I have found the Messiah, the Christ. I do not ask you to take it on my word. I ask that you come and see for yourself." After the Samaritan woman found Christ at the well, she ran to her people and said, "Come, see a man who told me all that I ever did. Can this be the Christ?" That night when they came back, they said to her, "Now we believe, not because you told us: for we have seen and heard Him ourselves, and know that this is indeed the Savior of the world!"

Faith is an experience of God, a living relationship of love with Him, in, with, and through His Son, Jesus. Listen to the Apostle John: "That which . . . we have heard, which we have seen with our eyes, which we have looked upon and touched with our hands . . . (this) we proclaim to you" (I John 1:1-3). Our Orthodox Christian faith is based on the Bible and on Sacred Tradition, but let us not forget that the Bible and Tradition become real when we experience God's presence and power and love personally in our lives. "We have seen . . . we have heard . . . we have touched." We have experienced!

Being an Orthodox Christian is far more than being able to produce a baptismal certificate; it is a personal experience of the Risen Christ, living and reigning in our lives. It is inner peace and freedom, a new sense of direction and purpose in our lives.

We can have experience long before we have explanation. In fact, experience always comes before understanding. Without the experience first, we have nothing to reflect on but abstractions and theories. All of man's attempts to describe beauty are nothing compared to seeing and smelling a beautiful rose. As Orthodox Christians we believe in the Holy Trinity, i.e., that God is Father, Son and Holy Spirit. But first, man *experienced* God as Father. He experienced God as Son in Jesus. He experienced God as Holy Spirit on Pentecost. After the experience came the explanation that we call Holy Trinity. If we separate the experience from the explanation we are talking of empty abstractions. "One thing I know," said the blind man who had been healed by Jesus, "that whereas I was blind, now I see." The experience changed his life. The experience led to faith—a faith that was unshakable as it was real.

How do we gain this personal experience of God that we have been talking about? How did the apostles gain it? It came to them on the day of Pentecost. Jesus commanded them "not to depart from Jerusalem, but to wait for the promise of the Father, which he said, you heard from me, for John baptized with water, but before many days you shall be baptized with the Holy Spirit . . . you shall receive power when the Holy Spirit has come upon you; and you shall be my witnesses in Jerusalem and in all Judea and Samaria and to the end of the earth" (Acts 1:4-5,8).

When the Holy Spirit came on Pentecost, He brought a new and powerful experience of God's presence and power in their lives. They were never the same again. The experience of God in their lives through the presence of the Holy Spirit was powerful and personal.

"I *know* him in whom I have believed," said Paul. I *know*. "*I am persuaded* that nothing shall separate me from the love of God in Christ Jesus." "I *know* that all things work together for good, to make men Christ-like, when the heart loves God." "I *know* that if the earthly tent we live in is dissolved, we have a building of God, a house not made with hands, eternal in the heavens. . ." "I *know*." Here is a faith that was born not of argument or discussion but in the inner experience of living by faith and prayer, obedience and love in the Holy Spirit.

It is not enough that the Christian believe that Jesus Christ or the Holy Trinity live in him, said St. Symeon. That presence must be operative in a way that is consciously experienced. We should be aware of that divine life moving and operating in us just as a pregnant woman is aware that new life stirs within her.

What people want to hear is not God's lawyers presenting logical arguments for His existence but God's witnesses sharing from personal experience what God has done for them. And this is what the early Christians were: *witnesses, martyres*. As someone said of the early Christians: "God? They knew Him! Miracles? They themselves were miracles! Resurrection? They had gone through it! Heaven? They were living in it! Hell? They had escaped it! Reconciliation? They rejoiced in it! Eternal Life? They possessed it!"

Pentecost was the day on which the apostles experienced God's powerful presence in their lives through the Holy Spirit. Through prayer every day can be Pentecost.

C. A RICH HERITAGE OF MEMORIES

A great deal of our Orthodox Christian faith is made up of memories. Memories of Christ. Memories of the apostles. Memories of the Fathers. But memories are museum pieces unless they come alive in us today to fill us with the love, the power and the presence of God. The One Who makes these memories come alive is the Holy Spirit. He is the power of God in action in our lives, the Great Awakener of faith and love, the One Who arouses our memories. As Jesus said, ". . . the Holy Spirit, whom the Father will send in my name, he will teach you all things, *and bring to your remembrance all that I have said to you"* (John 14:26).

That is why the Fathers of the Church keep telling us that the whole purpose of the Christian life is nothing more than the receiving of the Holy Spirit. In the words of St. Seraphim of Sarov: "Prayer, fasting, vigils and all other Christian acts, however good they may be in themselves, certainly do not constitute the aim of our Christian life: they are but the indispensable means of attaining that aim. *For the true aim of the* Christian life is the acquisition of the Holy Spirit of God. As for fasts, vigils, prayer and almsgiving, and other good works done in the name of Christ, they are only the means of acquiring the Holy Spirit of God. . . Prayer is always possible for everyone, rich or poor, noble and simple, strong and weak, healthy and suffering, righteous and sinful. *Great is the power of prayer; most of all does it bring the Spirit of God and easiest of all is it to exercise."*

It is the Holy Spirit Who not only makes the memories of Christ come alive but also helps us *experience* the presence and power of God in our lives so that we speak not *about* Christ but *for* Christ as Christians who know Him personally as the Church Fathers did.

D. THE PEARL OF GREAT PRICE

For the Church Fathers, life with God was the pearl of great price; to possess it they gladly sold all and followed Jesus. Modern man does not recognize the claim of these spiritual ventures that summon all our reserves and strength and endurance in a quest for the Eternal One. We readily grant that the dedicated soldier, the arctic explorer, the artist in the South Seas, the pioneer in space research, the scientist in his laboratory, shall endure unmeasured self-denial, shall risk everything—even life itself—for his own satisfaction or for the enrichment of mankind. Only God is not deemed worthy of such sacrifice.

The dispelling of this error is one of the major messages of the Church Fathers. They gladly forsook all to follow Christ. For example, when St. Anthony was twenty, his parents died, leaving their land and wealth to him. One day in church he heard the priest read Christ's command to the rich young ruler: "One thing you lack; go, sell all, and give to the poor." He felt that the word was addressed to him, and he obeyed. Leaving behind all his possessions, he began not long after, the hermit life in desert solitude which was to contine for about eighty years. He died when more than a hundred years old. By that time thousands had followed his example. He himself had been the counselor of bishops and emperors. His friend, the great St. Athanasius, wrote his biography. It was soon translated and brought to the West where it became an important link in the conversion of St. Augustine.

The example of the Fathers in forsaking all for the Pearl of Great Price—Jesus—points the way for us today. No one deserves the total commitment God deserves. The modern "Christian" who gives his all for his business or profession, neglecting his family and his church—and, in the end, losing both his family and his soul—needs to hear the message of the Fathers.

E. ELDERS AND THE EMPHASIS ON LOVE

The Monastic tradition and literature emphasized greatly the necessity of having an elder. St. Cassian (5th Century) says that it is foolish for someone to think that it is not necessary to have a teacher for the spiritual profession, since for every worldly profession we need one. Not only novices but also experienced monks were expected to follow obediently the advice of Elders, and not to become lawgivers unto themselves. The Elder, who was looked upon as God's instrument, was regarded as the only means by which one could reach the advanced stage of spiritual life (hesychia or quietness). An Elder could never be replaced by books, since his task was not simply to lecture but to know and analyze the inmost thoughts and acts of his disciples. The foremost requirement for the Elder was that he should be full of love for his disciples, to the extent that he should be ready and willing to die for them.

The concept of the importance of an Elder in the religious life of monks tells us something about the importance of priests, church school teachers, and the laity in general in the nurture of Christians today—young and old. The Christian faith is not only taught; it is—even more so—caught from someone who incarnates the love of Christ. When Augustine, for example, wrote about the person who was most instrumental in converting him to Christianity, Bishop Ambrose of Milan, he said, "That man of God received me as a father and showed me kindness. I began to love him, at first not as a teacher of truth, but as a person who was kind to me." Who can estimate the value of an Elder (any priest, monk, or lay person) who radiates the love and kindness of Christ?

F. THE JESUS PRAYER

The Church Fathers can never be understood without prayer. It was the source of their wisdom and power. In addition to prayer as a means of receiving the Holy Spirit, there was the Jesus Prayer whereby in the words of St. Chrysostom, "He (the Christian) should always live with the name of the Lord Jesus so that the heart swallows the Lord and the Lord the heart, and the two become one."

TM (Transcendental Meditation) urges people to meditate quietly on a meaningless word called the mantra. The mantra for the Orthodox Christian is not a meaningless or secret word. It is the Jesus Prayer. "Lord Jesus, Son of the Living God, have mercy on me a sinner." Here is the prayer that unites us to Christ. Here is the prayer through which, if mastered, Jesus actually prays in us. The heart of the prayer is the name "Jesus"—Who is our salvation: "You shall call His name Jesus, for He will save His people from their sins" (Matthew 1:21). The other part of the Jesus Prayer: "have mercy on me a sinner," expresses the bridging of the gulf between the righteousness of God and fallen man. It speaks not only of sin but of its forgiveness: the union of God and man through God's loving mercy in Christ Jesus our Savior.

As Fr. Kallistos Ware writes, "To mention a name prayerfully is to make it come alive. To invoke the name of Jesus with faith is to make Jesus effectively present with us. In the New Testament, devils are cast out in the name of Jesus, for the Name is power."

Prayer was the animating life-blood of the Church Fathers. Can it not be so for us today?

G. THEIR LOVE OF BOOKS

Another animating force of the Church Fathers was their love of books. Foremost among them, of course, was the Bible, great parts of which were often memorized. St. Isaac of Nineveh writes, "A true spirituality is drawn from the bottomless treasure of the Scriptures." Even during meal-time there were readings for the monks, providing them with food for the soul. The whole man was being fed. In some monasteries, where poverty was applied in the strictest sense, an allowance was made for books. A Syrian canon for nuns forbad visitors to give anything for the monastery except a book. When monks had read all the books they possessed, they usually borrowed more books from other monks. In the life of St. Daniel, the Stylite, (409-493), we read:

> "For it is a custom in monasteries that many different books
> should be laid in front of the sanctuary and whichever book a
> brother wants he takes and reads."

The monastic libraries did not contain only religious books, but many different kinds. Especially during the Byzantine period, they were repositories of the ancient knowledge to which many had access. Men who had a love for learning found monasteries to be the best places in which to fulfill their scholastic instincts, and they were always welcome by the monks.

St. Pachomius, the first monastic legislator, laid down rules protecting books and libraries. He wrote, "If someone takes a book and he does not take heed of it, but disdains it, let him make fifty prostrations." Voobus notes another interesting monastic canon which provides for the care of books:

> "Everyone who takes a codex to read or to collate and does
> not return it, or damages the copy, anathema will strike him,
> the leprosy of Gehazi on his soul and body, and the fate of
> Judas the traitor."

If the Church Fathers had such a great love and respect for books, can we today who are called on to carry their torch and pass it on to the coming generations do less?

APOPHEGMATA OR SAYINGS OF THE FATHERS

"The abbot Macarius said, 'If we dwell upon the harms that have been wrought on us by men, we amputate from our mind the power of dwelling upon God' "

"The abbot Mathois said, 'The nearer a man approaches to God, the greater sinner he sees himself to be. For the prophet Isaiah saw God, and said that he was unclean and undone' "

"Again he (abbot Anthony) said, 'That with our neighbor there is life and death: for if we do good to our brother, we shall do good to God: but if we scandalize our brother, we sin against Christ' "

"A brother asked a certain old man, saying, 'There be two brothers, and one of them is quiet in his cell, and prolongs his fast for six days, and lays much travail upon himself: but the other tends the sick. Whose work is the more acceptable to God?' And the old man answered, 'If that brother who carries his fast for six days were to hang himself up by the nostrils, he could not equal the other, who does service to the sick' "

" 'Tell me, Father, what is it to hate evil?' And the old man said, 'He hates evil who hates his own sins, and who blesseth and loveth every one of his brethren' " (p.144).

"They said that a certain old man asked God to let him see the Fathers and he saw them all except Abba Anthony. So he asked his guide, 'Where is Abba Anthony?' He told him in reply that in the place where God is, there Anthony would be"

"Abba Anthony said, 'A time is coming when men will go mad, and when they see someone who is not mad, they will attack him saying, 'You are mad, you are not like us' "

THE CHALLENGE TO ORTHODOXY TODAY

A challenge was addressed some years ago to Orthodox Christians by Krister Stendahl of Harvard. He said:

"The word 'gifts' comes easily to my mind when I think about the Greek Orthodox Church. It must be wonderful to be able to call one's own in a very special manner the Greek Fathers, to participate directly and by oneness of language in the world of the Apostles and the Apostolic Fathers. . .

"Great gifts, indeed, are yours in the Orthodox Church. So great that they may have overwhelmed you and given you the feeling that you can never hope to emulate the greatness of the greats. . . With fear and trembling, I must remind you of the manna in the wilderness. According to the Bible, we know that the manna could not be stored, not even from day to day. Israel had to trust that the gift would be renewed as needed, and those who worked to keep this lavish gift, preserving if for future use, found that is spoiled overnight. That is a word of warning, I think, for anyone who thinks that the gifts of the past, the gift of traditions, can save the Church and feed its people.

"Thus I would love to think that faithfulness to your Orthodox heritage must include a bold recapturing of the fearless and sometimes risky creativity of your great fathers. For their gift was not only their thoughts, but their very style of continuing creative exploration of the faith. I see no valid reason why we should not—by the help of the Spirit—expect your Orthodox theologians to become again the pioneers of theology. To be guardians of the faith is not enough . . . You can do it, and we others are eager for your gift."

As Goethe said, "What you have received from your fathers as an inheritance, you must now gain and develop in order to win it."

SUMMARY

Summarizing what we said about the Church Fathers:

1. They help us maintain a living connection with the early Church.
2. They remind us that we do not stand alone. Even today we are part of a great cloud of witnesses and martyrs extending all the way back to Christ.
3. What we believe today is based not on one person's interpretation or experience of God but on that of the whole redeemed community of God's people (Church Fathers) extending back to the apostles of Christ.
4. The Orthodox Church honors the Fathers not as witnesses of antiquity but as preservers of the complete and unaltered truth give us by Christ.
5. The Church Fathers have placed in our hands the flaming torch of the apostolic faith which our generation is to preserve and pass on the the succeeding generations.
6. To have Church Fathers is a permanent dimension of the Church. We are called to be Church Fathers and Mothers today begetting others and training them in the true faith of Christ.
7. The qualities that distinguished the Church Fathers were: their personal knowledge of God in Christ; their personal experience of the power and presence of God through the Holy Spirit; their faith in Jesus as the Pearl of Great Price; their great emphasis on love; their prayer life; their love of books, especially the Bible.
8. The inheritance we received from the Fathers cannot be hoarded. In order to be gained, it must be appropriated, developed and shared with the world.

What We Believe
About the Church Year

An atheist complained to a friend because Christians had their special holidays, such as Christmas, Easter and the like; and Jews celebrated their holidays such as Passover and Yom Kippur. "But we atheists," he said, "have no recognized national holiday. It's unfair discrimination."

To which his friend replied, "Why don't you celebrate April first?" (April first is Fool's Day in the U.S.A.)

THE CALENDAR TELLS MUCH

A great historian said once that a good way to start historical analysis is by asking of a particular people what holidays they celebrate on their calendar. If one wishes to understand, for example, the Greek people as over against the Jewish people, one can begin by studying what great events they celebrate on their national calendar every year. These events tell much about a people or a nation. To understand the United States, for example, we have to look first at its calendar and the great events it celebrates such as Thanksgiving Day and the Fourth of July.

In the same way, the religious calendar of the Orthodox Church reflects and expresses the whole history and faith of the Church. In the words of F. Heiler, "Its (the Orthodox Church's) liturgical year is . . . a sermon on the mystery of divine love, and this sermon is preached in words more powerful and sublime that any that could come from the mouth of a preacher." [1]

TO KEEP US FROM FORGETTING

A baby struggling to liberate itself from the womb reaches a crisis where he, not his mother, has to do the breathing. To encourage the lungs to make this radical adjustment, the physician gives the baby a sharp slap. The slap is the child's chance to live. The Holy Days of our church calendar are our annual sharp slap to keep us from forgetting events that are vital to our salvation and the abundant life that God wants us to have. It is so easy to forget. We become so immersed in our daily preoccupations that we forget our Lord and we begin to live as if He never came. We need constant reminders of His presence. One such reminder is the church calendar.

UNFOLDS BEFORE US THE LIFE OF CHRIST

The liturgical calendar unfolds before us annually the whole life of Christ from His birth to the ascension and the coming of the Holy Spirit on Pentecost. By bringing into daily focus the great events of the life of Christ, the church year enables the Church to revolve around Him as a satellite around its star. It helps us remember the great events in the history of our salvation and makes them present again mystically so that we may re-live them and participate in them. With the regularity of the yearly cycle, the church calendar reminds us of what God has

[1] *"Urkirche and Ostkirche"* pp 363f.

said and done for us in Christ. The liturgical year is a most effective instrument for the religious education of all, both the literate and the illiterate. It sanctifies time.

THE PRESERVATION OF ORTHODOXY

Thomas Smith was able to discern the real reason for the survival of the Orthodox Church under centuries of Moslem oppression when he wrote:

"Next to the miraculous and gracious providence of God, I ascribe the preservation of Christianity among them to the strict and religious observation of the Festivals and Fasts of the Church. . . This certainly is the chiefest preservative of Religion in those Eastern countries against the poison of the Mahometan superstition. For Children and those of the most ordinary capacities know the meaning of these holy Solemnities, at which times they flock to the Church in great companies, and thereby retain the memory of our Blessed Saviour's Birth, dying upon the Cross, Resurrection, and Ascension, and keep up the constant profession of their acknowledgment of the necessary and fundamental points of Faith, as of the doctrine of the Blessed Trinity, and the like. And while they celebrate the sufferings and martyrdoms of the Apostles of our Lord and Saviour Jesus Christ, and other great saints, who laid down their lives most joyfully for His name, and underwent with unwearied and invincible patience all the Torments and Cruelties of their Heathen Persecutors, they take courage from such glorious examples, and are the better enabled to endure with less trouble and regret the miseries and hardships they daily struggle with." [2]

ITS IMPACT OF RELIGIOUS EXPERIENCE

Describing the impact of the liturgical year on the religious experience of the Orthodox Christian, Peter Hammond wrote:

"Nobody who has lived and worshipped amongst Greek Christians for any length of time but has sensed in some measure the extraordinary hold which the recurring cycle of the Church's liturgy has upon the piety of the common people. Nobody who has kept the Great Lent with the Greek Church, who has shared in the fast which lies heavy upon the whole nation for forty days; who has stood for long hours, one of an innumerable multitude who crowd the tiny Byzantine churches of Athens and overflow into the streets, while the familiar pattern of God's saving economy towards man is re-presented in psalm and prophecy, in lections from the Gospel, and the matchless poetry of the cannons; who has known the desolation of the holy and great Friday, when every bell in Greece tolls its lament and the body of the Saviour lies shrouded in flowers in all the village churches throughout the land; who has been present at the kindling of the new fire and tasted of the joy of a world

---

[2] "An Account of the Greek Church," pp 18-19. Quoted by G. Every in "The Byzantine Patriarchate", pp ix-x.

released from the bondage of sin and death—none can have lived through all this and not have realized that for the Greek Christians the Gospel is inseparably linked with the liturgy that is unfolded week by week in his parish church. Not among the Greeks only but throughout Orthodox Christendom the liturgy has remained at the very heart of the Church's life." [3]

THE USE OF THE WORD "TODAY"

The constant use of the word "today" in the hymns of the Orthodox Church has profound meaning. For example, on Good Friday we sing:

Today He who hung the earth upon the waters is hung on a Tree.
The King of the angels is decked with a crown of thorns.
He who wraps the heavens in clouds is wrapped in false purple.
He who freed Adam in the Jordan accepts buffeting.
The Bridegroom of the Church is affixed to the Cross with nails.
The Son of the Virgin is pierced by a spear.
We venerate Thy passion, O Christ.
Show us also Thy glorious Resurrection.

(From the Ninth Hour of Holy Friday)

On Christmas we sing:

Today He who holds the whole creation in the hollow of His hand
is born of the Virgin.
He whom in essence none can touch is wrapped in swaddling
clothes as a mortal.
He who in the beginning established the heavens lies in a manger.
He who rained down manna on the people in the wilderness is fed on
milk from His Mother's breast.
The Bridegroom of the Church calls unto himself the Magi.
The Son of the Virgin accepts their gifts.
We venerate Thy birth, O Christ.
Show us also Thy divine Epiphany.

(From the Ninth Hour on the Eve of Christmas)

On Epiphany we pray:

Today the grace of the Holy Spirit has descended . . . .
Today the shining stars adorn the universe . . . .
Today the sins of mankind are blotted out . . . .
Today paradise has been opened to mankind . . . .
Today have we escaped from darkness . . . .
Today the whole of creation is lighted from on high . . . .
Today the Lord comes to baptism to elevate mankind . . . .

---

[3] *"The Waters of Marah,"* pp 51-2.

On Easter:

"Today brings salvation to the world, for Christ has risen as Almighty . . ."

On Palm Sunday:

"Today Christ enters the city . . ." etc.

MAKES PRESENT AGAIN THE MYSTERIES OF SALVATION

The word "today" is an important liturgical word replete with meaning. Fr. Alexander Schmemann writes: "For someone to whom worship is a living experience, the frequently used *today* is not merely a rhetorical 'figure of speech'. For it is indeed the proper function of liturgy that in and through it everything that Christ accomplished *once* always returns to life, is made present again, actualized in its relation to us and our salvation." [4]

Fr. Sergius Bulgakov wrote in the same vein:

"The life of the Church, in these services, makes actual for us the mystery of the Incarnation. Our Lord continues to live in the Church in the same form in which He was manifested once on earth and which exists forever; and is given to the Church to make living these sacred memories so that we should be their new witnesses and participate in them." [5]

THE NOW MOMENT

Thus, the word "today" is not merely a quaint expression peculiar to Orthodox hymnology. It expresses the essence of liturgical consciousness. For, everything that Chirst accomplished once, returns to life eternally. It becomes present mystically in the now moment. It transcends time, joining the past with the present. It places each of us in the sacred acts of history. They become events in our lives. Salvation is aimed at each one of us personally.

AN EXISTENTIAL ENCOUNTER

Through the events of the liturgical year, then, we actually relive with Christ the great events of His life. Unlike a movie or a play, however, which merely re-enacts the events in the life of a great person, the liturgical year not only re-enacts those events but also places us in each event. An existential encounter takes place between us and Christ in the events of His birth, crucifixion, resurrection, etc. These sacred events are mystically present in the Church here and now. We re-enter each event in such a way that it becomes a unique and refreshingly new act of salvation for us today. Thus, far from being a cold and lifeless representation of the events of the past, the liturgical year is a living and personal encounter with Jesus today. Today He comes to be born in the manger of my soul and yours to bring us new life. Today He offers me His precious Body and Blood for my salvation. Today He hangs on the cross for me. Today He is resurrected and I am resurrected with Him. Today He is transfigured and I am transfigured with Him.

---

[4] *"Liturgy and Life,"* Dept. of Religious Education, Orthodox Church in America, p 19.
[5] *"The Orthodox Church,"* London. 1935.

Today He ascends into heaven and I ascend with Him. So it is that the beautiful word *today* tears down the walls of the past and the future and makes Christ the eternally present One, Who is "the same yesterday and today and forever" (Hebr. 13:8).

Each year the liturgical calendar relives and makes present again the sacred events of our salvation so that we are there when they happen. The past reaches out and joins the present. The acts of God for His people are not buried in the past. They live in the present. History does not exhaust grace. God is present through the centuries. He never ceases accomplishing the work He has begun.

George Mantzarides writes,

> *"The body of Christ surpasses time and space and joins all its members in the triadic communion where all things are present and live in the Lord. Within the body of Christ, namely in the Church, there is neither lost time nor lost people. Whatever God did in the past for the salvation of the world exists always as present and can be made accessible to each person. . . Distance of time and place are annihilated, and all things become present in Christ. Just as Christ as the Lord of glory is beyond time and place, so too whatever belongs to his body or whatever relates to it also surpasses time and place and is preserved eternally present."* [6]

SCRIPTURE WOVEN INTO CALENDAR

Important Scriptural truths have been woven into the church calendar. Take, for example, the words of John the Baptist concerning his relationship to Jesus, "He must increase, but I must decrease" (John 3:30). The birthday of Jesus was fixed at December 25. This is at the beginning of the winter solstice after which the days grow longer, i.e., Jesus, the Light, has entered the world; He must increase. John the Baptist's birthday, on the other hand, was fixed on June 24 which is at the very beginning of the summer solstice, after which the days grow shorter, i.e., John was not the light; he must decrease. "He (John the Baptist) was not the light, but came to bear witness to the light" (John 1:8).

THE HINGE ON WHICH THE YEAR SWINGS

The liturgical year revolves around the crucified and risen Christ. It has been said that Easter is the hinge on which the whole church year swings. It is the greatest and most exalted feast, the feast of feasts in the Orthodox Church. In the words of Fr. Schmemann: "The entire worship of the Church is organized around Easter, and therefore the liturgical year . . . becomes a journey, a pilgrimage towards Pascha, the End, which at the same time is the Beginning—the end of all that is "old"; the beginning of the new life, a constant 'passage' from 'this world' into the kindgom already revealed in Christ." [7] It has been said that an Orthodox Christian is one who lives from Easter to Easter.

---

[6] *"The Divine Liturgy and the World"* The Greek Orthodox Theological Review, vol. XXVI, Number 1 and 2 Spring-Summer 1981. Brookline, MA.

[7] *"Great Lent."* St. Vladimir Seminary Press. Scarsdale, New York.

Dedicated to God, all the days of the year are bathed in the rays of the Risen Son of God and reflect them to us daily. The liturgical year becomes "a garland of the beauties of the Lord" (Ps. 65:11).

The liturgical year is not so much a collection of special days as much as it is a Christ-centered whole repeatedly reminding us of events in the saving work of Christ.

INSPIRES A RICH HYMNOGRAPHY

An eminent Orthodox theologian, Dr. Bratsiotis, writes, "This rich and powerful drama which is played against the suggestive background of Byzantine church architecture has inspired a host of great poets in the Greek East and produced a rich and magnificent hymnography." [8]

In fact, whereas the services of most other Christian churches are contained in one or two volumes, the services of the Orthodox Church are so extended and elaborate that they require a small library of about twenty volumes, comprised of some 5,000 pages in double columns.

These twenty volumes contain the services for the entire Christian year and constitute one of the great treasures of the Orthodox Church.

THE TWELVE GREAT FEASTS

The liturgical year begins on September 1. Following Easter, which is the pre-eminent festival, come the TWELVE GREAT FEASTS which are divided into two groups, i.e., the Feasts of the Mother of God and the Feasts of our Lord.

The Feasts of the Mother of God are:
1. The Birth of the Theotokos (September 8).
2. The Entry of the Theotokos into the Temple (November 21).
3. The Meeting of Our Lord (February 2).
4. The Annunciation (March 25).
5. The Dormition of the Theotokos (August 15).

The Feasts of Our Lord are:
1. The Exaltation of the Cross (September 14).
2. Christmas (December 25).
3. Theophany (January 6).
4. Palm Sunday (one week before Easter).
5. The Ascension of Our Lord (40 days after Easter).
6. Pentecost (50 days after Easter).
7. The Transfiguration of Our Lord (August 6).

Easter is not one of the Twelve Great Feasts because it is considered to be the source of all of them.

Because three of the Twelve Great Feasts depend on the date of Easter, they are movable; the remainder are fixed. Benjamin Franklin said once, "All mankind are divided into three classes: those who are immovable; those who are movable; and those who move." The purpose of all great feasts—movable and fixed—is to move us to greater devotion and commitment to our Lord, to make these sacred

---

[8] "The Greek Orthodox Church," University of Notre Dame Press.

events present again so that we might provide our personal response to them. As George Mantzarides writes, "Each one of these feast days is not a mere rememberance, but a liturgical repetition of that day on which the celebrated event actually took place" [9]

PERIODS OF FASTING

In addition to the Twelve Great Feasts (seven of which are feasts of our Saviour and five of the Theotokos), there are also periods of fasting in the liturgical year. Just as Jesus fasted, so did the early Christians. Regarded as a means of disciplining the body and overcoming the passions, fasting is built into the church year. The periods of fasting are:

1. Each Wednesday and Friday, in memory of the betrayal (Wednesday) and crucifixion (Friday) of our Lord, except between Christmas and Epiphany, during Easter week and Pentecost week.

2. The Christmas fast—40 days, from Nov. 15 to Dec. 24.

3. The Great Fast of Lent which begins seven weeks before Easter.

4. The Fast preceding the Feast of the Holy Apostles on June 30.

5. Two fasts which closely follow each other: the first from August 1 to 6 (before the Feast of the Transfiguration of Christ); the second from August 7 to 15 (before the Feast of the Falling Asleep of the Theotokos).

6. The fasts on the Exaltation of the Cross, the Beheading of St. John the Baptist, and the eve of Epiphay.

THE DAYS OF EACH WEEK

Each day of the week has its own memory.

1. The first day of the week is Sunday, which is a "little Easter," commemorating the resurrection of Jesus. We begin each week with the resurrection. As Easter is the center of the year, so Sunday is the center of the week. Thus, a positive mood of victory is established at the very beginning in order to carry us through the entire week. The Christian week begins on the note of the celebration of life. We work all week long in order to get to Sunday. We begin each new week with the remembrance and celebration of the greatest victory this world has ever known.

2. Monday is dedicated to the archangels, angels and the hosts of invisible powers.

3. Tuesday is dedicated to the memory of St. John the Baptist, the last of the Old Testament prophets, the first and greatest saint (after the Theotokos), and the greatest man who was ever born of woman (Matt.11:11).

4. Wednesday is dedicated to the Theotokos and to the passion of Christ. Considered to be the day on which Judas betrayed Jesus, it is a day of fasting.

5. Thursday is dedicated to the apostles and all the Church Fathers.

6. Friday is remembered as the day on which Jesus was crucified. It is a day of fasting.

---

[9] "The Divine Liturgy and the World," Greek Orthodox Theological Review. Vol. XXVI. Number 1 and 2. Spring-Summer 1981. Brookline, Mass. U.S.A.

7. Saturday is dedicated to the holy martyrs and to the faithful who have departed from this world. It is the day on which Christ resurrected Lazarus. It is also the day on which Christ the Lord lay dead in the tomb, "resting from all His works", and "trampling down death by death." All Saturdays of the church year receive their meaning from these two decisive Saturdays. Thus, Saturday became the proper day for remembering the dead and offering prayers in their memory. This is why prayers for the dead are offered on the various Memorial Saturdays during the church year, i.e., before Lent and Pentecost.

THE DAILY CYCLE

As the year and week are broken into cycles, so is each day.

The New Testament follows a system of telling time according to which the first hour of the day is hour one after sunrise or 7 a.m. Hour two is eight a.m. Hour three is 9 a.m., etc.

Using this time schedule the early Christians would pause for prayer and meditation every third hour during the day and night. For example, we know that the apostles Peter and John "went up together into the temple at the hour of prayer, being the ninth hour" (Acts 3:1). We find St. Peter praying on Simon's housetop "at the sixth hour" (Acts 10:9).

The monastic orders devised prayer services for common worship around the system of "hours." Their life became a constant balance between prayer and work. They would enter the sanctuary for prayer at the third hour (9 a.m.), the sixth hour (noon), the ninth hour (3 p.m.), the twelfth (6 p.m.), and midnight. They paused for prayer in the morning, noon, afternoon and evening. We still celebrate "the service of the hours" in every Orthodox parish every Holy Friday, Christmas and Epiphany. This New Testament way of telling time is still in use today in the monasteries of Mt. Athos.

Each of the six hourly cycles of prayer had a special theme related to something in the history of salvation that happened at that hour. The worship service composed by the Church Fathers for that hour usually included scripture readings, psalms and hymns relating to that event.

Let us examine each hour with the special purpose of helping us to pause briefly on these hours each day to meditate and pray.

THE FIRST HOUR

The first hour (hour one after the rise of the sun or 7 a.m.), has as its central theme the coming of the light in the dawn of a new day. The coming of the physical light reminds the Christian of the coming of Him Who is the Light of the World. The physical light is but an icon or image of Christ. Thus, the Christian begins the day by praising God for the dawn of the physical light as well as for the Light of the World which shines brightly in the face of Jesus. We pray that His light will guide us and show us the way for the day, blessing also the work of our hands which begin daily at this hour.

THE THIRD HOUR

The third hour (three hours after sunrise 9 a.m.), was the exact time the Holy Spirit descended upon the apostles on the day of Pentecost (Acts 2:15). This single theme dominates the third hour. One of the three psalms that are read is the 51st which contains petitions for the sending of the Holy Spirit: "Create in me a clean heart, O God; and renew a right spirit within me . . . take not thy holy spirit from me . . . and uphold me with the free spirit" (Ps. 51:10-12).

Special prayers are said to thank God for sending the Holy Spirit on Pentecost, beseeching Him also to bestow the gift of the Spirit's presence upon us for the works of that day. The third hour is a daily reminder that the life of the faithful Christian remains empty without the inner presence of the Spirit. He is the One Who provides inner peace and power. He is the One "in Whom we live and move and have our being" (Acts 17:28).

THE SIXTH HOUR

The sixth hour, six hours following sunrise (noon), coincides with the hour the Lord Jesus was crucified (Matt. 27:45, Luke 23:44, John 19:14). Each day at noon the Church tries to focus our attention on this great event in the history of our salvation. We offer Him prayers of gratitude for so loving each one of us that He gave His only begotten Son so that we who believe in Him may not perish but have life everlasting (John 3:16). Our noontime prayers (sixth hour) include petitions that He save us from the sins and temptations of that day.

THE NINTH HOUR

The ninth hour, nine hours following sunrise (3 p.m.), is the time when Jesus died on the cross. "And at about the ninth hour Jesus cried with a loud voice, saying, 'Eli, Eli, lama sabachthani? That is to say, 'My God, my God, why hast thou forsaken me?' . . . When he had cried again with a loud voice (Jesus) yielded up the ghost" (Matthew 27:46,50). At this time prayers of thanksgiving are offered to Him Who by His death destroyed death. The prayers of the ninth hour conclude with a petition that we put to death the old sinful nature within us to enable us to live the new life in Christ Jesus with Whom we were not only crucified but also resurrected through baptism.

VESPERS

Morning and evening were always considered to be proper times for prayer. Worship services were held every morning and evening in the Temple of Jerusalem and were continued by the early Christians even after they separated themselves from the worship of the Temple. The old Jewish psalms are still used. The theme of vespers takes us through creation, sin and salvation in Christ. It includes thanksgiving for the day now coming to an end and God's protection for the evening. In the Orthodox Church the liturgical day begins in the evening with the setting of the sun. The coming of darkness reminds us of the darkness of our sin and death and makes us long for the light. One of the great themes of vespers is the coming of Christ the Light to dispel the darkness. Jesus is praised as "The gladsome light of the holy glory of the Immortal Father" and "a light for revelation to the Gentiles." Vesper services are offered daily in monasteries and usually only on Saturday evenings in parishes. Evening prayers may be offered in private by Orthodox Christians daily by praying the Psalter and the other vesper prayers at home.

MIDNIGHT

The hour of midnight was designated as a time for prayer for three reasons. First, the Jewish people were led out of Egypt at midnight (Exodus 12:29). In remembrance of this event, the Messiah at the time of Jesus was expected to come at midnight. This expectation was fulfilled when Jesus was resurrected in the early morning while it was still dark (Matthew 28:1). Midnight also became associated in early Christian thought with the hour of the Second Coming of Jesus (Mark 13:35). He was expected to come "as a thief in the night" (I Thess. 5:2,4). This hour of prayer is kept today only in certain monasteries where monks rise at midnight, as if from the grave of death, to meet the risen Lord in prayer. The prayers offered at this hour remember those who have died in Christ and also invoke God's mercy upon us for the coming judgment. Although we do not live in monasteries, we may use midnight as an hour of prayer if we happen to waken during the night. Instead of counting sheep, we can use the time to speak and pray to the Shepherd of our souls.

PRAYING THE HOURS TODAY

The service of the hours was not able to survive outside the monastic environment. People simply did not have the time to flock to the monasteries three or four times a day. Yet how much we need the inspiration and the power that comes to us today from the prayerful observance of these hours:

the FIRST HOUR, 7 a.m., to thank Jesus for the physical and spiritual light as a new day dawns:

the THIRD HOUR, 9 a.m., the hour of Pentecost, to thank God for the Holy Spirit beseeching Him for the Spirit's presence with us throughout that day;

the SIXTH HOUR, noon, to pause at that, the moment of His crucifixion, to thank Him for His great love for us;

the NINTH HOUR, 3 p.m., to remember Him Who expired in our behalf at that very hour, repeating the words of the dying thief: "Remember me, Lord, when You come into your kingdom."

the TWELFTH HOUR, 6 p.m., to remember Him Who came to be "a light for revelation to the Gentiles."

the MIDNIGHT HOUR, to remember Him Who will come again as "a thief in the night" to judge the living and the dead.

LENT, HOLY WEEK AND EASTER

The most inspiring and meaningful periods of the liturgical year in the Orthodox Church are Lent, Holy Week and Easter.

The main purpose of Lent in the early Church was to prepare the catechumens, i.e., the newly converted pagans, for baptism which was administered at the Easter liturgy. Even though today we do not train catechumens during this period, the basic meaning of Lent remains the same. Fr. Schmemann observes, "For even though we are baptized, what we constantly lose and betray is precisely that which we received at Baptism. Therefore, Easter is our return every year to our own Baptism, whereas Lent is our preparation for that return—the slow and sustained effort to perform, at the end, our own 'passage' or 'pascha' into the new life of Christ." [10]

During Holy Week the Church re-enacts before us the entire passion of Christ. We do, within the confines of the church building, what the early Christians did in Jerusalem every year during this week. They visited and prayed at each site where the events of Holy Week originally took place. This sacred Holy Week Pilgrimage is acted out before us through the service and processions of this week. We are mystically present with Christ at each stage of His passion and death. At no other time of the year do we have the opportunity to experience the love of Christ as powerfully as during Holy Week.

Easter in the Orthodox Church is the feast of feasts, the festival of festivals. It radiates the tremendous joy of Christ's victory over death. At the stroke of midnight the Paschal Candle is illuminated at the altar—the candle that represents Christ, the Light of the World. The door to the sanctuary swings open, representing the opening of Christ's tomb. The priest appears holding the unwaning light of Christ. "Come, receive light from the unwaning light," he sings, "and glorify Christ Who is risen from the dead." The worshippers light their candles from the Paschal candle passing on the light to their neighbors until the whole church is ablaze with the new light of the resurrection, proclaiming to the world that Christ is risen, that through His resurrection our darkness has been changed into light, our death has become life, our midnight has become dawn, a dawn of victory.

The brightness of Easter spills over into the following week which is celebrated as the Bright Week, a week of unbounded joy during which no fasting is permitted. For forty days following Easter, Orthodox Christians greet one another with the words, "Christ is risen" and hear the joyful response, "Truly He is risen."

SYNAXIS

The Orthodox calendar celebrates a synaxis (Greek: an assembly or gathering). This is a feast on which we commemorate those saints who are a vital part of the feast that was celebrated on the previous day. For example, on the day following the Nativity of the Mother of God, we celebrate the feast of her parents, Joachim and Anna. On the day following the presentation of our Lord, we honor St. Simeon and St. Anna who acknowledged the Christ Child as the Expected Saviour when His Mother brought Him to the Temple. On the day following the Annunciation we celebrate the feast of St. Gabriel the Archangel who brought the good news to the Theotokos the day before. On the day after Epiphany we celebrate the memory of St. John the Baptist who baptized Jesus on Epiphany, etc. In the early Church, according to tradition, the bishop would have an actual synaxis (synod) with his clergy on the day after certain important feast days.

---

[10] *"Great Lent."* St. Vladimir Seminary Press, New York.

PRE-FESTIVE AND POST-FESTIVE PERIODS

To celebrate a sacred event on one single day is not enough to help us remember it. The one day quickly passes and hardly leaves an impression. There is no permanent spiritual benefit

For this reason the Church Fathers decided that there should be a preparatory period before certain Feasts in order to help place us in the proper spiritual mood and excite in us a greater interest in the feast. This is called the pre-festive period.

To make certain that the fervor generated by a feast day outlasted the actual one-day celebration of the feast, it was felt that in addition to the pre-festive period, a post-festive period was required as a sort of aftermath or echo of the feast day. The pre-festive period builds up interest in the feast through special services, prayers and hymns. The post-festive period is designed to maintain our interest in the facts of the feast just celebrated and help us see its abiding relevance to our lives. The last day of the post-festive period is called *Apodosis,* a Greek word which means the ''giving up'' or the ''conclusion'' of the feast. The services on the day of *Apodosis* are almost the same as those on the day of the feast.

All the major feast days (except four) are anticipated with one pre-festive day. Easter, one of the exceptions, is anticipated by ten weeks of preparation (Pre-Lent, Lent and Holy Week) and forty days of post-festive celebration (until Ascension Day). Christmas has five pre-festive days while Epiphany has four.

The length of the post-festive period varies from year to year especially with those feasts whose date depends on Easter. A typical post-festive period will last from one to eight days.

RICHNESS OF LITURGICAL YEAR BESTOWS LIFE

In the words of the German scholar, Kirchoff, ''Just as the sun bathes the earth in the rays which she sends out and bestows fertility and growth upon her, so the heavenly sun, Christ the giver of light and life, enters into the liturgical year of the Church of God with His gifts and the riches of His goodness in order to fill her with the divine light of His grace.''

Thank God for the liturgical year! More than a teacher, more than a reminder, more than a life-giving slap to help us breathe on our own, it places us in the sacred events of the history of salvation that we may experience personally their relevance and power. That which time tends to erase from memory, the liturgical year keeps re-writing.

SUMMARY

1. As the secular calendar of holidays expresses the national history and heritage of a people, so the church calendar expresses the history and faith of the Church.

2. The liturgical year helps us remember annually events that are vital to our salvation and the abundant life that God wants us to have.

3. The Church year unfolds before us every year the whole life of Christ. It makes the events of His life present again in a mystical way so that we may re-live them and participate in them. This is expressed through the constant use of the word ''today'' in the hymns of the Church.

4. Easter is the hinge on which the whole Church year swings. It is the greatest and most exalted feast of the Orthodox Church.

5. There are twelve great feasts annually, five relating to the Mother of God and seven to the Lord Jesus. Periods of fasting are associated with many of the feast days.

6. Each day of the week has its own memory and is dedicated to some event in the history of our salvation. Sunday is a "little Easter," Monday is dedicated to the angels, etc.

7. Each day is broken down by hours to the remembrance of an important event in our salvation history that happened at that hour. For example, during the first hour (7 a.m.), the rising sun reminds us of the coming of the Light of the World; the third hours (9 a.m.), the actual time of Pentecost, reminds us to pray for the coming of the Holy Spirit, etc.

8. A *synaxis* is a feast on which we commemorate those saints who are a vital part of the feast that was celebrated on the previous day. On the day following the Nativity of the Theotokos, for example, we celebrate the feast of her parents, Joachim and Anna, etc.

9. Since a single day is not enough to help us remember a sacred event, the Church has established pre-festive and post-festive periods before and after major feast days culminating in the *apodosis*—the "giving up" or "conclusion" or a feast.

What the Walls
of the Orthodox Church
Teach Us

The idea of the saints on earth communing with the saints in heaven, is greatly emphasized in the Orthodox Church. This communion is expressed very effectively in the iconography of the Eastern churches. Cecil Stewart describes the role of sacred pictures on the walls of our churches as follows:

"The pictures seem to be arranged in a way which instills a feeling of direct relationship between the viewer and the pictures . . . each personality is represented facing one, so that one stands, as it were, within the congregation of saints. Byzantine art, in fact, puts one in the picture. Thus is achieved a spatial dynamic relationship across the volume of the church. The beholder belongs within the artistic envelope, and is linked visually with the heavenly host. He observes and is observed."

To illustrate this interdependence between the worshipper and the icon a little further, let us look for a moment at the interior of an Eastern Church. At the highest point of the church, i.e., the top of the dome, there is an icon of Christ Pantocrator—the Ruler and Redeemer of the universe. Immediately below He is surrounded by angels and archangels who serve Him and execute His commands. The remaining part of the ceiling and walls are decorated with episodes illustrating the redemption of the world, with pictures of saints who not only look at the worshippers but also converse with one another and form their own sacred circle. In the eastern apse, the most significant place after the dome, stands the Virgin Mother, the link betweeen Creator and Creation. The whole story of the Incarnation is depicted on the walls of an Orthodox Church. It begins with the Old Testament patriarchs and prophets. Then come the apostles, martyrs, doctors, teachers, saints and finally on the floor level of the congregation, i.e., the members of the church militant on earth. Thus around the figure of the all-ruling Christ in the dome is gathered in a circle the communion of saints, the members of the church triumphant in heaven and the church militant on earth, all conversing with each other and all together offering the sacrifice of the liturgy to their Lord.

We now proceed with a detailed explanation of the interior of an Orthodox Church where the walls indeed speak to the worshipper.

THE INTERIOR OF AN ORTHODOX CHURCH . . .

is designed to speak to the worshipper, to establish the mood for worship, to preach the Gospel through architecture and icons, to elevate one's mind to the God one comes to praise and worship.

THE NARTHEX . . .

or vestibule of the church, represents this world in which man is called to repentance. The nave represents the kingdom of heaven. Passing from the narthex into the nave of the church symbolized the Christian's entrance into the kingdom of heaven. Paul Evdokimov wrote, "Architecturally speaking the temple has a cubic form or that of an elongated rectangle, always turned toward the East whence Christ came, like a ship (nave from *navis*) it floats in the eschatological dimension and sails towards the East, towards Christ."

THE ICONS AT THE ENTRANCE TO THE NAVE . . .

remind the Orthodox Christian that Christ and the saints are his invisible hosts when he comes to Church. His first act upon entering church is to salute them by making the sign of the cross. Often the worshipper also lights a candle upon entering the sanctuary as a reminder that he is to reflect the light of Christ in the world.

ARCHITECTURALLY . . .

Orthodox churches vary. Many are built in the form of a cross. Above the middle of the cross is a dome. This represents that in order to receive the many blessings that descend upon us from heaven through the open dome, it is necessary first to accept the cross, or salvation through Jesus Christ.

Eastern Christians set up their church buildings in such a manner that the whole theology of the Orthodox Church can be conveyed within a single church building. Each church becomes a complete expression of the complete cosmos. Jerusalem is where? Right in the parish church. Where is Mt. Tabor? Right in the parish church. Where is the Garden of Eden? Right in the parish church; the Mount of Olives—right in the parish church. Thus, to a person going through his own parish church, all these are present realities—not just facts in the past.

THE CHURCH EDIFICE . . .

is considered to represent the universe. The ceiling represents heaven. The opening in the ceiling (dome) on which is usually painted an icon of Christ Pantocrator, i.e., the all-ruling Christ, represents Christ looking down through heaven upon the assembled congregation hearing their prayers, reminding them of His all-pervading presence in the universe. The floor of the church represents this world. The altar uplifted from the floor by four or five steps and suspended, as it were, between heaven and earth gives expression to the fact that its purpose is to lift us up to heaven through the teachings of the Gospel and the grace of the Sacraments. both of which emanate from the altar.

THERE IS A HIERARCHICAL PLAN . . .

in the way the icons are arranged in the Orthodox Church. The highest point, the dome, is reserved for our Lord. Then comes the figure of the Mother of God on the front wall. Next there are the icons of the angels, apostles and saints on the iconostasion. These constitute the Church Triumphant in heaven. The floor level of the church is reserved for us—the members of the Church Militant. Thus around the figure of Christ is gathered His entire Church both that in heaven and that on earth.

THE CHURCH IS A PALACE . . .

for the King of Kings. This explains the extensive use of royal colors: gold, blue and white. The fact that the church is the palace of God's presence gives expression to our faith that even now earth is changed into heaven whenever the Eucharist is celebrated and divine grace is received.

THE VICTORIOUS CHRIST (PANTOCRATOR)

The victory of Christ is central to our Orthodox Christian faith. It is to dramatize this victory that the figure of Christ is placed at the highest point of the church, i.e. the top of the dome. It gives full expression the to great victory hymn of the early Church, quoted by Paul in his letter to Philippi:

". . . He lowered His dignity still more becoming obedient even unto death to the death of the cross.

Therefore God has raised Him up and has given Him that name which is above every name

so that all things, at the name of Jesus must bend the knee— those in high heaven and upon the earth, and under the earth

and every tongue must proclaim of Jesus Christ, that He is the Lord in the glory of God the Father."

THE SANCTUARY WALL (APSE)

A large painting of the Child-Holding Theotokos is usually depicted above the holy table on the sanctuary wall of many Orthodox Churches. The purpose of this icon is to express the incarnation. Out of the infinite heaven the Theotokos is presenting the new-born Child to the multitudes of believers standing below. It is a visual expression of Scripture: "Today a Savior is born to us; a Child was born to us, and a Son was given to us."

THE TWO LARGE CANDELABRA . . .

before the icon screen, represent the column of light by which God guided the Jews at night to the promised land. When the light appeared the Jewish people followed it until it eventually led them to the promised land. During the day God used a cloud. These two candelabra remind us that we, too, have a promised land, i.e., the kingdom of heaven. Just as God guided the Jews to their promised land, so today He guides us to ours through the teachings of the Gospel and the grace of the sacraments.

THE ICONOSTASIS OR ICON SCREEN . . .

separates the nave from the altar. It is symbolical of the temple veil in the Old Testament which separated the Holy of Holies from the remainder of the temple. On the screen are placed icons or religious pictures of Christ, of Mary the Theotokos, and of various other saints. All these invite the faithful to a worshipful meditation of God. The icon screen, screening off the holy of holies from the full view of the worshipper, reminds us of the mystery of God who can never be fully understood by finite man.

on the icon screen depicts the major scenes in the life of our Lord from the Annunciation to His Ascension. This serves as a visual Gospel to the worshipper. Not all churches may have this second tier of icons.

THE ROYAL DOORS . . .

on the icon screen are called "royal" in view of the fact that Christ the King is carried through them in the Sacrament of Holy Communion as the priest carries the precious Body and Blood out to the congregation. They remind us that Christ alone is the door leading to communion with the Holy Trinity.

THE ROLE OF ICONOGRAPHY

The Christian people need to realize that they belong to a pilgrim people en route to heaven. Here we have the role of iconography in our churches: to represent some of the major phases of salvation history to the worshippers and provide a reminder that the small local parish is in communion with the angels and saints.

LIVING ICONS

Druing the services of our Church the priest censes first the icons and then the entire congregation. In so doing the Church honors not only the angels, saints and martyrs, but also the *living icon* (image) of Christ which every faithful Christian bears.

THE HOLY ALTAR

From the very beginning Christians honored the memory of those who died in the persecutions. The tombs of the early martyrs were held in high veneration. On the anniversary of their deaths the liturgy was celebrated on their graves and a sermon was preached. This was practiced especially during to first 300 years of Christianity when worship was underground, in the catacombs, where the tombs of these early martyrs were easily accesible. From this early Christian custom has come the practice of placing the relics of some martyr in the holy altar of each church upon its consecration.

THE TABERNACLE . . .

is kept on the center of the holy altar. In the Old Testament the tablets on which God had written the Ten Commandments were kept in the tabernacle. In the New Testament it is the Lord Jesus Himself who dwells in the tabernacle. His precious Body and Blood are ever kept in the tabernacle. The church, then, is truly the house of God. God is ever present there in a very real way. This is why the Eastern Orthodox Christian makes the sign of the cross whenever he or she passes before the holy altar.

THE ETERNAL LIGHT . . .

is the votive light that is suspended above the tabernacle. It burns constantly to denote that the Lord Jesus Who is "Light of the World" is present in the tabernacle.

which are found in many Orthodox Churches are called in Greek "exapteriga" (six winged). Engraved on these are the six-winged angels which, according to Isaiah's vision of God, surrounded the throne of God in heaven. They remind us that these same angels surround the throne of God on earth—the holy altar—where God's precious Body and Blood are ever present in the tabernacle. They are used in sacred processionals during the liturgy.

THE GOSPEL BOOK . . .

is enthroned constantly on the holy altar where Christ is constantly present as the Word of Life in the Gospel book and as the Bread of Life (Eucharist) which is kept in the tabernacle.

THE FOUR GOSPEL WRITERS . . .

Matthew, Mark, Luke and John are usually depicted at the four corners of the base of the dome to express the fact that through their writings the Gospel of Jesus was spread to the four corners of the earth.

A CHANDELIER . . .

is usually suspended from the dome or ceiling to signify the majesty of the firmament and the glory of God's heavenly bodies i.e., the sun, the moon and the planets. "The heavens declare the glory of God" (Psalm 19:1).

THE TABLE OF PREPARATION . . .

is a small altar to the left of the main altar behind the icon screen. Here the peoples' gifts of bread and wine are prepared before the liturgy and later carried in a solemn procession to the main altar. An icon of the Nativity is usually found on the altar of preparation to signify that it represents the manger of Bethlehem. Just as Jesus was born in Bethlehem so through the Eucharist He comes to be born and dwell in our lives today.

A SEVEN-BRANCHED CANDLABRA . . .

is usually found in Orthodox churches to represent the seven sacraments and the seven gifts of the Holy Spirit.

THE BISHOP'S THRONE . . .

is usually found to the right of the iconostasis. It is set apart for the bishop or archbishop who is considered to be the head of the local Church and represents Jesus Christ. For this reason and icon of Christ, the High Priest, is usually painted somewhere on the throne. The Bishop occupies the throne during the liturgy and other church ceremonies.

is usually located to the left of the iconostasis near the center of the nave. Used for the reading of the Gospel and the preaching of the sermon, it symbolizes the stone used to seal the entrance to Christ's tomb from which the angel proclaimed the good tidings of the Resurrection to the women who had come to anoint His body. Often the pulpit is decorated with icons of the Lord and the four Gospel writers.

HEAVEN ON EARTH

In the film *The Deer Hunter* a Russian Orthodox parish church stands as a monument of riches and finery in the midst of an otherwise dreary Pennsylvania steel-town. Its gold encrusted "onion" towers and ornate Byzantine chancel are in stark contrast to the grim lives of the people it serves.

Rather than being offended by it, one gets a sense of purpose in the contrast. This parish church represents an alternative in the lives of the people. Rather than just more of the same, a mirror of what they already know and struggle with, it proclaims something *else,* as an active and saving force. It is erected not only to the glory of God, but as a sign of the presence of His glory. It is an invitation to experience heaven on earth.

The Orthodox church building represents God in the midst of His people, in their joys as well as their sorrows; God calling us to the other alternative, to the "more excellent way" (I Cor. 12:31), to the more fulfilling life for which we were created.

What We Believe
About the Saints
and the Theotokos

In the Orthodox Church we invoke and venerate saints. They are an essential part of religious life. In fact, it has been said that warm veneration of the Theotokos and the Saints is the soul of Orthodox piety. We shall devote this chapter to a study of why we honor saints and what role they play in the story of our salvation.

THE CELEBRATION OF GOD'S SALVATION

In honoring the saints we celebrate God's accomplished work of salvation. Archbishop Paul of Finland writes, "In glorifying the saints' spiritual struggle and victory, the Church is in fact glorifying God's work of salvation, the work of the Holy Spirit; it experiences the salvation already accomplished in them, the goal towards which the members of the Church militant are still pressing on (Phil. 3:12,14)." [1] Thus, by remembering the saints we celebrate what the Holy Spirit has done in their lives.

How greatly God honors our nature through the saints. Father John of Kronstadt, a saintly Russian priest, emphasized this when he wrote:

> "How the Creator and Provider of all has honoured and
> adorned our nature! The saints shine with His light, they are
> hallowed by His grace, having conquered sin and washed
> away every impurity of body and spirit; they are glorious
> with His glory, they are incorruptible through His incorrup-
> tion. Glory to God, Who has so honoured, enlightened, and
> exalted our nature" [2]

The saints show us what a glorious destiny we have in God. Through the glorious example of their lives, they point the way to our becoming "partakers of divine nature."

WHAT IS A SAINT?

Let us share some inspiring definitions of sainthood.

A saint is one who makes God's goodness attractive.

Saints are forgiven sinners living out their lives in the forgiveness God has given them.

Saints are people who make it easier for others to believe in God.

A little girl said once as she looked at a saint in a stained glass window: "A saint is a Christian who lets God's light shine through."

---

[1] "*The Faith We Hold,*" p. 28. St. Vladimir's Seminary Press. Crestwood, N.Y. 1980.
[2] "*The Spiritual Counsels of Father John of Kronstadt,*" p. 63. James Clarke Company. London. 1967.

St. Symeon the New Theologian says that the reason vigil lights are placed before the icons of the saints is to show that without the Light, Who is Christ, the Saints are nothing. It is only as the light of Christ shines on them that they become alive and resplendent.

A saint is one who is constantly conscious of being a sinner and rarely, if ever, conscious of being a saint. In fact, it has been said that there are two kinds of people in the world: sinners who think they are saints, and saints who know they are sinners. The most outstanding personalities in Orthodox spirituality, those who saw the uncreated light of God, never said they had reached that high level of spirituality. The people around them detected it from the distinct radiance they generated.

It has been said that when a saint gets to heaven, he will be surprised by three things. First, he will be surprised to see many he did not think would be there. Second, he will be surprised that some are not there whom he expected to see. Third, he will be surprised that he himself is there.

A saint is one who sees himself in the sins of others.

A saint is one in whom Christ lives; one who opens his life to Christ and lives as Christ wills him to live.

A saint is one who has been made actually what Baptism declares him to be, one set apart for God.

God's saints are not those who wear the biggest halos. They are ordinary people who go to work, pay taxes, talk to friends. But when God speaks, they obey.

God's saints are often afraid but they count on God's promise, ''Fear not.'' They know they are weak, but they depend on His strength. They sin, but grieve over every lapse. The never feel they have attained, but constantly press on toward their goal (Phil. 3:14).

''The saints show the way and are forerunners. The world is not yet with them, so they often seem in the midst of the world's affairs to be preposterous. Yet they are impregnators of the world, vivifiers and animators of potentialities of goodness which but for them would lie forever dormant'' (William James, 1842-1910).

Saints are the most convincing answer to atheism and agnosticism.

A saint is someone who shows us what the Christian life is really all about.

A saint is a sinner who keeps trying.

Francis R. Line wrote these words entitled ''A Saint?'':

''What made Francis a saint?

It was simple.
Love of God and love of neighbors—
That was all.
He lived the two great commandments.

He really loved.

He loved God
    With all his heart,
    With all his mind,

> With all his soul,
> With all his strength.

> As for his neighbors—
> He gave his whole life to them
> In loving word and deed and service.

> It is simple, being a saint.
> There are only two rules.
> It is simple
> But it isn't easy.''

Saints are people who have consecrated themselves wholly to strive to express in their daily lives the love of God as revealed in Jesus.

The Greek word for saint *hagios* comes from a root word that means *not like anything else, different*. Saints are different from the people of the world. They march to the tune of a different drummer. They are conformed to the will of God in Christ.

As members of the Body of Christ, the Church, saints are the hands of God by which He accomplishes His work in the world today. Even after their deaths they perform works of love as intercessors in heaven who pray for us.

After a Christian missionary surgeon had operated on an African woman for cataracts and restored her sight, she said to him as she was leaving, ''Good-bye, God.'' The doctor hastily explained that he was not God only a poor weak servant of His. That he was—but the woman saw God in him. So, a saint is one who makes God real to people today.

After visiting the home where a saint had lived, a person said, ''There was an aroma of God in that room that 200 years could not erase. I think I'm better because I visited there.'' A saint is ''the aroma of Christ to God among those who are being saved'' through whom Christ ''spreads the fragrance of the knowledge of Him everywhere'' (2 Cor. 2:15-16).

All of us are involved in the process of deification, i.e., becoming like God in Christ. The saints are those who, having advanced closer to that goal, can help the rest of us through their example and prayers.

Listen to this beautiful definition of a saint as a mirror of Christ:

> ''Francis of Assisi was poor,
> Frail in purse and body.
> No excess possessions,
> No surplus muscles or strength.
> Plain sandals, rude cloak, rough cowl.
> Not much to look at.
> But
> No one saw *him* when they looked.
> They saw the *one* he reflected.
> He was a *mirror of Christ*.''
> — by Francis R. Line

A saint is a mirror who reflects not himself but Christ.

St. Paul wrote to the Romans: "To all God's beloved in Rome, who are *called to be saints . . .*" (Romans 1:7). To the Corinthians he wrote: "To the church of God which is at Corinth, to those sanctified in Christ Jesus, *called to be saints . . .*" (I Cor. 1:2). When Paul was writing to the Christians in Rome and Corinth, reminding them they are "called to be saints," he was not writing to people likely to figure in stained-glass windows, but to a motley collection of shop-keepers, minor civil servants, converted prostitutes, prizefighters and slaves. These were the people he called God's "holy ones"—called to be like Christ their Lord, agents and instruments of His continuing work in the world. These were the "saints". And so, by God's grace, are we.

Every Christian is called to perfection and is capable of revealing the image of God hidden in him. But only a few become so transfigured through the Holy Spirit during their earthly life that they can be recognized as saints by other Christians and officially canonized as such by the Church. This should not draw our attention away from the fact that every baptized Christian is called to be a saint. In the New Testament the saints were not a spiritual elite but the whole body of Christians. That never meant that all Christians were regarded as having reached a sinless perfection. In that sense there are no saints in the New Testament, for even the best of Christians are far from perfect. The only saints the New Testament knows are forgiven sinners who are always ready to place their utter dependence on God's mercy and grace.

Thus, there are the Saints, with a capital "S", those officially recognized and canonized by the Church, and there are the saints with a small "s", who are the whole body of Christians—you and I included. We, too, are called to be men and women in whom others can in some way meet the living Christ. We can appreciate our call to be saints when we realize that saints become saints not so much because of the unusual things they do but rather because of the unusual degree to which they give themselves to Christ. By our daily faithfulness to Christ, each of us is a saint in the making. Made in the image of God and baptized in the Trinity, every Christian has the potential of sainthood.

Fr. Kallistos Ware writes, "It must not for one moment be thought that there are no saints except those publicly honoured as such. Those who are mentioned in the calendar form but a small fraction of the whole Communion of Saints; besides them there is a great host whose names are known to God alone, and these are venerated collectively on the Feast of All Saints (observed on the first Sunday after Pentecost)" [3]

FROM EVERY CLASS AND OCCUPATION

Saints come from every class and occupation, every temperament and background. They show us how Christ can be imitated in everyone's life including our own. As we have models in business, science, homemaking, etc., so we have faith models. We have soldier-saints, scholar-saints, politician-saints, missionary-saints, parent-saints, praying-saints, healer-saints, worker-saints, and most im-

---

[3] *"The Communion of Saints"* article by Fr. Ware in *"The Orthodox Ethos"* by A. J. Phillippou.

portant of all, sinner-saints. Saints are not perfect people: to be a saint is to be the best one can be by God's grace. That is why every saint is different and why every Christian can be one.

FULLY HUMAN

The Saints were people who were just as human as we are. They were jealous, spiteful, scheming, lustful, often depressed and utterly discouraged. They did not walk through life with halos gleaming, with kindness and love streaming from them 24 hours a day. There were strong disagreements among them. St. Paul and St. Barnabas, for example, had a strong difference of opinion as to whether to take John Mark along with them on a missionary journey. Their disagreement was strong enough to make them agree to go their separate ways. Writing to the saints at Corinth, St. Paul reminds them that some of them had been fornicators, idolaters, adulterers, thieves, covetous, extortioners . . . *but now in Christ they were washed and sanctified,* he tells them. Thanks be to Christ Who washes our soiled humanity and transforms it into an attractive image of Christ that serves as an inspiration to others.

GOD'S FAMILY

St. Paul wrote to the Ephesians: "So then you are no longer strangers and sojourners, but you are fellow citizens with the saints and members of the household of God. . ." (Eph. 2:19). Every Christian has status. He or she belongs. We are fellow citizens with the Saints and members of the household of God! Christians should be taught from infancy to have the right kind of family pride: the kind that makes us want to live up to the family standard. The Head of our family is Christ Himself. Some of our brothers and sisters are the Theotokos, John the Baptist, the Apostles, St. Basil, St. Chrysostom and countless others. We belong to them, and they to us. It is a distinguished family tree.

A Christian does not walk alone as if sealed in a space capsule. We are members of God's family. As such, we must help and be helped by others. Orthodox Christianity does not espouse a narrowly individualistic "God-and-me" relationship. The Church is a family, God's family, in which we are concerned for one another. In the words of St. Paul: "If one member suffers, all suffer together; if one member is honored, all rejoice together" (I Cor. 12:26).

The Russian theologian Alexis Khomiakov (1804-60) said, "We know that when one of us falls, he falls alone; but no one is saved alone. He is saved in the Church, as a member of her and in union with all her other members."

As members of the household of God, Orthodox Christians feel that they can call upon their brothers and sisters in the faith—the Saints—for family support. This they do through prayers, beseeching the prayers of the Saints in their behalf.

The late Fr. George Florovsky, eminent Orthodox theologian, wrote:

"The final purpose of the Incarnation was that the Incarnate should have a 'body', which is the Church . . . Christ is never alone. He is always the Head of His Body. In Orthodox theology and devotion alike, Christ is never separated from His Mother, the Theotokos, and His 'friends', the Saints. The Redeemer and the redeemed belong together inseparably. In the daring phrase of St. John

Chrysostom, inspired by Ephesians 1:23, Christ will be complete only when His Body has been completed." [4]

Speaking on the concept of the Church as the family and household of God, Nicolas Zernov wrote:

"The Orthodox . . . regard the saints . . . as teachers and friends who pray with them and assist them in their spiritual ascent. Jesus Christ during His earthly ministry was surrounded by disciples who did not prevent others from meeting Him, but on the contrary helped newcomers to find the Master. In the same manner fellowship with the saints facilitates communion with God, for their Christ-like character brings others nearer to the divine source of light and life." [5]

THE HEROES OF OUR FAITH

At Yankee Stadium, the home of the New York Yankees, there is a "Yankee Hall of Fame." One can spend a number of hours reading about all the great Yankee stars of the past. By putting on earphones one can hear their voices on recordings; telling among other things what their greatest thrills were as Yankee players.

God has a "Hall of Fame." In Hebrews chapter 11, He has listed some of the heroes and heroines of faith—men and women who trusted in God for their salvation. It is a thrilling chapter to read.

The Saints are in God's "Hall of Fame." They are the heroes of our faith. Carlyle said once, "Show me the man you honor, and I will show you the kind of man you are." It has been said that we are fresh out of heroes for our young people today. We are exalting punks. Saints make excellent heroes for children. They are powerful allies for parents and ideal heroes for children. It is for this reason that an Orthodox Christian is given the name of a saint at Baptism. In fact, the great St. John Chrysostom said, "Let us afford our children from the first an incentive to goodness from the name that we give them. Let none of us hasten to call his children after his forebears, his father and mother and grandfather and grandmother, but rather after the righteous—martyrs, bishops, apostles. Let one be called Peter, another John, another bear the name of one of the saints. Let the names of the saints enter our homes through the naming of our children."

It is not only the names but also the exemplary Christ-centered examples of the Saints that can enter our homes if parents will encourage children to learn about their patron saints. It is the custom among Orthodox to keep an icon of one's patron saint in one's room, to invoke his prayers and to celebrate the festival of one's patron saint as his/her *Name Day*. To many Orthodox this is a date even more important than one's actual birthday.

It is not just children who need heroes; adults also need them. In fact, in the early Church the veneration of saints was not imposed on the people by the hierarchy or the Church Councils. It was a practice that the people themselves began. It was a spontaneous act of the local community. They began to venerate certain exemplary Christians and often petitioned the Church to canonize them.

---

[4] *"Aspects of Church History"* G. Florovsky, p. 25. Nordland Publishing Co.

[5] *"Eastern Christendom,"* N. Zernov, P. 233. G. P. Putnam's Sons. New York.

Hero worship is part of human nature. Most of us want someone to look up to and admire. We need role models in our Christian faith. We grow to be like the people we admire. If the desire for holiness is to be encouraged, one must see, not only its perfection in Christ, but approximations to it in the Saints. In fact, if we see such holiness only in our Savior and not in His people (the Saints), we may be disposed to consider holiness as an impossible ideal which we imperfect humans can never attain. We learn best when we see concrete examples of how to live the life of Christ in the world today. This is why the Saints are a challenge to us. They can shake us out of our complacency with our mediocre way of following Christ. Each saint shows us some particular aspect of the life of Christ and in imitating them we imitate Christ. Thus, St. Paul could tell his converts, "I urge you, then, be imitators of me" (I Cor. 4:16).

Looking back to his childhood, a noted author wrote:

"We grew up with the strength of the tribe. If anyone were to attack me, he'd have to take on all my uncles and aunts. Families were secure. . . I had bleachers all around me, filled not only with family, but with all the grown-ups in the township, cheering me on when I did well and groaning when I failed. . .

"All sorts of young people today run the race with only silence from the bleachers. It's a lonely race. Grandparents are a thousand miles away, uncles and aunts scattered to both coasts and overseas, parents often busy with double jobs, harried by their own affluence, or casualties of the divorce courts." [6]

"A CLOUD OF WITNESSES"

The Bible also speaks of bleachers. The author of the book of Hebrews writes, "We are surrounded by so great a cloud of witnesses" (Hebrews 12:1). The "cloud of witnesses" are the Saints who have passed on to the Church Triumphant. They are with us in the stadium as we run the race of life. They fill the bleachers. They applaud us and cheer us on to victory. They pray for us to attain our goal. They have advice to give. For they have run on the very same track and have won the garland of victory. They offer us more than applause and prayers; they offer us evidence. They can tell us how they ran the race and won, how they trained for it, how they maintained their strength. We are surrounded by these witnesses. The air is thick with them. They are like a cloud in their multitude. The walls of Orthodox churches are filled with them. And every one of them has a story to tell, a story of grace and divine mercy, a story that is full of encouragement for the runners of today, if only we will listen to them. David, Daniel, Isaiah, Jeremiah, Matthew, Mark, Luke, John and millions of others. "We are surrounded by a great cloud of witnesses"—not one of them silent or indifferent; all of them eager to share with us what the Lord did for them, how they found Him, what grace they received.

It is because we are "surrounded by so great a cloud of witnesses" that we are exhorted to "lay aside every weight and sin which clings so closely" (Hebrews 12:1).

---

[6] Reprinted from *"Book of Comfort"* by Alvin Rogness, copyright 1979, by permission of Augsburg Publishing House.

It is because we are "surrounded by so great a cloud of witnesses" that we are challenged to "run with perseverance the race that is set before us" (Hebrews 12:1).

It is because we are "surrounded by so great a colud of witnesses" that we are admonished to look "to Jesus the pioneer and perfecter of our faith" (Hebrews 12:2).

The Saints are more than just watching us. They are surrounding us with their prayers, their cheers and the challenging stories of their victories in Christ.

We are not alone as we proceed on the journey to the kingdom. We are part of God's great family which includes those who have gone on before us. Just as it makes a difference in the lives of children when the bleachers are filled with uncles, aunts, and grandparents, so it makes a difference when we know that the bleachers of heaven are filled with Saints, cheering us on with their prayers and challenging us with the examples of their lives.

ONE MEDIATOR

Orthodox Christians believe that there is only one Mediator between God and man, Jesus: "For there is one God, and one mediator between God and men, the man Jesus Christ" (I Tim. 2:5).

The Orthodox theologian Kritopoulos explains why Orthodox Christians invoke the prayers of Saints. He writes:

"We do not say to a Saint, 'Saint N., save, redeem, or see that I obtain such and such goods' . . . but 'Saint N., pray for us' . . . Nor do we call Saints 'Mediators', for there is only one Mediator between God and man, . . . Jesus Christ, Who only is able to mediate between the Father and us . . . Not as mediators do we call upon Saints, but as intercessors . . . before God for us, who are our brethren . . . The Holy Spirit makes known unto them the needs of those who invoke them . . . and they intercede saying, 'not in our own deeds or merits—for we have nothing worthy in Thy sight—but in the deeds and merits of thy Only-Begotten Son, . . . do we pray to Thy Majesty, O thou Most High God' . . . Whence the Church asks nothing more from the Saints than that they intercede to God for us and beseech Him for all things useful to us." [7]

Just as we pray for each other in this life so we continue to pray for one another in the other life. As Archbishop Paul of Finland writes, ". . . life continues after death. It would be strange to think that the prayers of a devout Christian reach God during his temporal life in this world, but not afterwards when he has 'departed and is with Christ' (Phil. 1:23)." [8] Indeed, early inscriptions, as in the Roman catacombs, show that the first Christians prayed for those who had died, and also asked their prayers.

Orthodox Christians do not ask for the prayers of Saints because they feel that they are more accessible to us, more human, more understanding, more merciful.

[7] "Some Aspects of Contemporary Greek Orthodox Thought" Gavin, p. 401.
[8] "The Faith We Hold," p. 27 S.V.S. Press. Crestwood, N.W. 1980.

This would be an insult to God's love and a denial of His Incarnation through which God emptied Himself and took on our human nature because He cared so much for us.

Jesus is not some awesome Power in heaven Who looks down at us from a distance—too holy and too great to be approached. He is most approachable. Did He not say, "Come to me all you who labor and are heavy laden and I will give you rest"? (Matt. 11:28). And, "Him that cometh to Me, I will in no wise cast out" (John 6:37)? And do we not read in Hebrews: "For we have not a high priest who is unable to sympathize with our weaknesses, but one who in every respect has been tempted as we are, yet without sinning. Let us then with confidence draw near to the throne of grace, that we may receive mercy and find grace to help in time of need" (Hebrews 4:15-16)? No Saint can ever be more accessible or approachable than Jesus.

THE COMMUNION OF SAINTS

Although Saints are not substitutes for Christ, Orthodox Christians believe firmly in the communion of saints. By this we mean that the Church Triumphant in heaven is not insensitive to the needs and sufferings of the Church Militant on earth. The two churches remain connected through the bond of love which is expressed through prayer. The communion of saints is a communion of never-ending prayer.

Thus, besides our Church Family on earth, we belong to a larger family of God, which includes those who have gone before us. We are united with those in heaven. We call this the Communion of Saints, that is, the union of all who share in the life of Christ, whether on earth or in the other world.

Commenting on this, Fr. Kallistos Ware writes:

"In God and in His Church there is no division between the living and the departed, but all are one in the love of the Father. Whether we are alive or whether we are dead, as members of the Church we still belong to the same family, and still have a duty to bear one another's burdens. Therefore just as Orthodox Christians here on earth pray for one another and ask for one another's prayers, so they pray for the faithful departed and ask the faithful departed to pray for them. Death cannot sever the bond of mutual love which links the members of the Church together." [9]

Fr. John of Kronstadt writes on the communion of saints: "We live together with them (the Saints in heaven), in the house of the Heavenly Father, only in different parts of it. We live in the earthly, they in the heavenly half; but we can converse with them, and they with us." [10]

How effectively the Communion of Saints is expressed on the walls of Orthodox Churches where the angels, prophets, apostles, martyrs and saints are all gathered together with the worshippers around the figure of the All-Ruling Christ in the dome. The entire Church, that in heaven and that on earth, converses with each other and lifts its heart in praise to God.

---

[9] "The Orthodox Church" p. 258. Viking-Penquin Press. New York, NY.
[10] "The Spiritual Counsels of Father John of Kronstadt." James Clarke and Co. London.

Sergius Bolshakoff caught this when he visited the Monastery of Dionysiou on Mt. Athos. He writes: "The church had its own air of mystery. A few red lamps burned before the golden iconostasis and the icons on the stand. Hieratic saints solemnly looked down from the blue walls. It seemed as though they, too, had come to assist at the Liturgy, representing the church triumphant." [11]

Noting the small congregation in church one Sunday morning, a cynic said to the priest, "Not many in church this morning, Father. Not many at all." The old priest replied, "You are wrong, my son. There were thousands at church this morning. Thousands and thousands and tens of thousands." For, the priest had just read in the prayers of the liturgy: "Therefore with angels and archangels and all the company of heaven we laud and magnify thy glorious name, evermore praising Thee . . . ." It was the Communion of Saints in action!

THE THEOTOKOS

Among all the Saints, the Orthodox Church reserves a special position of honor for the Blessed Virgin Mary, who is venerated as the most exalted among God's creatures, "more honorable than the cherubim and incomparably more glorious than the seraphim."

The titles given to Mary by the Orthodox Church: *Theotokos* (Mother of God), *Aeiparthenos* (Ever-Virgin), and *Panayia* (All-Holy) serve a theological purpose. Far from elevating her to a position as a fourth person of the Trinity, such titles seek to protect and proclaim the correct doctrine of Christ's Person. The Mother is venerated because of the Son and never apart from Him. Too often a refusal to honor the Theotokos goes hand in hand with an incomplete faith in the Incarnation, i.e., the mystery of God becoming man in the Person of Jesus. Nicholas Cabasilas has written: "The Incarnation was not only the work of the Father, of His Power and His Spirit . . . but it was also the work of the will and faith of the Virgin. . . Just as God became incarnate voluntarily, so He wished that His Mother should bear Him freely and with her full consent." Mary stands as the greatest example of man's free response to God's offer of salvation. She stands as an example of synergy, or cooperation between man and God. God does not force His will on Mary but waits for her free response which she grants with those beautiful words: "Behold the handmaid of the Lord; be it done to me according to your word" (Luke 1:38). Thus, Eve's disobedience is counterbalanced by Mary's obedience. She becomes the New Eve as Christ is the New Adam, lifting by her obedience the curse that the first Eve brought upon the human race by her disobedience.

The Immaculate Conception of Mary is not recognized as a dogma (official teaching) by the Orthodox Church. According to this Roman Catholic dogma, Mary was cleansed of original sin by God while still in her mother's womb in order that the All-Pure Son of God might be born through her. Since such a teaching denies the free response of man to God, the Orthodox Church believes that Mary was cleansed of all sin at the Annunciation after she had agreed to accept God's offer. It was at that point that the Holy Spirit came upon her to make

<hr />

[11] *"In Search of True Wisdom."* Bolshakoff and Pennington. Doubleday and Co. 1979.

her fit to receive the Word in her womb. At that moment she became "blessed" and "full of grace".

The Bodily Assumption of Mary to heaven which was formally declared as official dogma of the Roman Catholic Church in 1950, remains a pious belief in the Orthodox Church based on tradition. According to this belief Mary's body was taken up to heaven after her death, as will our body at the Second Coming of Jesus. Thus, in Mary's case, the Resurrection of the Body has been anticipated. Although the hymns of the Church that are sung on the Feast of the Falling Asleep of the Theotokos (August 15) clearly affirm such a belief, the Orthodox Church has not declared the Bodily Assumption of Mary to be a dogma since in the words of Vladimir Lossky, "The Mother of God was never a theme of the public preaching of the Apostles; while Christ was preached on the housetops . . . the Mystery of His Mother was proclaimed only to those who were within the Church. . . It is not so much an object of faith as a foundation of our hope, a fruit of faith, ripened in Tradition. Let us therefore keep silence, and let us not try to dogmatize about the supreme glory of the Mother of God." [12]

Summarizing what the Orthodox Church believes about the Theotokos, we may say that the Virgin sits in the first pew leading us in our prayers to her Son. Her whole life and purpose are simply to bring us to Him. In the words of the Greek Orthodox theologian, Dr. N. A. Nissiotis:

"As shown in the icon, Mary is never alone but always with Christ. Thus prayer to her is the prayer of the Church with her to the incarnate Son. One should rather see in Mary, the 'Most Holy' (Panaghia), the first and the fullest of the Saints, leading them in a continuous intercession to her Son. The worshipping Church is not praying to the 'Theotkos' but praying with her to God. She is the animating power, the leader of this continuous intercession of the Community of Saints to the Trinitarian God." [13]

VENERATION

Orthodox Christians do not worship the Theotokos and the Saints; rather they venerate them. God alone is worshipped. Anyone who claims that the Orthodox worship Saints is guilty of bearing false witness against his neighbor since we clearly do not believe this. The Saints are reverenced as reflections of the Christ image. It is God Who is glorified through His Saints. They are praised for what God has done in and through them.

Reverence for Saints is enhanced through the use and veneration of icons which are ever-present in Orthodox homes. The icon becomes a meeting place, an existential encounter, a window through which we look on the Saints not as shadowy figures from a remote past but as contemporary brothers and sisters in Christ, members of the same household of God. We feel free to call on them through prayer for family support as they intercede to God in our behalf. For example, St. Basil writes, "I accept the saintly Apostles, prophets, and martyrs,

---

[12] V. Lossky, "*Panagia*," in "*The Orthodox Church in the Ecumenical Movement.*" W.C.C. Publications.
[13] "*Interpreting Orthodoxy*," N.A. Nissiotis, Light and Life Publishing Company, Mpls. MN.

and in my prayer to God I call upon them and through their prayer I receive mercy from our God who loves all humanity" (Epistle to Amphilochios).

There is in man an innate sense of reverence for moral greatness. In Orthodox Christianity this reverence finds expression in the veneration of the Saints, the moral giants of our faith. The Orthodox believer's daily association with the Saints, whose lives glorified Christ, serves to form the Orthodox lifestyle.

The veneration of Saints serves also as a safeguard of the true faith and as a test of Orthodoxy. Any teaching that is not in harmony with the lives and faith of the Saints is rejected as false. All that is in harmony is welcomed for the enrichment it brings.

"HAVING REMEMBERED ALL THE SAINTS"

As we have said, we do not pray alone during the liturgy. We pray together with all the Saints. This is expressed when the priest says, "Having remembered all the Saints, again and again in peace let us pray to the Lord." The saints here refer to both the living and departed members of the Church.

More than once during the liturgy the deacon calls on us to pray with the similar exhortation; "Calling to remembrance our most holy, pure, blessed and glorified Lady, Theotokos and ever-Virgin Mary together with all the Saints, let us commit ourselves and each other to Christ our God." Here we see clearly that the purpose of bringing to mind the Theotokos and all the Saints is to lead us to a deeper commitment "to Christ our God." The focus is not on the Saints but on Christ. After we have remembered the Saints, we move on "to commit ourselves and each other to Christ our God." Having fixed our gaze on others in the family of God who have rendered perfect service to His excellent glory, we are properly inspired to offer ourselves in total surrender and commitment to Christ, our Lord.

CANONIZATION

The names of the Saints, i.e., those who rejoice in heaven in fellowship with their Lord, are legion. They are known only to God. Of these countless Saints, the Church on earth remembers only a few whose holiness struck the imagination of the Christians of their era. The process of canonization in the Orthodox Church is described by Nicholas Zernov:

"Canonization in the Orthodox Church begins locally. Its first requisite is continuous and increasing love and veneration . . . by members of his community. The next step is reached when the hierarchy of a local church undertakes to examine all the records left by the holy man or woman, and if these prove satisfactory, then the last part of the act is performed and canonization is announced and other autocephalous churches are informed. This considered judgement of the Church is essential, for sometimes people of exceptional spiritual gifts, but not necessarily of sound moral life and Orthodox faith, attract admiration and can mislead their followers." [14]

---

[14] "Eastern Christendom" by N. Zernov. G. P. Putnam's Sons. New York. 1961.

RELICS OF SAINTS

The veneration of the relics of Saints dates back to the early Church. According to the Orthodox belief the body remains a Temple of the Holy Spirit even after death. Redeemed, cleansed, sanctified by the blood of Jesus, consecrated by the indwelling Spirit, the bodies of Saints are drenched, as it were, to their very bones with divinity. St. Cyril of Jerusalem (4th century) writes:

"Though the soul is not present, a power resides in the bodies of the saints because of the righteous soul which has for so many years dwelt in it, or used it as its minister" (Catechetical Lectures (XVIII, 16).

Fr. Kallistos Ware reminds us that the veneration of the relics of Saints in the Orthodox Church proceeds from a highly developed theology of the body:

"Belief in the deification of the body and in its eventual resurrection helps to explain the Orthodox veneration of relics. Since the body is redeemed and sanctified along with the soul, and since the body will rise again, it is only fitting that Christians should show respect for the bodily remains of the saints. Reverence for relics is not the fruit of ignorance and superstition, but springs from a highly developed theology of the body." [15]

We read in "The Martyrdom of Polycarp": "So we later took up his bones, more precious than costly stones and more valuable than gold, and laid them away in a suitable place. There the Lord will permit us, so far as possible, to gather together in joy and gladness to celebrate the day of his martyrdom as a birthday, in memory of those athletes who have gone before, and to train and make ready those who are to come hereafter."

SAINTS TODAY

Canonized saints are but a tiny fraction of those who are with God in heaven. They are merely a few whom the Church projects as examples to spur us on to holiness. They are proof that holiness and heaven are attainable. Such Saints circulate through the Church Year assuring us again and again: "I made it. So can you. So must you!"

A cartoon in "The New Yorker" some time ago pictured a couple in a midtown Manhattan apartment drinking martinis while the man said to the woman: "So what if Albert Schweitzer did escape the rat-race! Name three others!" The Church names more than three others! It points to a host of others—not only the Saints of the past but also the saints of the present. For, Scripture and the Liturgy call every baptized Christian a saint. When the priest says in the Divine Liturgy: "The saintly things (agia) to the saints (ayiois)," he is speaking not to the Saints on the iconstasis but also to the contemporary saints who are participating in the liturgy. The saintly things (the Body and Blood of Jesus) are offered to them (the living saints) to nourish their life in Christ. We are saints from the moment of baptism. We continue to be saints testifying and shining for Jesus in the world today as we maintian our fellowship with Him through prayer and the sacraments.

---

[15] *"The Transfiguration of the Body"* by K. Ware. And article in *"Sacrament and Image"* edited by A. M. Allchin. Fellowship of St. Alban and St. Sergius. 1967.

In the words of D.M. Prescott: "Each of us, the most unsaintly as well as the most spiritually minded, has a next step (to take) which will take him nearer to God; and all He asks of us is that we take that step."

A person once came to a religious teacher and exclaimed rather excitedly that someone had invented a robot, an artificial man. The great teacher was not impressed. "Show me someone who can create a saint," he said, "and I shall be impressed."

Our Lord Jesus specializes in creating saints!

> "If man is not rising upwards
>   to be an angel,
>   depend on it.
>   he is sinking downwards
>   to be a devil.
>   He cannot stop the beast."
>   Samuel Taylor Coleridge
>   "Table Talk"

SUMMARY

1. By remembering and honoring the saints we celebrate what the Holy Spirit has done in their lives. God is praised in and through His saints.

2. The saints are those who, having advanced closer to the goal of theosis (becoming like God in Christ), can help the rest of us through their example and prayers.

3. Made in the image of God and baptized in the Trinity, every Christian has the potential of sainthood and is called by God to be a saint. Just as there are Saints with a capital "S", those officially canonized by the Church, so there are "saints" with a small "s", all baptized and committed Christians.

4. Saints are our brothers and sisters in the household of God. We pray to God not only as individuals but also as members of God's family together with the saints. We may call upon them for family support beseeching their intercession in and through Christ.

5. The Saints are the heroes of our faith, God's "Hall of Fame", who offer all of us a great incentive to virtue.

6. As a great "cloud of witnesses", the saints fill the bleachers of heaven cheering us on with their prayers and challenging us with the example of their lives.

7. Since Jesus Christ is the "one mediator between God and man", saints are not mediators but intercessors. We do not pray *to* Saints; rather we ask them to pray *for* us.

8. The Theotokos (Mother of God) is venerated and honored because of her Son and never apart from Him. She is the *Panaghia,* the first and fullest of the Saints, leading the Church in a continuous intercession to the Trinity.

9. Saints are not worshipped; they are venerated. Only God is worshipped.

10. Orthodox Christians respect and venerate the relics of the Saints (bodily remains) because the body along with the soul is redeemed and sanctified; one day it will rise from the grave to be with God forever.

What We Believe About Eschatology or Life After Death

A few years ago a significant number of books were written on what happens after we die. Dr. Elizabeth Kubler-Ross' book "On Death and Dying" and Dr. Raymond Moody's best seller "Life After Life" brought the subject of life after death to the attention of many people. It was common to hear people on the street and in social gatherings talking about a subject that for many years was taboo, i.e., what happens after we die.

For Orthodox Christians the only real evidence for life beyond the grave is to be found in God's word, not in Kubler-Ross or Moody or anyone else. Many of these authors have been involved in mystical experiences and the occult which are tools of Satan according to the teachings of our Church. The promise of life after death is assured solely by the resurrection of Jesus. "Because I live, you shall live also," said Jesus. No Christian should ever base his faith on anything but the word of God as interpreted by the Church. We should never allow human experience to speak with more authority than the Scriptures on this issue.

In addition to all the talk about life after death, not since the Middle Ages has eschatology been so popular a subject of discussion. Eschatology is just another one of those Greek words for how the world will end. There are those who believe that in the end civilization will emerge perfected after some kind of world-wide calamity. Then there are those who predict that civilization will disappear altogether. Whereas a few years ago we used to believe in evolution, i.e., that the world was getting better and better, most people now believe that things are so bad they can't go on this way much longer. They believe more in a coming catastrophe than in evolution.

The story is told about Bishop Eivind Berggrav, the famed Norwegian war-resister of the Second World War, that when he saw the devastated ruins of London, he exclaimed, "If there is a Third World War, there will be nothing left." "Nothing but God!" Berggrav's British host rejoined.

President John Kennedy once said to the famous evangelist Billy Graham, after playing a round of golf with him in Florida, "I want to ask you a question. Where do you think history is going? What is going to be the climax, the end?"

It is a question that is being asked by many today; a question to which many false and misleading answers are being given; a question which affects each one of us. It is an important question that we shall endeavor to answer on the basis of God's word and the Sacred Tradition of the Orthodox Church.

WHAT IS ESCHATOLOGY?

What we shall be talking about is called in theology *eschatology*.

It comes from a Greek word, *eschatologia*, which means the doctrine or study of the last things. *Eschata* in Greek means the last things. It refers to the study of such events as death, the end of the world, the particular or intermediate judgment, the Parousia, the second coming of Jesus, the resurrection of the dead, the final judgment, heaven and hell.

Christian eschatology tells us that the life we now live will not come to an end. It is headed somewhere. Our years on earth, however many or few, are not the whole story. There is more ahead.

We cannot escape eschatology. If we reject Christian eschatology, we will replace it with another version of eschatology. For example, the statement, "Eat, drink, and be merry, for tomorrow we die," is an eschatological statement. It is talking about the end of your life and mine. It is telling us that death is supreme. It will get all of us in the end. So it behooves us to enjoy ourselves to the fullest before death catches us and puts an end to us.

In a similar way, our Christian faith is eschatoglogical. In contrast to the secular eschatology of "Eat, drink, and be merry . . .," our Christian faith tells us: God is more powerful than death. In fact, He sent His Son, Jesus, to destroy death. In Christ, death does not destroy life. It fulfills life. God confronts each one of us in Christ to offer us life. In the words of the Apostle John, "He who has the Son has life; he who has not the Son of God has not life" (I John 5:12). The decision we make about Christ, i.e., whether we receive Him, ignore Him, or reject Him, determines whether we spend eternity with God in heaven or without Him in hell. For the unbeliever the end of the world may mean annihilation, destruction, catastrophe; for the Christian, however, the end of the world means the beginning of eternity, the inauguration of a new and better life, the coming of the Kingdom of God for each of us personally.

So whether we are believers or unbelievers we are involved in eschatology. Something is going to happen to us at the end of our lives. Depending on what we do now it can be either the greatest good or the greatest calamity.

To see how eschatology fits into God's plan of salvation let us examine the four stages of grace:

1. *Preparation,* which, simply stated, means God calls us to be converted, to change the whole direction of our life so that it is headed toward God.
2. *Justification,* which is our being cleansed of sin through baptism and after baptism through repentance. We become justified, just-as-if-we-had-never-sinned.
3. *Sanctification,* which is the process of being sanctified or made holy. This is the Christian's gradual growth in Christ. It includes the putting on of Christ and the receiving of the Holy Spirit. Here prayer and the sacraments play an important role.
4. *Glory,* which refers to what will happen to us after death, i.e., we shall see God's glory and share in it. This is the last, or the eschatological stage. The first three stages: preparation, justification, and sanctification culminate in the glory stage. "When Christ who is our life appears, then you also will appear with Him in glory" (Col. 3:4). This is what lies ahead for the believer.

THE WHOLE PURPOSE OF THE CREED

Because Christ has overcome sin and death, because He is the living Lord of our lives, we have a future: death is not the last word in human destiny. This powerful theme of unquenchable hope runs through the whole New Testament and is expressed so effectively in the Nicene Creed.

The Creed delineates exactly what we are waiting for in the future. We are waiting for the second coming of Jesus. We are waiting for the resurrection of the dead. We are waiting for the life of the ages to come. To use the words of the Creed, "And I wait for the resurrection of the dead, and the life of the world to come. . . He (Jesus) shall come again with glory to judge both the living and the dead, of Whose kingdom there shall be no end."

This is the end. This is the purpose. This is the great goal toward which the entire creed is marching. If you drop the end of the Creed which talks about the coming of Jesus and the life of the world to come, you might as well stop reciting the rest of it, because it has no meaning left in it.

"I believe . . . in Jesus Christ His only Son our Lord." Why is Jesus one of the focal points of the Creed? The answer is to be found again in the Creed: "Who for us men and our salvation came down from heaven." That is what it is all about. He the beloved Son of God, of the same essence with the Father, came down from heaven, was crucified, died and buried. He rose on the third day and is now sitting at the right hand of God, the Father Almighty. But why? What for? Why this strange expedition all the way from heaven to earth? Why this incredible story of God become man? Why does God have to die and rise again? Why any of this but for one reason? God did it in order to come and take us with Him to a specially prepared place so that we might be with Him forever. This is what God desires for each of us as the end point, the omega, of our lives. This is our Christian eschatology—yours and mine—which Jesus expressed so beautifully in His priestly prayer to the Father, "Father, I desire that they also, whom Thou hast given me, may be with me where I am, to behold my glory which Thou hast given me in thy love for me before the foundation of the world" (John 17:24). This is why Fr. Florovsky stated that "eschatology is not just one particular section of the Christian theological system, but rather its basis and foundation, its guiding and inspiring principle, or, as it were, the climate of the whole of Christian thinking. . . The Christian perspective is intrinsically eschatological." [1]

THE LAST CHAPTER

Life is complex. Things never seem to turn our right. Many times it is like a detective story where the plot seems very confused. One is not at all certain what the outcome will be. But in the last chapter the detective summons all the suspects into a room, proceeds to unravel the mystery, shows the pattern running through it, and reveals how he knew the guilty man. It is only in the light of the last chapter that the rest of the book makes sense.

Now if one had read the last chapter first, then one would be able to make a good deal more sense out of the story. Knowing what happens in the last chapter, one would see meaning and significance in the events as they took place.

---

[1] *"Aspects of Church History"* Georges Florovsky. Nordland Press. Belmont, Mass.

In His great love God has allowed us to read the last chapter. He has allowed us to see that we live in a world where the final victory has been won. The cross was not the end for Jesus; neither will it be the end for those who believe in Him. The Risen Christ will have the last word. And the last word is:

"In the world you have tribulation but be of good cheer, I have overcome the world."

The final chapter is the Parousia, the Second Coming of Jesus, the resurrection of the dead, the final judgment and the establishment of the endless Kingdom of God. If we know this in advance, what a profound difference it should make in our attitude toward suffering, toward evil, toward death, toward everyday life.

DEATH

One of the very vital and existential truths with which Christian eschatology confronts us is death—your death and mine. We do everything to try to repress the reality of death. But Jesus talks about it repeatedly. He talks about it because He has the greatest good news to share with us about how He defeated death, actually trampled upon it by His own death, in order to grant those who are in the tombs, and to each one of us as we face our own death—the promise of everlasting life.

When St. Paul talks about death he uses a figure of speech which compares the earthly body to a tent that is used for a time and which at death is exchanged for a heavenly house (see 2 Cor. 5:1-4). This reminds us of the words of our Lord Jesus when He spoke of heaven as a place where there would be many rooms for His people to live in. "Let not your hearts be troubled; believe in God, believe also in me. In my Father's house are many rooms; if it were not so, would I have told you that I go to prepare a place for you? And when I go and prepare a place for you, I will come again and will take you to myself, that where I am you may be also" (John 14:1-3). All this means that when the moment of death comes for the believer he will move from the tent he is presently living in—his earthly body—and will take up residence in a permanent home Jesus has prepared for him.

One of the most beautiful illustrations of what death really is like for the Christian believer is the following. There was a little boy who had an incurable illness. Month after month, the mother tenderly nursed him. But as the time went by, the little fellow gradually began to realize he would not live. One day he asked his mother: "Mom, what is it like to die? Does it hurt?"

Tears filled the mother's eyes as she fled to the kitchen to see about something on the stove. She knew the question had to be faced. She leaned against the kitchen cabinet, her knuckles pressed white against the wall, and breathed a quick prayer: "Lord, tell me how to answer him." And the Lord did tell her. Immediately she knew what to say.

She returned to his room. "Kenneth," she said, "You remember when you were a tiny boy you used to play so hard, when night came you would be too tired even to undress, and you would tumble into mother's bed and fall asleep? That was not your bed. It was not where you belonged.

"In the morning you would wake up and find yourself in your own bed in your own room. Your father had come with big strong arms—and carried you into your own bed. Kenneth, that's what death is like. We fall asleep. Then our heavenly Father picks us up with His mighty hands and carries us to heaven. Later, when morning comes, we wake up and find ourselves not in a strange place but in our own room—in a place where we belong.''

That is what death is for the Christian: moving day. We move from one room in our Father's house (a temporary room which St. Paul calls a tent) to a permanent room which shall be our very own in heaven. It is, in effect, a true homecoming. As the door closes on this life, God opens a new door to a heavenly life.

As surely as God sent us to earth, He has given us a return ticket. As Jesus said, ''I come from God and I go to God.'' Life is like a round-trip journey. We come from God and ultimately we go back to Him.

Aristides, a pagan Greek, in 125 A.D., wrote to one of his friends about the new religion, Christianity, and its attitude toward death. A sentence from one of his letters reads, ''If any righteous man among the Christians passes from this world, they rejoice and offer thanks to God, and they escort the body with songs and thanksgiving as if he were setting out from one place to another nearby.''

St. John Chrysostom summarized the Christian's attitude toward death when he wrote:

> ''When a dear one dies, the unbeliever sees a cadaver, but the Christian sees a body asleep. The unbeliever says that the dead person has 'gone'. We agree, but we remember where he has gone. He has gone where the apostle Paul is, where Peter is, where the whole company of the saints are. We remember that he will rise, not with tears of dismay, but with splendor and glory.''

Thus, physical death, the separation of soul and body, which occured as a result of sin and as punishment for it, loses its fearful aspect for those who have been redeemed in Christ. It opens the door to a glorious new life with God in heaven. Death is now swallowed up in victory (I Cor. 15:54). ''For since by man came death, by man came also the resurrection of the dead. For as in Adam all die, even so in Christ shall all be made alive'' (I Cor. 15:21-22).

Let us apply this faith to a specific example.

What if you had an eight-year-old boy and the doctor told you that he had only a few minutes to live, what would you say to him?

Or, what if you were a priest, and the parents of that child came to you, and said, ''Father, won't you say something to Johnny? He has only a few minutes left.'' What would you say? What would I say?

Well, this actually happened once. A splendid Christian woman who happened to be a scrubwoman in the hospital where little Johnny was a patient had come to know him well. Upon learning that he did not have much longer to live, she walked calmly into Johnny's room, sat on his bed, took his thin hands between her calloused palms, and said, ''Listen, Johnny, God made you. God loves you. God sent His Son to save you. God wants you to come home with Him.''

With great difficulty Johnny raised himself up on his elbow and said, "Say it again." She repeated: "God made you. God loves you. God sent His Son to save you. God wants you to come home with Him." Johnny looked into her beautiful face and said, "Tell God, 'Thank you.' "

These beautiful words of the Christian scrubwoman summarize our theology of death.

THE PARTICULAR OR INTERMEDIATE JUDGMENT

Now we face the question: what happens immediately after a person dies? Is there immediate judgment? Do we just sleep until the Second Coming of Jesus? What lies ahead for us the moment after we die? The Orthodox Church teaches that immediately after death a person is judged. He or she experiences a foretaste of the punishment or reward that will be received in its entirety as the Second Coming of Jesus. It is much like a runner who has come in first in a track meet. He knows he has won. He basks in the satisfaction of victory. He is already in heaven, as it were, but he has to wait until the banquet in the evening to receive the trophy. It is then that he will be granted his reward officially.

The Synod of Constantinople (1672 A.D.) expressed our belief regarding the Particular Judgment as follows:

> "We believe that the souls of the departed are either in bliss or in torment as each one wrought, for immediately after the separation from the body they (the souls) are pronounced either for bliss or suffering and sorrow, yet we confess that neither the joy nor the condemnation are as yet complete. After the General Resurrection, when the soul is united to the body, each one will receive the full measure of joy or condemnation due him for the way in which he conducted himself, whether for good or bad."

Thus, after death we begin to experience a real foretaste of heaven or hell, but we shall have to wait for the Second Coming before we can receive the fullness of our reward.

The judgment that takes place after death is called the Particular or Intermediate Judgment. It is clear that the soul does not sleep during this time. The word "asleep" applies only to the body. This is why the place where the body is placed is called "cemetery" from the Greek word *Kimitirion,* a place where one sleeps. The soul, however, does not sleep after death. It is fully conscious, experiencing its reward.

Can there be anything like repentance after we die? The Orthodox Church teaches that the state of the soul at the Particular Judgment (immediately after death) is fixed and unchangeable, that is, there can be no moral improvement or repentance beyond the grave. The place for such improvement is in this life. "We must work the works of him who sent me, while it is day," said Jesus, "night comes, when no man can work" (John 9:4). In His mercy God gives us many chances to repent and return to Him. But this should not lead anyone to presume upon God's goodness. One day there will be a last chance.

THE RICH MAN AND LAZARUS

We see much of what we believe about the Particular or Intermediate Judgment illustrated in the story of the rich man and Lazarus as told by Jesus. When Lazarus died ''he was carried by the angels to Abraham's bosom.'' That is rabbinic language for paradise. This parable tells us that we are not alone at the moment of death. God sends His angels to carry us, to escort us, into His Presence.

In that life beyond death, Lazarus and the rich man are not asleep. They are very much alive. They recognize each other. They remember their life on earth. ''Son, remember that you in your lifetime received your good things, and Lazarus in like manner evil things; but now he is comforted here, and you are in anguish.'' The rich man in his great affluence had been ignoring poor Lazarus, dying of starvation on his doorstep. Now he was paying the price for his lack of love. ''Being in torment . . . he called out, 'Father Abraham, have mercy on me, and send Lazarus to dip the end of his finger in water and cool my tongue; for I am in anguish in this flame.'' To show that there can be no repentance, no moral improvement, no salvation beyond the grave, Abraham tells the rich man, ''. . . between us and you a great chasm has been fixed, in order that those who would pass from here to you may not be able, and none may cross from there to us.''

One cannot pass from hell to heaven beyond the grave. The time and place for that is in this life. Jesus calls us to faith and repentance today. For today, *now* is the day of salvation.

JUDGMENT TODAY

Already in this life God prepares us for the Particular Judgment. Whenever we choose God's will, we experience a bit of heaven in the satisfaction that God bestows on us through the voice of conscience. We enter already by anticipation into eternal life. Likewise whenever we deliberately disobey God's will, we experience a foretaste of hell through the terrible pangs of conscience. The moral order of God's universe keeps breaking in on us constantly to prepare us for the judgment to come.

Thus, we may distinguish three stages in life:

1. Our life on earth which is the arena of grace and the preparation for heaven; 2. the particular judgment which takes place after death during which time, while the body sleeps, ths soul experiences a foretaste of heaven or hell and 3. the Resurrection of the dead and the Final Judgment at the coming of Jesus when the soul and the body will be reunited for eternity to receive in full their crown of glory or punishment.

This is the faith we live by. This is the faith we die by. When the end comes, we too will be able to say together with St. Paul: ''The time of my departure has come. I have fought the good fight, I have finished the race, I have kept the faith. Henceforth there is laid up for me the crown of righteousness, which the Lord, the righteous judge, will award to me on that day, and not only to me but also to all who have loved his appearing'' (2 Tim. 4:6-8).

The Scriptures mention six events that will occur before the Second Coming of Jesus:

1. The preaching of the Gospel to all nations (Matt. 24:14).
2. The return of Israel to Christ (Rom. 11:25-26).
3. The coming of Elijah and Enoch in the last days (see Rev.11).
4. The appearance of the Antichrist.
5. A mass apostasy or falling away from the true Christian faith led by false teachers (Matt. 24:4-5).
6. Wars, revolutions, famines and earthquakes (Matt. 24:6-8).

Commenting on the meaning of these six events that will precede the Second Coming, Fr. Kallistos Ware writes:

"Scripture and Tradition speak to us repeatedly about the Second Coming. They give us no grounds for supposing that, through a steady advance in 'civilization', the world will grow gradually better and better until mankind succeeds in establishing God's kingdom upon earth. The Christian view of world history is entirely opposed to this kind of evolutionary optimism. What we are taught to expect are disasters in the world of nature . . . warfare between men . . . apostasy . . . tribulation . . . (the) Antichrist who . . . will be . . . not Satan himself, but a human being . . . in whom all the forces of evil will be concentrated and who will for a time hold the entire world under his sway. The brief reign of Antichrist will be abruptly terminated by the Second Coming of the Lord, this time not in a hidden way, as at His birth in Bethlehem, but 'sitting on the right hand of power' (Matt. 26:64). So the course of history will be brought to a sudden and dramatic end, through a direct intervention from the divine realm." [2]

The six signs that will precede the Second Coming are sufficiently vague as to keep the exact time of His coming a mystery. How many times, for example, in history have Christians thought that the Antichrist had come in the person of Nero, Hitler or Stalin? How many times have there been mass apostasies from the Christian faith led by false teachers? How many times have there been revolutions, famines, and earthquakes which made many believe that the Coming of Jesus was imminent? Despite these six signs we have no exact timetable from God regarding the Second Coming of Jesus. We know neither the day nor the hour. "But of that day and hour no one knows, not even the angels of heaven, nor the Son, but the Father only. . . Watch therefore, for you do not know on what day your Lord is coming" (Matt. 24:36,42). He will come "as a thief in the night" (I Thess. 5:2).

You ask, why did not God tell us when Jesus will come again? For very good reason. He wants us to be constantly prepared, to maintain constant purity in our lives. Augustine put it this way: "This one day God has concealed from us that we may keep a better and closer watch over the other days of life."

When company comes to your home, you like to know the exact hour of their arrival so that you can have the house clean and ready for their arrival. If you do not know when they are coming, you will have to keep the house clean and neat all the time.

---

[2] *"The Orthodox Way"* Fr. Kallistos Ware. St. Vladimir Seminary Press. Crestwood. N.Y.

I read recently of a conversation between two of our Roman Catholic brethren:

"Oh, my Lord! He's coming!"

"Who?"

"Jesus, you idiot. O, Lord! Where's the nearest confessional?"

"Why?"

"Because I'm not ready, that's why! What a way to run a world. Doesn't He know I've been too busy lately? Why didn't He give us a little advance warning?"

"He did."

"When?"

"About two thousand years ago."

WATCHFULNESS

The whole theme of the Christian's life is watchfulness, preparedness, expectant faith. The end is always imminent, always spiritually close at hand. We are constantly only a heart beat away from judgment. "And just as it is appointed for men to die once, and after that comes the judgment . . . (Heb. 9:27). How well this sense of urgency is captured by the words of St. Andrew of Crete, recited each Lent in the Great Canon:

"My soul, O my soul, rise up! Why art thou sleeping!

The end draws near, and soon shalt thou be troubled.

Watch then, that Christ thy God may spare thee,

For He is everywhere present and fills all things."

The Lord Jesus said,

"Let your loins be girded and your lamps burning, and be like men who are waiting for their master to come home from the marriage feast, so that they may open to him at once when he comes and knocks. Blessed are those servants whom the master finds awake when he comes; truly, I say to you, he will gird himself and have them sit at the table, and he will come and serve them. . . You also must be ready; for the Son of Man is coming at an hour you do not expect" (Luke 12:35-40).

God will one day step into history in the Person of Jesus to judge the living and the dead. "We must all appear before the judgment seat of Christ; so that each one may receive good or evil, according to what he has done in the body" (2 Cor. 5:10). The purpose of Judgment is not to make us afraid but to drive us to repentance so that we may become truly "His people" by faith, hope and love. God's judgment is redemptive. He wants all to be saved and to come to the knowledge of truth.

THE VICTORY MADE MANIFEST

The Second Coming of Jesus is the goal toward which all of life is moving, the harbor toward which the ship of life is sailing. The victory of Christ achieved by His resurrection remains to the world a hidden victory, seen only through the eyes of faith. The Second Coming of Jesus will be that point in history when the victory of Christ will be seen and made manifest to all eyes, and the world will come to know what the Church already knows: that Jesus Christ is Lord!

The Second Coming of Jesus shows us that God has a plan for the world, that history is not a haphazard collection of chance events which are going nowhere. The Second Coming tells us that the world is going somewhere. It has a supreme purpose. The whole of creation is marching toward the time when Jesus will come again as Judge and Lord of all. Every one of us will appear before Him to give an account of our life. This is how much God cares for each one of us personally; this is how much what we do in life today and every day matters to Him. At the end of life each of us will have a personal and private audience with the Lord of the Universe! Every liturgy reminds us of this when it invites us to pray for "a good defense before the awesome judgment seat of Christ." The whole of life, then, for the Christian is a preparation for the parousia, the Second Coming of Jesus. When the perfect comes, the imperfect will pass away; we shall see Him not as in a mirror darkly but face to face (I Cor. 13:9-12). We shall be looking upon His glory forever (I Thess. 4:17) in a "new heaven and a new earth" (2 Peter 3:3-13).

WHAT WILL HAPPEN ON THAT DAY?

1. The Bible tells us that when the Lord returns: "All the tribes of the earth will . . . see the Son of man coming on the clouds of heaven with power and great glory: and He will send out His angels with a loud trumpet call, and they will gather His elect from the four winds, from one end of the earth to the other" (Matt. 24:30,31).

2. At the return of the Lord the dead are to be raised up. "For the Lord Himself will descend from heaven . . . and the dead in Christ will rise first; then we who are alive . . . shall . . . meet the Lord . . ." (I Thess. 1:16-17).

3. At the return of the Lord, judgment will take place. St. Paul writes, "This judgment will issue in . . . Christ's personal coming from Heaven with the angels of His power. It will bring full justice in dazzling flame upon those who have refused to know God or to obey the Gospel of our Lord Jesus Christ. Their punishment will be eternal exclusion from the radiance of the Face of the Lord, and the glorious majesty of His power. But to those whom He has made holy His coming will mean splendor unimaginable. It will be a breath-taking wonder to all who believe—including you, for you have believed the message that we have given you" (2 Thess. 1:7-10).

Fr. Kallistos Ware writes, "The Orthodox attitude toward the Last Judgment and Hell is clearly expressed in the choice of Gospel readings at the liturgy on three successive Sundays shortly before Lent. On the first Sunday is read the parable of the Publican and Pharisee, on the second the parable of the Prodigal Son, stories which illustrate the immense forgiveness and mercy of God towards all sinners who repent. But in the Gospel for the third Sunday—the parable of the Sheep and the Goats—we are reminded of the other truth: that it is possible to reject God and to turn away from Him to Hell." [3]

---

[3] "The Orthodox Church" by Ware. Viking-Penguin Press. N.Y.

Judgment means that we shall be seen by God one day as we truly are, with all our masks and pretension stripped away. This is what happened to Peter after he denied Jesus. He saw Jesus once. Jesus looked at him and Peter couldn't return the look. He was judged, seen as he truly was. It was that look that helped Peter realize the great sin he had committed. It led him to repentance and forgiveness.

We may expect mercy from God. There is no sin He will not forgive if man repents. It is only for unrepented sin that there is no forgiveness—not because God refuses to forgive but because man does not seek forgiveness. We would all like to be given a second chance after death. But God gives us a second chance—a thousand second chances—in this life. He became man in the Person of Jesus; He died on the cross to forgive us; He rose from the grave to destroy death for us; He forgave the penitent thief just before he died to show how many second and third chances He is willing to give us. He continues to plead with each one of us personally with His Spirit through the voice of conscience. His love and mercy are continually offered to us through the Church and the Bible, but even God cannot 'force' people to love Him or it is not true love. Part of the meaning of human freedom is that it gives us the awful privilege of saying "No" to God and refusing His love.

THE RESURRECTION OF THE BODY

One of the events that will occur at the Second Coming of Jesus is the resurrection of the dead. By resurrection of the dead we mean the raising of the bodies of all those who have died and the reunion of the body with the soul by the power of the Almighty. St. John of Damascus tells why the resurrection of the body is necessary: "If the soul alone exerted itself in the battle for virtue, then it alone should be crowned. If it alone was defiled . . . in justice it alone should be punished. But since neither soul nor body had existence the one apart from the other, nor did the soul apart from the body exercise itself in virtue or vice, quite rightly are both to receive their due reward together."

The Greek Orthodox theologian Androutsos called the resurrection "a creative act of divine greatness and might, dissolving the rule of death and raising up all the dead along with the living before the divine bar of judgment. Just as God created all things out of nothing, so, through the same creative power He restores human bodies to their first essential form." According to St. Paul the bodies of the dead, when raised, will be incorruptible and spiritual bodies like the body of the Risen Christ during His appearances to the disciples following the resurrection. As a spiritual body it will no longer need the marriage relationship and will not be susceptible to death. It must be borne in mind that the Scripture passages of the New Testament that deal with the Resurrection of the dead and the General Judgment do not give all the details about what will occur. In the words of one respected Orthodox theologian, "nor must they be taken literally, since they are pictures portraying to us the inconceivable grandeur of that day."

When trying to describe the resurrection of the dead, St. Paul uses an analogy from nature. He reminds his readers that when they sow grain, the seed must first "die" before it can produce new life. Though the "body" of the seed is different from the "body" of the full-grown wheat, there is still continuity between them.

What is reaped is different than what is sown, and yet it comes from what is sown.

He goes on to explain that the same is true with the resurrection of the dead. It is "sown" a physical body, he says, but it is raised a spiritual body.

"What is sown is perishable, what is raised is imperishable.

It is sown in dishonor, it is raised in glory.

It is sown in weakness, it is raised in power.

It is sown a physical body, it is raised a spiritual body."

(I Cor. 15:42-44).

In the resurrection we shall not have our weak earthly bodies but new bodies, fashioned by God. Yet there shall be continuity between them. It will be our present body but transformed and renewed as St. Paul describes in Phil. 3:20.

"But our commonwealth is in heaven, and from it we await a Savior, the Lord Jesus Christ, *who will change our lowly body to be like his glorious body,* by the power which enables him even to subject all things to himself" (italics added).

In the final analysis the questions of "How the dead are raised? With what kind of body do they come?" (I Cor. 15:35) remain beyond human understanding: "Lo! I tell you a mystery" (I Cor. 15:51), says Paul. The main truth is that God, in His own way and fashion, will transform us so that we may continue to live in constant fellowship with Him, glorifying Him through all eternity.

Speaking of the continuity between the earthly and the resurrected body, St. Cyril of Jerusalem writes,

"It is this selfsame body that is raised, although not in its present state of weakness; for it will 'put on incorruption' (I Cor. 15:53) and so be transformed . . . It will no longer need the foods which we now eat to keep it alive . . . for it will be made spiritual and will become something marvellous, such as we cannot properly describe."

Both the Old and New Testaments agree that body and soul cannot be split apart. We are both *psyche* (soul) and *soma* (body). We are a unity (psychosomatic). We are not just one or the other; we are both, and God will keep body and soul together for all eternity. Thus, eternal life is a transforming rather than a junking of life on earth. When God came to earth to save man, he took on not only a human soul but also human flesh. He came to save the whole man, body and soul.

God created man to be a unified being of body and soul and to remain so for all eternity. It was the fall of Adam that brought about the separation of body and soul in death: "Dust thou art and unto dust thou shalt return" (Gen. 3:19). Through the Resurrection of Jesus God's original plan for man is restored. At the Second Coming the body will be resurrected to be reunited with the soul.

This is the faith of the New Testament. This is the faith of the early Christians. This continues to be the faith of the ancient Orthodox, Catholic and Apostolic Church: that through His Resurrection the Lord Jesus has completely conquered death. As a result of His victory the dead will rise again *"in Christ"* to enjoy eternal life in spiritualized and transfigured bodies and in a totally new creation. St. Gregory Palamas said, "When God is said to have made man according to His image, the word 'man' means neither the soul by itself nor the body by itself, but both together.'' Both together will be saved. Both together will be transfigured. Both body and soul will spend eternity together in a new heaven and a new earth.

St. Athanasius speaks of the resurrection of the body as the great monument of Christ's victory over death:

"The supreme object of his coming was to bring about the resurrection of the body. This was to be the monument to his victory over death, the assurance to all that he had himself conquered corruption and that their own bodies also would eventually be incorrupt; and it was in token of that and as a pledge of the future resurrection that he kept his body incorrupt.''

THE GENERAL JUDGMENT

Following the resurrection of the dead at the Second Coming of Jesus, the General Judgment will take place. As Jesus said, "When the Son of man comes in his glory, and all the angels with him, then he will sit on his glorious throne. Before him will be gathered all the nations, and he will separate them one from another as a shepherd separates the sheep from the goats, and he will place the sheep at his right hand, but the goats at his left. Then he will say to those at his right hand, 'Come, O blessed of my Father, inherit the kingdom prepared for you from the foundation of the world; for I was hungry and you gave me food. . . Then he will say to those at his left hand, 'Depart from me, you cursed, into the eternal fire prepared for the devil and his angels; for I was hungry and you gave me no food. . . And they will go away into eternal punishment, but the righteous into eternal life'' (Matthew 25).

The same Jesus who came humbly in Bethlehem to be our Savior will come again at the end of time to be our Judge. The purpose of His first coming was to prepare us for the Second Coming. The One who will meet us at the end of the road is the One with Whom we may walk hand in hand on the road of life right now. In fact, we may even minister to Him in the persons of the hungry, the thirsty, the naked, the imprisoned, the sick. The single most important criterion by which we shall be judged is the royal virtue of love: love of God and love of neighbor. ''As you did it to one of the least of these my brethren you did it to me'' (Matt: 24:40).

Remember that the Lord Jesus as Judge on the last day will not condemn those who have sinned, but those who have sinned without repenting. He forgives and saves those who have repented of their sins. For this reason He came into the world: to SAVE. That was the purpose of His coming; that was the dream of His heart; to save us all so that we might be with Him in His glory forever—not one missing!

Fr. Kallistos Ware writes,

''The Last Judgment is best understood as the *moment of truth* when everything is brought to light, when all our acts of choice stand revealed to us in their full implications. When we realize with full clarity who we are, and what has been the deep meaning and aim of our life. And so, following this final clarification, we shall enter—with soul and body reunited—into heaven or hell, into eternal life or eternal death.'' [4]

Daniel Webster was once asked, ''What is the greatest thought you have ever had?'' Pondering a moment, he replied, ''The greatest thought I have ever had was my accountability to God.'' Without this fact of the ultimate justice of God, when all the inequities will be balanced and the injustices corrected, life would be a ''tale told by an idiot.'' Nothing would make sense. Everything would by unreasonable, nonsensical, meaningless.

There have been those in the history of Christianity who have believed in the so-called millenium. This is a teaching that holds that when Christ returns He will reign on earth with His disciples for one thousand years. Based on a literalistic interpretation of Revelation 20, and espoused by heretics in the early Church (Gnostics and Montanists), the idea of an earthly millenium was rejected by the Church. It is mentioned neither in the Nicene Creed nor its doctrines as are the Second Coming and the General Judgment.

HEAVEN

What is heaven?

Orthodox theology teaches that the bliss of heaven consists (1) in deliverance from suffering, pain, grief, corruption, etc., (2) the enjoyment of the vision of God, (3) the reunion with all other righteous souls. There is also a gradation of blessedness corresponding to the moral state of each soul.

Heaven is spoken of in Scripture as ''Kingdom of God,'' ''everlasting life,'' ''bosom of Abraham,'' and ''paradise.''

In 2 Corinthians 12, St. Paul used guarded language to speak of a contact he had with the glorious heavenly reality. He writes:

''I know a man in Christ who fourteen years ago was caught up in the third heaven—whether in the body or out of the body I do not know, God knows. And I know that this man was caught up into Paradise— whether in the body or out of the body I do not know. God knows—and he heard things that cannot be told, which man may not utter'' (vv 2-4).

St. Paul is speaking here about himself. He speaks as carefully as he does because he continued to be so astonished by the memory of the event that he could scarcely believe that it actually happened. Above all, he did not wish to fall into the trap of boasting to others about it. Paul had been given a vision of Paradise, and he knew something special about the future beyond the grave; and what he knew gave him reason to tell us that the future of believers is glorious beyond imagination. ''Eye has not seen, ear has not heard, nor has it ever entered into man's imagination what things God has prepared for those who love Him'' (I Cor. 2:9).

One great Christian said once that if the Lord told us too much about heaven in the Scriptures, we would be so homesick for heaven we wouldn't do any work here. God is wise not only in what He tells us but also in what He does not tell us.

---

[4] "The Orthodox Way" St. Vladimir's Seminary Press.

One of the great characteristics of heaven will be joy. Jesus Himself compared the Kingdom of God to a marriage feast. Christian joy results from the marriage of God to His people, from His constant presence in their midst. The joy of the final stage of the Kingdom of God overflows in the Gospels. For example:

— at the birth of Christ, the angels proclaim: ''I bring you good news of of great joy'' (Luke 2:10);

— in His final discourse with the apostles at the Last Supper, Jesus says, ''These things I have spoken to you that my joy may be in you and that your joy may be full'' (Jn 15:11);

— in the early Church we read, ''And the disciples continued to be filled with joy and with the Holy Spirit'' (Acts 13:52).

This joy is not something that will pass. It will continue eternally in heaven.

''Blessed are the pure of heart,'' said Jesus, ''for they shall see God.'' Heaven is where this promise will be fulfilled. We shall enjoy the open vision of God. ''We shall see Him as He is'' (I John 3:2). The vision begins on earth. At the Transfiguration the disciples were able to see the divine light which shone from the Person of Jesus. St. Paul says that we are like spiritual mirrors that receive and reflect the glory of God. The Church Fathers tell us that man's purpose in life is to be able to see the divine light as much as we are able. We too become transfigured and progress slowly from glory to glory until we attain to the likeness of Christ (2 Cor. 2:18). Already in this life Christians can experience the vision of God. The ascetic Fathers sought to experience this vision of the divine light through prayer and meditation. We call this *theosis* or participation in the divine glory. ''For now we see in a mirror dimly, but then face to face'' says Paul (I Cor. 13:12). Heaven is to be with God ''face to face.'' Our eyes are destined to gaze upon the fullness of God's glory forever.

Fr. John Meyendorff holds that this ''face to face'' vision of God is not to be as Origen believed, ''a static contemplation of divine 'essence', but a dynamic ascent of love, which never ends, because God's transcendent being is inexhaustible and . . . contains new things yet to be discovered through the union of love.'' [5] As St. Irenaeus wrote, ''Not only in this present age but also in the Age to come, God will always have something more to teach man, and man will always have something more to learn from God.'' In other words, we shall not be idle in heaven; we shall be constantly learning and growing.

''I consider that what we suffer at this present time *cannot be compared at all with the glory that is going to be revealed to us*'' (Romans 8:18). This is what lies at the end of the road for the believer. ''To him who overcomes,'' says the Risen Christ. ''I will grant to eat of the tree of life, which is in the paradise of God'' (Rev. 2:7).

The believer who walks with Jesus on the road of life already has eternal life. ''He who eats my flesh and drinks my blood has eternal life,'' said Jesus (John 6:54). Not *''will have''* but *''has''*! Heaven is a continuation of our communion with Jesus that begins on earth. As Fr. Stavropoulos writes:

---

[5] *''Byzantine Theology''* John Meyendorf. Fordham University Press.

"When a person receives the holy sacrament, he receives concurrently the promise of an indescribable communion with Christ in the age to come. . . The Kingdom of God, as a communion of Christ with human beings in the Holy Spirit, is already realized in this life through the mystery of the Eucharist. The Kingdom of the age to come will be the complete and perfect form of the communion which already exists between Christ and the faithful." [6]

HELL

As heaven begins on earth so does hell. An outstanding psychologist has written, "There is a very tangible and a very present hell on this earth. It is this—the hell of neurosis and psychosis—to which sin and unexpiated guilt lead us." We are the ones who create hell when we use the gift of free will that God gave us to say "No" to Him. To exclude God from our lives is to be in hell. God did not create us for hell. He created us for the Kingdom of heaven. We are the ones who create hell for ourselves through our prideful rebellion and disobedience. God came in the Person of Jesus to set us free from hell. We see the Risen Christ in the Easter icon smashing the gates of hell to smithereens. Not one of us can enter hell without first passing over the hill where there is a God-man enthroned on a cross, with arms outstretched to embrace, with head bent to kiss, with heart open to love and forgive. The question that bothers me most is not, "How can God's love tolerate the existence of hell" but "Why should God die on the cross to save unworthy me from a hell which my sins so rightly deserve?" This is the great mystery.

Having been created free, man cannot be forced into a union with God. He is allowed the privilege of facing the eternal consequence of either his "yes" or his "no" to God. To deny hell is to deny free will. God does not forgive those who do not want to be forgiven. Fr. Kallistos Ware writes, "If anyone is in hell, it is not because God has imprisoned him there, but because that is where he himself has chosen to be. The lost in hell are self-condemned, self-enslaved; it has been rightly said that the doors of hell are locked *on the inside.*" [7]

Aristotle taught that the ultimate nature of a thing is determined by its telos or end. So it is that the ultimate meaning of man is to be found in his end. And man's destiny, man's end, is to return to God, to spend eternity with Him, to see Him "face to face." Because the Christian is secure in his eschatological hope, he can live in this world with a kind of abandon, not fearing "what might happen" to him. St. Paul expressed it this way:

"If we live, in the Lord, and if we die, we die in the Lord; so then, whether we live or whether we die, we are the Lord's. For to this end Christ died and lived again, that He might be Lord both of the dead and of the living" (Rom. 14:8,9).

Our Christian eschatology offers us great perspective for living. It revises our whole attitude toward our possessions:

---

[6] *"Partakers of Divine Nature"* C. Stavropoulos. Translated by S. Harakas. Light and Life Pub. Co., Mpls, MN.
[7] *"The Orthodox Way"* by Fr. Kallistos Ware. St. Vladimir Seminary Press, Crestwood, NY.

"If you buy anything, you should remember that you do not have it to keep. If you make use of this world's goods, remember that you have no chance to use them up, for the structure of the world is passing away" (I Cor. 7:30-31).

To see the direction toward which the whole of life is moving is to see more clearly exactly what our true mission in life is:

"The end of all things is at hand; therefore, be sane and sober and say your prayers; above all, have intense love for one another; be hospitable; and use you gifts in the service of God that He may be glorified in everything" (I Peter 4:7-11).

"But the day of the Lord will come like a thief, and then the heavens will pass away with a loud noise, and the elements will be dissolved with fire, and the earth and the works that are upon it will be burned up. Since all these things are thus to be dissolved, what sort of persons ought you to be in lives of holiness and godliness, waiting for and hastening the coming of the day of God . . . (for) we wait for new heavens and a new earth in which righteousness dwells" (2 Peter 3:10-13).

Poetically speaking, history began in a garden and it will end in a garden. Once, by sin, man cut himself off from the garden and the tree of life (Gen. 3:23), but in the end God will bring him back to his proper home and he will find the tree of life freely offered for his use (Rev. 22:2).

Eschatology forces us to ask ourselves some very basic questions: What is the direction of my life right now? If I keep following this way, where will I end up? Am I headed toward God or away from Him? Is my relationship to my Savior a living one? or one of lip-service only? If I should die right now, where would I find myself? What would be my personal eschatology? Where would I spend eternity?

SUMMARY

1. Eschatology is the study of the last things, i.e., death, the end of the world, the Second Coming of Jesus etc.

2. Simply stated, our Orthodox Christian eschatology is expressed in the Nicene Creed when it says that Jesus "will come again with glory to judge the living and the dead, of whose kingdom there shall be no end. . . I wait for the resurrection of the dead, and the life of the world to come".

3. The end of life for the Christian is moving day. We move from a temporary room in our Father's house (which St. Paul calls a tent) to a permanent room in heaven.

4. At the Particular Judgment, which takes place immediately after death, we receive a foretaste of our reward or punishment which will be received in its entirety at the Second Coming of Jesus.

5. God never told us exactly when Jesus will come again. He wants us to maintain a constant state of watchfulness and purity.

6. On the last day: Jesus will return, the dead will be raised, judgment will take place, the new heaven and new earth will be established.

7. The resurrection of Lazarus is a living image of the general resurrection of the dead which will occur on the last day. Every dead body will be resurrected and united again with the soul as a spiritual body similar to the one Jesus had after the resurrection.

8. Life continues eternally beyond the grave in the same direction as in life. If we lived with Christ on earth, we shall continue to live with Him in heaven. If we lived without Him on earth, we shall continue to live without Him in the life beyond.

9. Having been created with free will, man is allowed the privilege of facing the eternal consequence of either his "yes" (heaven) or his "no" (hell) to God. To deny hell is to deny free will.

10. Christian eschatology offers us great perspective for living. To see the direction toward which the whole of life is moving is to see more clearly exactly what our true mission in life is.

What We Believe
About the Sacraments

INTRODUCTION

Man needs power—spiritual power to get off the ground. We have many jokes on the failure of our missiles to get off the ground as planned. But when a human life does not get off the ground with spiritual power it is no joke.

It is an exhilarating experience to stand at the brink of Niagara Falls watching that tremendous water-power thundering over the cliff, knowing that millions of kilowatt—hours of electric power are right in front of us. Exhilarating yet sad if none of it lights our way in darkness; none of its heats our homes in the cold; none of it supplies energy for our work. But when the power of the Falls is channeled to where we need it: to light up our darkness, to dispel the damp cold from our homes and supply energy for our work, what a difference it makes! In Christ, God does just this. He brings God's grace and power to each one of us. The means He uses to do this are the Sacraments which are like seven power lines from God's Niagara to each Christian.

WHAT IS A SACRAMENT?

If it is true that Christ has been invisible ever since the Ascension, it is also true that He has remained visible in the Church which is His Body, through which He is made present in the world today. From the Church, Christ reaches out to us with the Sacraments to bring to us His grace and love.

Every sacrament puts us in touch with Christ and applies to us the power of the Cross and the Resurrection.

St. Leo the Great said, "He who was visible as our Redeemer has now passed into the Sacraments."

It has been said that the blood and water on the Cross, flowing from the Body that was pierced by the lance, represent the Sacraments. These flow from Christ's love for us, which led Him to give His life in our behalf.

The Sacraments are the kiss of God where He pours out the riches of His love. They communicate to us the very life of God.

Every Sacrament is a theophany, the appearance of God to us for a specific purpose and need.

The Sacraments are the way to theosis (becoming like God) since they make us partakers of divine nature.

The Sacraments are the means by which "the same graces are present nowadays which were formerly imparted in the Upper Room, or at the waters where the disciples of Jesus baptized." [1]

The Sacraments are the ways by which we come into intimate personal contact with Jesus today.

---

[1] "Orthodox Spirituality" by a Monk of the Eastern Church. S.P.C.K. 1968.

The Sacraments are like the hands of Jesus reaching out over the expanse of time to touch us with His love and power and to let us know that He is still with us.

Through the Sacraments we go to Christ to appropriate the fullness of life that is in Him.

A Sacrament is a divine rite instituted by Christ and/or the Apostles which through visible signs conveys to us the hidden grace of God. The basic requirements are: divine institution, visible sign, and the hidden power of God.

NUMBER OF SACRAMENTS

The Orthodox Church numbers among the Sacraments the following:
1. Baptism;
2. Chrismation or Confirmation;
3. The Eucharist;
4. Confession or Repentance;
5. Holy Orders;
6. Holy Matrimony;
7. Holy Unction or The Anointing of the Sick;

We must realize, however, that traditionally the Orthodox never limited the Sacraments to seven. The number seven is rather symbolic and is used to indicate the perfection of grace. For example, the gifts of the Spirit are seven (Isaiah 11:2-4). The number seven was adopted only in the seventeenth century under the influence of the Roman Catholic Church. It was at that time that the Council of Trent officially affirmed the Sacraments as seven. This was done in opposition to the Protestant Reformers who recognized but two Sacraments, Baptism and the Eucharist.

To place a limitation on the number of sacraments is to view them from a very narrow perspective. If a sacrament happens whenever God's grace is mediated to man through matter, then there is no limit to the number of Sacraments. Indeed the whole of creation becomes a sacrament, a theophany, through which we see God. Fr. Thomas Hopko states: "Traditionally the Orthodox understand everything in the church to be sacramental. All of life becomes a sacrament in Christ who fills life itself with the Spirit of God" [2]

Orthodox writers vary as to the number of Sacraments. Joasaph, Metropolitan of Ephesus declares, "I believe that the number of sacraments are not seven, but more." He proceeds to list ten. Others give exclusive and prominent importance to the two Sacraments that initiate us into the new life of Christ: Baptism and Chrismation. For example, Gregory Palamas proclaims that "in these two (sacraments), our whole salvation is rooted, since the entire economy of the God-man is recapitulated in them." Another great Orthodox writer, Nicolas Cabasilas, wrote an entire book "The Life of Christ" as a commentary on the three sacraments of Baptism, Chrismation and the Eucharist. Thus it is evident that not all sacraments are of equal importance. There is a hierarchy among them with the Eucharist occupying the position of greatest importance.

---

[2] *"Meeting the Orthodox"* Dept. of Religious Education. O.C.A. Syosset, N.Y.

OTHER SACRAMENTS

Some of the other sacraments or sacramentals listed by Orthodox writers are:

1. Monastic Profession;
2. The Great Blessing of Waters at Epiphany;
3. The Funeral Service;
4. The Consecration of a Church;
5. The Anointing or Crowning of an Emperor or King;
6. Preaching through which we commune with Christ as the Word of God;
7. The Icon, which is not only an image of the divine world but also its real presence on earth;
8. The Relics of Saints;
9. The minor Sanctifications of wine, bread, oil, fruits, homes, fields etc.
10. Prayer through which we commune with God;
11. Charity. St. John Chrysostum states, "Charity is a sacrament . . . For our sacraments are above all God's charity and love of mankind."

It may be said that Jesus Christ is the original sacrament of God's presence in the world. The Church itself is a sacrament making real the presence of the Trinity in the world today. The entire universe is a sacrament, a sort of "cosmic Burning Bush, filled with the divine Fire yet not consumed," to use the words of Fr. Kallistos Ware. All nature becomes transparent and we look through it to see the Creator. Events can also be sacramental. It is not blind chance but God Who works through the events of our lives. Illness, a setback, a great success or whatever, can be a message from God or a bearer of His grace. God knows how to use everything for the benefit of those He loves. In like manner, we can turn every experience of life into a sacrament, so that everything we do is done for His glory. Somebody coming to see you when you're sick can be a sacrament. A meal with people you love can be a sacrament. Looking into a stranger's eyes and finding out he's not a stranger can be a sacrament. Christ looks at us through the eyes of all His living images, even "the least of my brethren," He says. Once we recognize His Universal Presence, all our acts of love and service become sacraments. In fact, when Jesus calls us "light" and "salt" and "yeast", is He not calling us to be sacraments of His presence in the world? We would have to be blind not to see that all of life is sacramental. As Fr. Kallistos Ware writes, "The whole Christian life must be seen as . . . one great Sacrament, whose different aspects are expressed in a great variety of acts, some performed but once in a person's life, others perhaps daily." [3]

THE VISIBLE SIGN

Most of the sacraments use material things as vehicles of the Spirit. Water, oil, bread, wine etc. are used regularly in the worship services of the Orthodox Church to remind us that matter was created by God to be good. In fact, in so

---

[3] "The Orthodox Church" Viking-Penguin Co. New York, N.Y.

doing, the Church was inspired by the Incarnation whereby God Himself did not hesitate to become flesh for our salvation.

Knowing that we have a body as well as a soul, God chose not to communicate His life to us invisibly. He willed to give us His grace under the symbol of some material sign so that by seeing water we would know that something was being washed away; by seeing bread we would know that we were being nourished. The day will come when it will no longer be necessary to use material signs, for then we shall see Him face to face and partake of Him in the nightless day of His kingdom. But that day is not yet.

Through the use of material things in the sacraments nature participates in the salvation of man. Bread, water, wine etc., become bearers of spiritual meaning and God's saving power. Nature and the Spirit become united in Salvation.

St. John Chrysostom invites us to look beyond the material signs to the reality of what is occuring. For example, he writes about baptism: "When you come to the sacred initiation, the eyes of the flesh see water; the eyes of faith behold the Spirit. Those eyes see the body being baptized; these see the old man being buried. The eyes of the flesh see the flesh being washed; the eyes of the spirit see the soul being cleansed. The eyes of the body see the body emerging from the water; the eyes of faith see the new man come forth brightly shining from that new purification. Our bodily eyes see the priest as, from above, he lays his right hand on the head and touches (him who is being baptized); our spiritual eyes see the great High Priest (Jesus) as He stretches forth His invisible hand to touch his head. For, at that moment the one who baptizes is not a man but the only-begotten Son of God."

G. P. Fedotov writes concerning the material elements used in the sacraments of the Orthodox Church: "In this sacramental religion the Deity ceases to be transcendent. It takes up its abode in the temple. The Church becomes 'heaven on earth', according to a classical Orthodox saying. The Divinity is accessible through water, that of the sacraments and sacred objects; it can be not only seen, but even smelled, tasted, kissed." [4]

Thus it is that Orthodox liturgical worship makes its appeal to the total person through all five senses. The eyes behold the beauty of the icons. The incense surrounds us with the fragrance of God's presence. The ears hear on earth the songs of the angelic choirs that constantly praise Him in heaven. The palate tastes of the fruits of the earth now sanctified. The entire person is lifted into the kingdom of God. Indeed, we taste and see that the Lord is good (Psalm 34:8).

THE SACRAMENTS AS MYSTERIES

The normal word for sacrament in the Orthodox Church is the Greek word *mysterion,* from which the English word *mystery* is derived. Hence the Sacraments are called mysteries in Greek. Through the use of this word the Orthodox church emphasized the mystery of God's love and grace. Fr. Alexander Schmemann sees a spiritual message behind the word *Mystery.* He writes:

---

[4] *"The Russian Religious Mind"* G. P. Fedotov. Harper Torchbook. 1960.

". . . they (the Greek Christians) called 'mystery' the entire ministry of Christ, through Whose life, death, resurrection and glorification God saves man and the world. Christ thus both reveals and accomplishes the Divine plan of salvation, kept secret ('mystery') until His coming. And since the Church is to proclaim that mystery and communicate it to men, the essential acts by which she is accomplishing this are also called mysteries. . . Through all these acts (mysteries or sacraments) we are made participants and beneficiaries of the great mystery of salvation accomplished by Jesus Christ." [5]

IMPORTANCE AND PURPOSE OF SACRAMENTS

The sacraments constitute our life in Christ according to Nicolas Cabasilas. We cannot be truly Christian if we treat them merely as mechanical rituals of the Christian faith that are necessary for some but not for others.

The chief purpose of the sacraments is to impart to the believer the life of Christ. Through the Sacraments God shares His life with us, redeems us from sin and death and bestows on us the glory of immortality. The kingdom of God becomes accessible now in the sacraments through which "being in Christ" and sharing in the life of God are realized.

A PERSONAL ENCOUNTER WITH CHRIST

The sacraments are not the "machines of salvation," or magical contacts that work automatically; they are rather personal encounters with Christ in faith.

Fr. George Florovsky writes:

"The climax of the Sacrament (Eucharist) is in the Presence of Christ . . . and in the personal encounter of the faithful with their Living Lord, as participants at His 'Mystical Supper'. The utter reality of this encounter is vigorously stressed in the office of preparation for Communion, as also in the prayers of Thanksgiving after Communion. The preparation is precisely for one's meeting with Christ in the Sacrament, personal and intimate . . . personal emphasis in all these prayers is dominant and prevailing. This personal encounter of believers with Christ is the very core of Orthodox devotional life." [6]

The personal aspect of the sacraments as an encounter between the believer and Christ is expressed in the manner by which the Eucharist is administered in the Orthodox Church. It is always personal. The name of each communicant is mentioned by the priest as one receives the Eucharist, i.e., "The servant of God . . . (name) receives the holy and precious Body and Blood of our Lord for the forgiveness of sins and unto life everlasting." In administering the oil of Holy Unction the priest again addresses the believer by name.

As personal encounters with Christ, the sacraments are Jesus' way of continuing His presence with us on earth. They are like the hand of Jesus reaching out

---

[5] From an article that appeared in *UPBEAT MAGAZINE*.

[6] *"Aspects of Church History"* by George Florovsky, Nordland Publ. Co. Belmont, MA.

personally to each one of us today, now forgiving, now healing, now blessing, now consecrating, now empowering, and now uniting. Here we encounter Jesus and the power of His resurrection, as we do in prayer, in His word, through His Spirit within us and in the least of His brethren (Matt. 25:40). The sacraments are an important and vital part of our encounter with Christ today.

THE NEED FOR FAITH AND OBEDIENCE

The need for faith as we approach Christ in the personal encounter of the sacraments is obvious. In answer to the question whether those who approach the sacraments without sufficient contrition and faith are absolved from their sins, Bishop Innocent of Cherson says, "Without them (faith and contrition), you will not receive absolution from God, no matter how often the priest repeats, forgiven, absolved."

There were many people in the crowd that day who jostled about Jesus and touched Him. Yet it was only the sick woman who managed to get close enough to touch the hem of His robe who was healed. Of all the people in that crowd she was the only one who touched Jesus with faith. The touch of Jesus in the sacraments is not magical or mechanical. It is just as personal as the touch established by that sick woman in the crowd. Jesus knew that someone had touched Him with faith, and so did the sick woman. She felt a surge of healing power go through her body.

When shopping in certain countries, one must bring one's own bag with which to carry away the items purchased. So it is with the sacraments. We must bring our own receptacle of faith. In fact, the greater the receptacle, the greater the grace we receive.

In addition to faith, there is need for obedience and surrender as we approach the sacraments. If a straw is placed in line with the current of the Gulf Stream, all the essential quality of the stream will flow through it. So it is with human life. If we place our life in the direction of God's will through obedience and surrender, it is not unreasonable to expect that the very life of God with its great healing power will flow through our life, as does the Gulf Stream through the straw.

Thus, we must approach Jesus in the Sacraments with faith, love, obedience, and deep penitence for our sins. Through the grace of the Sacraments we come to share in the very life of God, yet, we come not just to be takers but also givers. We give ourselves to God and to our fellow humans with a deliberate act of love without which the sacraments themselves would be worthless. In the words of the Apostle John, ". . . love is of God, and he who loves is born of God and knows God. He who does not love does not know God; for God is love . . . No man has ever seen God; if we love one another, God abides in us and His love is perfected in us" (I John 4:7,8,12).

The greatest fruit of the grace that we receive through the Sacraments is love. Bishop Maximos Aghiorgoussis expresses this well when he writes:

> "The abundance of the gifts of the Holy Spirit are bestowed upon us Christians, who prove ourselves to be 'charismatics' when we become aware of the presence of these gifts in us. The highest gift is love (Cor. 13.13). Love, poured into

our hearts through the Spirit of God (Rom. 5.5), is the characteristic of Christians (Jn. 13.35), the proper attitude of members of the Kingdom of God. It is only through the practice of this unselfish love, and energy of God which comes to us from God, that we are in communion with God Himself and in communion with our brothers and sisters. It is through the practice of love that we achieve the purpose of our creation: salvation and theosis." [7]

THE SACRAMENTS OF INITIATION

The sacraments of initiation in the Orthodox Church are three: Baptism, Chrismation and Holy Communion. The newly baptized is immediately annointed with the holy oil of Chrism through which he receives the Holy Spirit. He is thus baptized "of water and the spirit" (John 3:5). The new life in Christ is immediately nourished with "the Bread of Life", the Holy Eucharist. Receiving all three sacraments, the newly baptized infant becomes a full member of the Church.

BAPTISM

Some time ago LIFE Magazine carried a photograph illustrating "A Baby's Momentous First Five Minutes." It was a photograph of a mother's hand reaching out to her newborn child. The photograph illustrated beautifully a mother's love reaching to embrace her baby. So it is that every time an infant is baptized, the hand of God's love reaches out to embrace that baby and bestow upon it the kiss of His love. It is divine love that stands behind the Sacrament of Baptism.

Baptizing infants before they know what is going on is an expression of God's great love for us. It shows that God loves us and accepts us before we can ever know Him or love Him. It shows that we are wanted and loved by God from the very moment of our birth. To say that a person must reach the age of reason and believe in Christ before he may be baptized is to make God's grace in some way dependent on man's intelligence. But God's grace is not dependent on any act of ours, intellectual or otherwise; it is a pure gift of His love.

We bring infants to baptism not *because* they believe but *in order that* they might believe. Baptism is like the planting of the seed of faith in the human soul. Nourished and fed by Christian training, or *catechesis,* in the family and in the church school, the seed of faith will grow to produce a mature Christian.

Baptism introduces the child to the love of God and opens him to the grace of the Holy Spirit. These are great riches even if the child is unaware of them at the beginning. To deny a child baptism is to deprive him of this inner grace that is so necessary to Christian growth.

Through baptism Christ cleanses us of sin. He calls us His own sons and daughters. He makes us heirs of His riches. He makes us members of His family. As members of God's family we are all related to each other and responsible for each other. Yet baptism is more than this. Through baptism we are attached to Christ. We become members of His body. Each baptized Christian becomes an

---

[7] *"The Theology and Experience of Salvation,"* an article in The Greek Orthodox Theological Review.

extension of Christ. We become other Christs in the world. We become His eyes, His hands, His tongue, His feet. Christ has chosen to work in the world through us—the members of His body. It is our special responsibility as baptized Christians to let Christ be present wherever we ourselves are stationed in the world as baptized Christians.

St. Chrysostom writes, "For this reason we baptize children, although they have no sins . . . in order to confer upon them sanctification, adoption, inheritance . . . that they may be members of Christ and become the abode of the Holy Spirit."

The baptismal font in the language of the Church Fathers is the Divine Womb whence we receive the second birth as children of God. Baptism is truly a birth. "But to all who received him, who believed in his name, he gave power to become children of God; who were born, not of blood nor of the will of the flesh nor of the will of man, but of God" (John 1:12,13). The baptismal font is not only a *womb* where we become "alive to God," but also a *tomb* where we become "dead to sin."

We believe that Christ died for our sins. To show that we, and not Christ, are worthy of death because of our sins, we are immersed in the baptismal font. The immersion in water symbolizes death, since a person cannot live long under water. Through baptism we share mysteriously in Christ's death. As St. Paul says, "We were buried therefore with him (Christ) by baptism unto death so that as Christ was raised from the dead by the glory of the Father, we too might walk in newness of life." The baptized person rises out of the baptismal font a new person, cleansed of every sin and promising, like St. Paul, to surrender his life to Christ, his Savior: "He died for all that they who live should not henceforth live unto themselves, but unto him who for their sake died and was raised" (2 Cor. 5:15). The triple immersion symbolizes the three days our Lord spent in the tomb as well as the Holy Trinity since the baptismal formula used in the Orthodox Church is: "The servant of God . . . is baptized in the name of the Father and of the Son and of the Holy Spirit."

Baptism is our own personal Easter. When we are plunged under the waters of baptism, we are not only washed, we *die* to sin. The old sinful nature is drowned. When we rise from the waters, we *rise* to new life in Christ. We share in Christ's death and resurrection.

In early times Baptism and Confirmation were not administered in the church but in a separate edifice called the *baptisterion* (baptistery). Following anointment with holy chrism the newly baptized, wearing their white robes and carrying candles, were led by the clergy to the church for the celebration of the Eucharist. Here they would receive their first Communion.

This is the origin of the present procession of the priest accompanied by the sponsor holding the newly baptized infant, around the baptismal font just before the neophyte is given the Sacrament of Communion. The purpose of Baptism and Chrismation is expressed by this procession to the Eucharist. The door is now open to full and complete communion with God. During the procession the priest sings, ". . . as many as have been baptized into Christ, have put on Christ. Alleluia" (Gal. 3:27).

In the words of Fr. Schmemann: "Thus baptism truly fulfills itself as *procession* to the Church and into the Eucharist: the participation in Christ's Pascha 'at the table, in His kingdom' " (Luke 22:15-16).

Baptism is God filling the emptiness in man with His life and presence.

In summary we may define Baptism as follows: It is God laying claim to you. St. Paul Says, "You are not your own, you are bought with a price, so glorify God in your body." God doesn't rent you. He buys you. He holds title to you. He owns you. Through baptism you become His child. And when God adopts you as His child, He does so for a purpose. He has a plan for you. You're saved *from* sin. You're saved *for* service, *for* love, *for* good works, *for* enlarging the kingdom. You're saved into significance. Your life has real worth and meaning. "I know my sheep," said Jesus. "And nobody can pluck them out of my hand."

Baptism is an act of liberation, a paschal experience, an exodus, a passage through the Red Sea of sin and death to the glorious freedom of the children of God.

Baptism is the transition from the world that is under the power of the evil one to the world that has been redeemed by Christ.

Baptism is a regeneration, a new life. It makes us partakers of divine nature.

After baptism man is a living member of the Body of Christ. He is no longer *mere* man, but man transformed, divinized, newly begotten as God's own son or daughter. He carries within him the very life of God.

The effect of baptism according to St. John Chrysostom is "to be set free from sins, to reconcile God to man, to make man one with God, to open the eyes for souls to perceive the divine ray—to sum it up, to prepare for the life to come."

Baptism in the Orthodox Church is far more than for the remission of sins. The dominant theme of baptism is positive. As Nicholas Cabasilas, a 14th century Byzantine theologian, points out all the scriptural and traditional terms applied to baptism point to a positive meaning: "birth", "new birth", "clothing", "annointing", "gifts", "washing", "enlightening", "refashioning", "seal", etc.

The following words, addressed by the priest to the newly baptized, capture the essence of baptism:

"You have been justified and illuminated . . .
   You have been baptized;
   You have been illuminated;
   You have been chrismated;
   You have been sanctified;
   You have been washed in the name of the Father and the Son
      and the Holy Spirit."

Because of Baptism, St. Gregory of Sinai could say to us who are baptized:

"Become what you already are,
   Find Him Who is already yours,
   Listen to Him Who never ceases speaking to you,
   Own Him Who already owns you."

THE SACRAMENT OF
CHRISMATION OR CONFIRMATION

In the Orthodox Church the Sacrament of Confirmation is administered immediately following baptism as in the early Church. It is considered the fulfillment of baptism. Human nature purified by baptism is made ready to receive the manifold gifts of the Holy Spirit. As Fr. Schmemann says, "Confirmation is thus the personal Pentecost of man, his entrance into the life of the Holy Spirit . . . his ordination as truly and fully man. . . His whole body is anointed, sealed, sanctified, dedicated to the new life: 'the seal of the gift of the Holy Spirit,' says the priest as he anoints the newly baptized 'on the brow, and on the eyes, and the nostrils, and the lips, and on both ears, and the breast and on the hands, and the feet'. . . The whole man is now made the temple of God. . ."

The Greek word for Confirmation is "chrisma," which means anointing. The one anointed with "chrisma" becomes "christos," that is, the anointed one, which is the meaning of the name Christ. Thus, by this sacrament we are made Christians or other Christs. Chrismation is the "ordination of the laity." According to Orthodox belief every lay person is "ordained" into the priesthood of the laity by this sacrament; he receives the gift of the Holy Spirit to become "light", "salt", and "yeast" for Christ in this world.

Chrismation is a participation in the annointing of Christ by the Spirit after His Baptism (Cyril of Jerusalem).

As in baptism we share in the death and resurrection of Jesus, so in Chrismation we share in the annointing of Christ by the Holy Spirit.

Chrismation is the fulfillment of baptism even as Pentecost is of Easter.

Chrismation is receiving the Holy Spirit Who will enable us to live the life of God into which we are born through baptism.

Just as the Eucharist is a personal Last Supper, so Chrismation is a personal Pentecost: the personal coming to man of the third Person of the Godhead, the Holy Spirit, as He came to the Apostles on Pentecost.

Chrismation is the newly baptized person's entrance into the new life in the Holy Spirit. It is the divine "wind," the *ruah* of God, invading our life, setting us ablaze with fire and love, filling us with hope and joy, making us instruments of His action in the world.

The Sacrament of Chrismation was administered in the apostolic era by two methods (1) the laying on of hands and (2) by annointing (Acts 19:1-7 and I John 2:20). In the East the practice of administering this Sacrament by annointing prevailed. The oil of chrism is consecrated by bishops of autocephalous churches and administered locally by presbyters. Baptized Christians of other churches entering the Orthodox Church are usually received through Chrismation.

THE SACRAMENT
OF PENANCE OR CONFESSION

The Sacrament of Penance (Confession) is a "new Baptism". It has also been called the Mystery of the Second Baptism since it involves the forgiveness of all sins committed after Baptism. Fr. Meyendorff writes: "Originally a public act, required from sinners who either had been officially excommunicated or had performed acts liable to excommunication, penance, gradually and especially after the fourth century, took the form of private confession, followed by a prayer of absolution pronounced by a priest. It then identified itself almost completly with the practice of private spiritual direction, especially widespread in monastic communities." [8]

Not every sin requires the necessity of sacramental forgiveness since we are never completly without sin. The Church has regarded sacramental penance as necessary for grave sins, i.e., murder, apostasy, adultery and for those sins of disobedience which serve to separate us from God and the love of our fellow humans. Christians who live in communion with Christ are expected to avail themselves of sacramental penance periodically as a form of spiritual check-up, as a means of humbling themselves before God and in order to receive guidance in the spiritual life from their pastor. Confession has never been viewed legalistically in the Eastern Church, i.e., as a way of sentencing and punishing guilt. On the contrary, the sinner is considered to be a prisoner of Satan and, as such, a morally sick person. Christ comes through the Sacrament of Penance to liberate and heal rather than to judge.

One can find in the Orthodox Church an important theology of tears. Just as in Baptism our sins are cleansed by water, so the sins committed after baptism are cleansed by water, i.e., tears of repentance. St. Symeon the New Theologian calls them the "Baptism of the Holy Spirit" and teaches that sins committed after baptism cannot be forgiven without tears. Thus St. John Climacus wrote: "Greater than baptism itself is the fountain of tears after baptism, even though it is somewhat audacious to say so. For baptism is the washing away of evils that were in us before, but sins committed after baptism are washed away tears. Because baptism is received in infancy, we have all defiled it, but we cleanse it anew with tears. And if God in His love for mankind had not given us tears, then few indeed would be saved."

There are two kinds of confession in the Orthodox Church: private confession by prayer and sacramental confession. Whereas our Roman Catholic brethren tend to hold to sacramental confession only, and our Protestant brethren to confession by private prayer only, the Orthodox Church, following the apostolic way, avoids both extremes. It holds that divine forgiveness may be received either by private prayer or by the Sacrament. In the case of a grave sin, confession by private prayer should be supplemented by sacramental confession. In case of uncertainty as to what constitutes a grave sin, one should consult one's priest. Sacramental confession before a priest even for lighter sins is a recommended practice in the Orthodox Church at least once a year. Whichever way of confession we choose, in any given situation, either private or sacramental, or both, must be followed by receiving Holy Communion since this is the sacrament by which our sins are forgiven and washed in the Precious Blood of Jesus.

The entire beauty and mystery of the Sacrament of Penance is expressed in the following exhortation which the priest addresses to the penitent in the Russian

---

[8] *"Byzantine Theology,"* John Meyendorff. Fordham University Press.

rite. It portrays the role of the priest in Confession as that of a witness rather than a judge. "Behold, my child, Christ stands here invisibly and receives your confession; therefore, do not be ashamed or afraid, and hide nothing from me; but tell me without hesitation all the things that you have done, and so you will have pardon from our Lord Jesus Christ. See, his holy image is before us; *and I am only a witness,* bearing testimony before him of all the things you have to say to me. But if you hide anything from me, you will have greater sin. Take care, then, lest having come to a physician you depart unhealed."

THE SACRAMENT OF HOLY COMMUNION

In the sixth chapter of John's Gospel Jesus said to His disciples:

> "Truly, truly, I say to you, it was not Moses who gave you the bread from heaven; my Father gives you the true bread from heaven. For the bread of God is that which comes down from heaven, and gives life to the world . . . I am the bread of life. Your fathers ate the manna in the wilderness, and they died. This is the bread which comes down from heaven, that a man may eat of it and not die. I am the living bread which came down from heaven, if anyone eats of this bread, he will live for ever; and the bread which I shall give for the life of the world is my flesh" (John 6:32-33; 48-51).

The disciples then turned to Jesus and said, "Lord, give us this bread always" (John 6:34).

Jesus complied with their request. He gave us the Bread of Life, Himself, in the Sacrament of the Eucharist:

> "For my flesh is food indeed, and my blood is drink indeed.
> He who eats my flesh and drinks my blood abides in me, and I in him" (John 6:55-56).

The Eucharist is a personal encounter with the living Christ. This is where we meet Him and invite Him into our soul.

The Eucharist has been called a nuptial encounter of the soul with her Lord, a marriage union between Christ and the soul. In the words of Cyril of Jerusalem: "Christ has given to the children of the bridal chamber the enjoyment of His body and His blood." Another ancient Christian writer, Theodoret, writes, "In eating the elements of the Bridegroom and drinking His blood, we accomplish a marriage union." The Eucharist, then, becomes the marriage relationship through which the Bridegroom, Christ, espouses the Church as His Bride, thus transforming a human community into the Church of God.

The Eucharist is a divine blood transfusion. God transfuses His own precious, sacred, royal and life-giving blood into our blood stream to give us new life, new strength and royal dignity. The Old Testament speaks of blood as life (Gen. 2:7; Lev. 17:11,14). In the New Testament the Eucharist becomes the way by which we receive the very life of God through the Precious Blood of His Son.

Someone said once, "I had been taught in Sunday School that 'God is everywhere.' But that was one of the things that made me angry. Everywhere was too vague. I wanted to find Him somewhere."

The God who is present everywhere is to be found somewhere in specific. "This *is* my body . . . This *is* my blood." When Jesus spoke these words He meant exactly what He said. The bread and the wine that are received at Communion are literally His Body and Blood. They are not merely symbols. For Jesus Himself said, "For my flesh *is* food indeed, and my blood *is* drink indeed" (John 6:55). St. John Chrysostom writes, "What is in the chalice is the same as that which flowed from Christ's side. What is the bread? Christ's body." ". . . the bread which I shall give for the life of the world *is my flesh*," said Jesus (John 6:51).

Meditating on the Last Supper, some might say to themselves: Would that I were there with those eleven apostles in the presence of the Master that evening in the Upper Room! How I wish I could have heard from His lips the words, "This is my body . . . This is my blood . . . Take, eat . . . drink . . ." Yet through the Eucharist *we are there*! The same Master is present. The same bread. The same cup. The same sacrifice. The same Upper Room. The same Last Supper. In the words of Nicolai Gogol, the Eucharist is "the eternal repetition of the great act of love performed on Calvary."

The Eucharist is a making present again of the sacrifice of Christ in a mysterious manner. The Sacrifice of Christ is presented in the New Testament as something that happened once for all, that can never be repeated and to which nothing can be added. The Sacrifice of Jesus may be made present again to us in Holy Communion today so that we may partake of its benefits, but still as that which happened once for all. It is not a new sacrifice. For this reason it is called an "unbloody sacrifice." It is equally clear that the Eucharist in Orthodox worship is the remembering not only of the death of our Lord but also of His burial, Resurrection, Ascension, and Second Coming as well.

St. Isaac the Syrian writes: "Blessed is he that has eaten of the Bread of love which is Jesus. While still in this world, he breathes the air of the resurrection, in which the righteous will delight after they rise from the dead."

Writing on the importance of the Eucharist, Nicholas Cabasilas says, "It is the completion of all the sacraments and not simply one of them. . . All human striving reaches here its ultimate goal. For in this sacrament we attain God Himself, and God Himself is made one with us in the most perfect of all unions. . . This is the final mystery: beyond this it is not possible to go, nor can anything be added to it."

St. Nilus writes, "It is impossible for the believer to be saved, to receive remission of sins and be admitted to the kingdom of heaven, unless in fear, faith and love he receives communion of the pure Mysteries of the Body and Blood of Jesus."

The Eastern Church has been willing to accept the mystery of the change that occurs in the elements of the bread and wine without trying to explain it with words such as "transubstantiation" as was done in the Western Church. As Paul

Evdokimov said, "The East has too strong a sense of mystery to attempt to explain the Eucharist."

One of the most important points of the Orthodox liturgy comes with the priest's invocation (epiclesis) of the Holy Spirit to consecrate the bread and the wine.

Just as the Holy Spirit descended to the womb of Mary and made the body of Jesus from the flesh of the Virgin, so the same Spirit descends upon the bread and wine on the altar, transforming them into the Body and Blood of Jesus.

St. John of Damascus writes, "And now you ask, 'How does the bread become Christ's Body, and the wine and the water become Blood?' I tell you, the Holy Ghost comes and makes these Divine Mysteries . . . to be Christ's Body and Blood."

The early Church Fathers never suggested that we not partake of Communion often because of personal unworthiness. To the contrary, one of the most ancient Christian documents, the Didache, says, "If anyone is holy, let him come; if he is not, let him repent (and come)."

We need to realize that no one is ever worthy to receive God within one's soul. It is not a matter of our worthiness but of God's grace. Communion is never a reward for holy living but always the gift of God's grace no matter how much we may have prepared. May we keep our sense of unworthiness so that it may keep leading us to the only One Who can make us worthy. The sense of unworthiness is just the right attitude with which to approach Communion, for it helps us accept the Eucharist as a completely free gift of God's supreme grace. An exaggerated sense of unworthiness needs to give way to humble gratitude for God's grace which accepts especially the unworthy to make them worthy. Is not the Eucharist Matthew's banquet all over again? To the horror of the "good" people, Jesus eats and drinks with sinners!

St. Nicodemus promoted frequent communion on Mr. Athos and in the Orthodox Church in general. In 1783 he published a booklet "On Frequent Communion". Although he was attacked by some, an official decree of the Synod of Constantinople (August, 1819) accepted his principle that the faithful should receive communion at every liturgy. This is now an official canon of the Church. So, let us "with the fear of God, with faith and love draw near" to receive the King of Kings in every liturgy. Every liturgy is Communion time. In the early Church not to receive communion at the liturgy was a sign that the individual was a lapsed member who was seeking readmission to the Church.

Ideally, preparation for Holy Communion is not something that is done hastily in a few days, or even weeks. The whole life of the Christian should be preparation for the Eucharist. We shall share some of the specific ways by which we may prepare:

> 1. St. Paul speaks of this when he writes, ". . . let a man examine himself and so eat of that bread and drink of that cup" (I Cor. 11:28). In a sense, self-examination is something that is practiced regularly in the life of the Christian as he prays daily, reads God's word devoutly and participates faithfully in the liturgy. He is constantly judging himself as

Jesus speaks to him, pruning from his life the dead branches that bear no fruit. The purpose of self-examination is not to make a person consider himself "worthy", but to bring him to an awareness of his unworthiness and lead him to repentance.

2. On the morning before going to the liturgy to receive Communion we do not eat or drink anything if our health allows. Just as one would not spoil his appetite by eating before a special meal, so we sharpen our spiritual appetite for Christ through such fasting. The general rule for fasting is that the more often one receives Holy Communion, the less one may fast. There can be some abstinence from meat the week before, especially on Wednesdays and Fridays. It is good to consult with one's priest as to the extent of one's fasting since it depends on the frequency of receiving the Sacrament. One thing we must remember is that there is no necessary connection between fasting and Communion. We must never allow an overemphasis on fasting to become a wall separating us from Christ Who wishes to come to us in every liturgy. Christianity is a relationship with a Person. We must never allow a self-righteous emphasis on so-called "rules of fasting" to destroy this all-important relationship. The Church Fathers keep emphasizing that true fasting is to abstain from sin and evil. They also suggest the more positive "fasting of love", i.e., to deny oneself of food in order to share that food with the hungry.

3. The Orthodox Prayer Book contains some very moving prayers written by the Church Fathers that are designed to be read before and after Communion. We may incorporate the reading of these prayers into our daily prayer life, reading one or two each day, morning and evening. All of these beautiful prayers contain the cry of humility, unworthiness, and penitence, as expressed by this sample:

> ". . . I am not worthy, Master and Lord, that You should enter under the roof of my soul. Yet inasmuch as You desire to live in me as the lover of men, I approach with boldness. You have commanded: let the doors be opened which You alone have made and You shall enter with Your love . . . You shall enter and enlighten my darkened reasoning. I believe that You will do this . . ."

4. One must always approach Jesus with a plea for mercy and forgiveness. It is sincere faith and repentance—not perfection—that make us worthy for frequent Communion. Although it is not necessary to go to Confession before each Communion, if we receive Communion regularly it is still necessary to seek forgiveness through prayer. The pre-Communion prayers of the Church are replete with pleas for forgiveness. If grave sins have been committed, one should avail oneself also of the Sacrament of Confession.

5. Forgiveness from those we have hurt should be sought before Communion. We must approach the Holy Table ''with the fear of God (filial reverence), with faith and with LOVE.'' We are bound to share with others the forgiving love we receive from Jesus. Love is the one thing we must pray for before coming to the Holy Table. No hostilities or grudges or dissension must be brought there. There must be penitence for lack of love. Thus, we prepare for Communion with self-examination, fasting, prayer, repentance and forgiveness.

The most wonderful thing about man is that he was created to contain God. This is the miracle of miracles! Each one of us was made to be a temple of God, a golden chalice, a tabernacle of God's presence. The infinitely great God Who revealed Himself in Jesus as the great God of love waits to take up residence in us. He stands at the door of our soul and knocks until we hear His voice and His knock to open and let Him come in to sup with us in the heavenly banquet. He will not rest until He has invaded our heart and made it His throne. If we allow Him to enter regularly through the Eucharist, He will transubstantiate and change our lives into the beautiful life of Jesus. ''I live, yet not I, but Christ lives in me'' (Gal. 2:20).

THE SACRAMENT OF HOLY MATRIMONY

For the Orthodox Christian, marriage is a sacrament. It is God blessing our love. ''Without Me you can do nothing,'' said Jesus. By itself, without God, true love is impossible. It cannot be what it was created to be. With God, love is perfected, completed, transfigured, sanctified, blessed, resurrected, and ultimately saved. This does not mean that having a Church wedding will automatically guarantee a successful marriage. But it does mean that the opportunity is now given in Christ for the completion and the perfection of our love. It means that we have invited the Lord Jesus to enter this all-important relationship to redeem it, to give us the grace and the power to be patient when it is so easy to be impatient; to be loving when it is so easy to be unloving; to be forgiving when it is so easy to be unforgiving; to be kind when it is so easy to be insulting; to be understanding when it is so easy to be critical. For all this we need His grace, His presence, His love and His power.

True love entails a life-long commitment to the person loved. Real love never says, ''I'll love you for a day or a month or a year or ten years.'' True love is forever. One of the purposes of the marriage ceremony is to acknowledge publicly this life-long commitment. The couple stands before God and the world, as represented by the friends invited to the ceremony, to pledge their commitment to each other not ''until some other prettier face comes along'' but ''until death do us part.'' ''What God has brought together let no man tear asunder,'' said Jesus. Two things are done during the Orthodox wedding ceremony to express the life-long commitment of love. The couple is asked to clasp their right hands and then to drink wine from the same cup, symbolizing the intimate cementing of their lives through the Sacrament of Holy Matrimony. Andre Maurois expressed beautifully the commitment of true love when he wrote, ''I bind myself for life; I have chosen; from now on my aim will be not to search for someone who will please me, but to please the one I have chosen."

It is our faith that all of the sacraments were instituted by Jesus Christ. But marriage is as old as the human race. It goes all the way back to creation. It was founded by the Creator Himself when He said, "It is not good for man to be alone." (Gen. 2:18). Then He created woman, and blessing them, said, "Increase and multiply and fill the earth." Jesus confirmed these words of the Creator in Genesis when he said, "Have you not read that He Who made them from the beginning made them male and female, and said, 'For this reason a man shall leave his father and mother and be joined to his wife, and the two shall become one'? So they are no longer two but one. What therefore God has joined together, let no man put asunder" (Matt. 19:4-6. quoting Genesis 1:27, 2:24).

Marriage is not merely a social and civil arrangement for the convenience of two people. It is undertaken in the presence of God before His holy altar. It is not simply matrimony but "holy" matrimony. It is the oldest of God's institutions. As a sacrament, it is not an estate instituted of man but of God. It is not regulated by man's commandments but by God's.

After God created the first couple, we read that He "blessed them, and said unto them, 'Be fruitful and multiply and replenish the earth' " (Gen. 1:28). Just as God blessed that first marriage, so He blesses ours today when we stand before His holy altar. This is why marriage is a sacrament in the Orthodox Church. It is a way by which Christ comes to us to bless us. The candles we hold during the wedding ceremony are like the oil lamps of the five wise maidens in the New Testament. They kept the lamps burning to greet the bridegroom as he came in the middle of the night. Another Bridegroom — Christ — comes to bless us during the Sacrament of Holy Matrimony. The burning candles we hold signify our spiritual eagerness to receive Him.

St. Paul calls marriage a *mysterion* or mystery. This is the same word that is used for sacrament in Greek: mystery. "This is a great mystery: but I speak of Christ and the Church" (Eph. 5:32). Marriage was considered a mysterion or sacrament in the early Church. Tertullian, writing in the second century, tells us that a Christian couple who desired to be married applied for a civil license and then went to Church on Sunday to receive Communion during the liturgy and the blessing of the bishop or priest. Thus the civil agreement became also a sacrament. After the blessing, their names, Tertullian tells us, were "inscribed in heaven" and not just in a government "registry." Their marriage was sealed in Christ and became an eternal union with Him. St. Ignatius (c. 100 A.D.) corroborates what Tertullian writes when he says, "Those who get married must unite with the knowledge of the bishop, so that marriage may be according to the Lord, and not by human desire."

When Scripture says that "the two shall become one", the oneness is not only physical. It implies a total unity: one spirit, one heart, one mind. Such total oneness is made possible by God through the Eucharist. He comes to dwell in both husband and wife making them truly "one flesh". This is why originally marriages were blessed during the Divine Liturgy where both bride and groom received Communion and became truly one in Christ. Homer wrote somewhere in

"Odyssey", "There is nothing mightier or nobler than when a man and wife are of one heart and mind in the home." This kind of oneness can come only from God.

BIRTH CONTROL

Is birth control allowed according to Orthodox doctrine? Two eminent Orthodox theologians share their views with us on this subject. The well-know Orthodox theologian, Fr. John Meyendorff, writes, "Straight condemnation of birth control . . . has never been endorsed by the Orthodox Church as a whole, even if, at times, local Church authorities may have issued statements on the matter identical to that of the Pope. In any case, it has never been the Church's practice to give moral guidance by issuing standard formulas claiming universal validity on questions which actually require a personal act of conscience. . . The question of birth control . . . can only be solved by individual Christian couples. They can make the right decision only if they accept their Christian commitment with ultimate seriousness . . . if they realize that children are a great joy and a gift of God, if their love is not a selfish and egotistic one, if they remember that love reduced to sexual pleasure is not true love. . . In any case, the advice of a good father confessor could help much in taking the right 'first step' in married life." [9]

Fr. Stanley Harakas, Professor of Orthodox Ethics at Holy Cross Seminary, writes, "In the Orthodox Church, the purposes of marriage are numerous. High on the list is the procreation of children. The couple is understood to be co-workers with God not only in the perpetuation of human life through the conception, birth and physical care of children, but also in the more profound sense of the spiritual nurture of new members of God's kingdom. That is why birth control methods which could frustrate this purpose of marriage deliberately are not approved by the Orthodox Church. But there are other purposes to marriage besides this. The emphasis on mutual support, and aid assistance and mutual fulfillment is strongly made by the Orthodox. . . That is why many Orthodox theologians believe that Birth Control methods may be used by Orthodox Christian couples when the other purposes of marriage are also respected." [10]

CHURCH BLESSING NECESSARY

An Orthodox Christian must seek the blessing and grace of Christ for his/her marriage through the Church. For example, the *Guidelines on Holy Matrimony of the Synod of Bishops of the Orthodox Church in America* state: "An Orthodox Christian who excludes his marriage from this gracious union with Christ in the Church certainly excludes himself from the communion of the Church." Fr. Stanley Harakas writes, "Orthodox Christians who have not been married in the Church and have been married civilly, or by a clergyman of another Church or Faith, should have their union sanctified in Christ through the Sacrament of Holy Matrimony in the Orthodox Church. Otherwise they are not in good standing with their Church and may not receive Holy Communion and other sacraments of the

---

[9] *"Marriage: An Orthodox Perspective,"* John Meyendorff. St. Vladimir's Seminary Press.
[10] *"Guidelines for Marriage in the Orthodox Church,"* S. Harakas. Light and Life Pub. Co.

Church." [11] A devout Orthodox Christian will not exclude Christ from such a vital and important area of life as marriage. For, in the words of the Psalmist, "Unless the Lord build the house, they who labor, labor in vain."

DIVORCE

The view of the Orthodox Church on divorce is stated succinctly by Fr. Kallistos Ware:

"The Orthodox Chruch permits divorce and remarriage, quoting as its authority the text of Matthew XIX, 9, where our Lord says, 'If a man divorces his wife, *for any cause other than unchastity,* and marries another, he commits adultery.' Since Christ also allowed an exception to His general ruling about the indissolubility of marriage, the Orthodox Church also is willing to allow an exception. Certainly, Orthodoxy regards the marriage bonds as in principle lifelong and indissoluble, and it condemns the breakdown of marriage as a sin and an evil. But while condemning the sin, the Church still desires to help the sinners and to allow them a second chance. When, therefore, a marriage has entirely ceased to be a reality, the Orthodox Church does not insist on the preservation of a legal fiction. Divorce is seen as an exceptional but necessary concession to human sin; it is an act of *oikonomia* (economy or dispensation) and *philanthropia* (loving kindness). . . In theory the Canons only permit divorce in cases of adultery, but in practice it is sometimes granted for other reasons as well. . . One point must be clearly understood: from the point of view of Orthodox theology a divorce granted by the State in the civil courts is not sufficient. Remarriage in Church is only possible if the Church authorities have themselves granted a divorce." [12]

There survives a medallion from a Byzantine golden marriage belt dating back to the sixth century. On this medallion Christ stands between the bride and the groom as they fondly gaze at each other. He joins their right hands in marriage while above their heads are two small crosses with the inscription: "From God, concord, grace (and health)." This beautiful medallion expresses the meaning of marriage according to Orthodox theology. It is a marriage that is sealed in the Lord with a love that comes ultimately from the splendor of God. St. Paul, drawing deeply from the wells of Christ, described it: "Love is patient and kind. . . It hopes, believes, endures all things. . . Love never ends. . ." It holds "till death us do part." And continues forever!

THE SACRAMENT OF HOLY UNCTION

Jesus gave His apostles the same power He had to heal diseases. We read in Luke 9:1-2, ". . . He gave them power and authority over all demons, with the power to heal diseases. And he sent them to proclaim the kingdom of God and to heal. . ." We read in Mark 6:13 that the apostles "anointed many sick persons with oil, and healed them."

From the beginning the apostles used the power Jesus had given them over sickness. They anointed the sick with oil to heal the body and forgive sins. We read in James 5:12-15:

---

[11] *"Guidelines For Marriage in the Orthodox Church,"* Light and Life Publishing Co. Minneapolis, MN. 1980.
[12] *"The Orthodox Church,"* Timothy Ware. Viking-Penquin Press.

"Is any among you sick? Let him call for the elders of the church, and let them pray over him, anointing him with oil in the name of the Lord, and the prayer of faith will save the sick man, and the Lord will raise him up; and if he has committed sins, he will be forgiven."

Holy Unction is one of the sacraments of the Church through which the healing power of Jesus is mediated to us today. The visible sign of Unction is oil.

Always used for healing in the ancient world, the oil is blessed by the Holy Spirit to bring us God's healing grace. As we come to be anointed with this consecrated oil, we bring with us our "prayer of faith", i.e., a living, personal faith that when we are anointed with this oil, the hand of Christ will touch us with His healing power. God speaks to us through the fourteen Scripture readings that are part of this Sacrament (seven Epistle and seven Gospel readings). He speaks to increase our faith in His power to heal. The fact that the presence of seven priests is recommended (but not required) for the celebration of this sacrament gives expression to our faith that the whole Church is present and praying for the sick person together with relatives and friends.

Through the Sacrament of Holy Unction, every Church becomes a healing shrine pervaded by the prayers of the clergy and the faithful, and hallowed by the presence of the Holy Spirit. Here we find our faith fortified and sustained as we grow in grace and understanding. Here we find the power and the presence of the Healing Christ.

During Holy Week when we are reminded how much God suffered on the cross to save our souls, we are reminded that God cares for our bodies also. This is why on Holy Wednesday evening every year the Greek Orthodox Church celebrates this Sacrament of healing. She invites us to come forth with faith to be touched by God's love through this sacrament of healing.

"The prayer of faith will save the sick," writes St. James. God's saving of the sick may include healing but not in every case. God does not always promise healing, but, if faith is exercised, God does always promise salvation. Sickness is often used by God to create faith and to strengthen it. Sickness may lead to panic and despair, but it can also lead to faith. And if, through sickness, one is led to faith, then that faith leads to the saving of the person.

Speaking on this aspect of Unction, Fr. John Meyendorff writes:
"Healing is requested only in a framework of repentance and spiritual salvation, and not as an end in itself. Whatever the outcome of the disease, the anointing symbolized divine pardon and liberation from the vicious cycle of sin, suffering and death, in which fallen humanity is held captive. Compassionate to human suffering, assembled together to pray for its suffering member, the Church through its presbyters asks for relief, forgiveness, and eternal freedom. This is the meaning of holy unction." [13]

The Sacrament of Anointing is a sacrament for the body. Many pagans looked upon the body as something evil. They considered it a prison in which the soul was kept a prisoner. Their whole philosophy of salvation centered in helping

_____
[13] "*Byzantine Theology,*" John Meyendorff. Fordham University Press.

the soul free itself from the chains of the body through extreme fasting and self-mortification.

Christianity, on the other hand, looked upon the body not as a PRISON but as a TEMPLE OF GOD. "Know ye not that your body is a Temple of the Holy Spirit," writes St. Paul.

The body is destined not for the earth: "dust thou art and unto dust shalt thou return;" it is destined for heaven. When we see Christ ascending into heaven with His physical body, we see humanity — ourselves — ascending there with Him. The body that dies is buried in a grave, but only temporarily. One day God will resurrect the body and re-unite it with the soul so that both soul and body may spend eternity together.

C. S. Lewis once said, "Christianity is almost the only one of the great religions which thoroughly approves of the body — which believes that matter is good, that God Himself once took on a human body, that some kind of body is going to be given us in Heaven and is going to be an essential part of our happiness, our beauty, and our energy."

The Sacrament of Anointing is thus an expression of God's love for the body which He created and has destined for eternity.

Unction should remind us that as members of Christ's Church we are members of a healing fellowship. We are healed in order to bring healing to others. We are forgiven in order to bring forgiveness to others. We are loved in order to love others. We are blessed in order to be a blessing to others. We are to be channels of God's healing in the world.

Like the Good Samaritan, we should never hesitate to stop on the road of life to pour the healing oil of God's love and forgiveness on our neighbor lying neglected and abandoned by the roadside. If the Church is the Body of Christ, then that kind of healing should be happening all the time. Whoever touches the Church, even in a tenuous way, should discover that he has touched the source of healing. For, the healing that is given us through Unction and prayer is given to us for the sake of all our neighbors in the world.

THE SACRAMENT OF HOLY ORDERS

Just as there were apostles at the time of Jesus, so we have their successors today. We use different names for them. Instead of apostles, we call them deacons, priests (or presbyters) and bishops. But they continue the work of the apostles.

You may recall how Jesus chose the apostles to be His co-workers:

"In these days He went out into the hills to pray; and all night He continued in prayer to God. And when it was day, He called His disciples, and chose from the twelve, whom He called apostles. . ." (Luke 6:12-13).

Jesus ordained the apostles to be His co-workers when He breathed the Holy Spirit upon them:

"Jesus said to them again, 'Peace be with you. As the Father has sent Me, even so I send you.' And when He had said this, He breathed on them and said to them, 'Receive the Holy Spirit. If you forgive the sins of any, they are forgiven; if you retain the sins of any, they are retained' '' (John 20:21-23).

We see from the above verses that the Sacrament of Ordination was instituted by Jesus Himself after His resurrection.

In the book of Acts we note that the first seven deacons were ordained by the twelve Apostles. The seven candidates were ''set before the apostles, and when they had prayed, the apostles laid their hands upon them'' (Acts 6:6). When presbyters or priests were ordained we read, ''Then after fasting and praying they laid their hands on them (Barnabas and Saul) and sent them off'' (Acts 13:3). Speaking of his ordination to the office of bishop, the Apostle Paul said to Timothy: ''I beseech you to rekindle the gift of God that is within you through the laying on of hands; for God did not give us a spirit of timidity, but a spirit of power and love and self-control'' (2 Tim. 1:6-7).

Jesus chose special persons to continue the work of the Church through the ages: to preach the Word, to administer the sacraments, and to govern the Church. As this ministry was to endure permanently, it needed to be transferable from one person to another. This was provided for by Jesus in the Sacrament of Ordination through which, by the laying on of hands and prayer, the special grace of God is bestowed on those selected to serve as Christ's Apostles. We recall that just before Pentecost, Judas was replaced by Matthias so that the number of Apostles was restored to twelve (Acts 1:23-26). That the Apostles kept ordaining others to carry on their work is amply testified by the Church Fathers in the writings of St. John Chrysostom, St. Basil, St. Gregory of Nyssa, St. Ambrose and others.

Ordination may be defined as the sacrament by which through the laying on of hands of a bishop, with prayer, the grace of the Holy Spirit comes upon the candidate for Orders sanctifying him and making him a worthy minister (leitourgos) of the Church, elevating him to one of three orders of ministry, (bishop, priest or deacon) empowering him to be a shepherd and minister of Christ, to teach His Word, to administer the sacraments, to guide God's people to salvation, and to govern His Church. Since the office of bishop is collegial, his ordination is performed by a college of three, or at least two, bishops.

Women are not eligible for Holy Orders in the Orthodox Church in keeping with Sacred Tradition and the example established by Jesus and His apostles. This practice conforms with the traditional Orthodox belief that men and women were designed by God to serve Him in different capacities.

Christ ordained the first apostles. They in turn ordained others to succeed them as bishops, priests and deacons. Each generation of bishops was succeeded by another down to the present. The succession can be traced directly back to the Apostles and Christ. This continuity of descent is called *Apostolic Succession.* It is important because it maintains a direct and unbroken historical link with the original Church established by Christ and the Apostles. It guarantees the unbroken continuity of the Church *in origin* as well as *in doctrine* with the early Apostles. It proves historically that the Church is authentically the one, holy, catholic and apostolic Church founded by Christ.

To help you understand your role as laypeople in the Orthodox Church, let me summarize a few main points.

1. There is not just one priesthood. There is the ''royal priesthood'' of all the baptized. This is the general priesthood of all the baptized and chrismated believers. Then there is the special priesthood of the ordained clergy. It is unfortunate that a *lay* person has come to mean non-professional in whatever field. It is assumed that the important work in any field is done not by the layman but by the professional.

This is a far cry from the meaning of the word layman in the early Church. Coming from the word *laos* which means *people*, it refers to the people of God, the Israelites, chosen and sanctified by God Himself as *His* people to serve Him in a special way. Later on, in the New Testament, the Church becomes the new Israel, the new people of God — again, called by God to serve Him in a special way.

In the practice of the Orthodox Church each Christian is ordained into the laity through Baptism and Chrismation. Whereas *Baptism* restores in us the image of God, obscured by sin, *Chrismation* gives us the power to be Christians, responsible participants in the work of the Church. It ordains us to serve and work for the Lord as His people in the world today.

Thus, the word *lay* or *laikos* is given a highly positive meaning. Moses said to the people of the covenant: ''You are a holy people to the Lord your God. The Lord your God has chosen you to be a people of his own possession, out of all the people that are on the face of the earth.'' St. Paul calls all baptized Christians ''fellow citizens with the saints and members of the household of God'' (Eph. 2:1). Addressing himself to the early Christians, St. Peter said, ''But you are a *chosen race, a royal priesthood, a holy nation, God's own people*, that you may declare the wonderful deeds of him who called you out of darkness into his marvellous light. Once you were no people; once you had not received mercy, but now, you have received mercy'' (I Peter 2:9-10). Lay people have a high calling in the Orthodox Church. If they are members of St. Nicholas Church or St. George Church, St. Peter says, they are ''members of *a chosen race, a royal priesthood, a holy nation, God's own people.*'' This is the Orthodox layman's identity; this is who he is. Having defined identity, St. Peter proceeds to give the layman his job description: to ''delclare the wonderful deeds of him who called you out of the darkness into his marvellous light.''

The place of the layman in the Orthodox Church is brought out in the liturgy. The very word *leitourgia* means a common, corporate action in which all those who are present are active participants. The prayers of the liturgy are all in the plural ''we''. The priest calls upon *the people* to pray: *''let us beseech the Lord''*, *''let us commit ourselves unto the Lord''*. Thus, it is not just the priest or just the people but the entire Church, the one Body of Christ, that performs the liturgy.

Fr. Schmemann finds a wonderful illustration of the co-celebration of the liturgy by priest and laity in the word *Amen:* ''. . . it is a crucial word. No prayer, no sacrifice, no blessing is ever given in the Church without being sanctioned by the Amen which means an approval, agreement, participation. To say *Amen* to anything means that I make it mine, that I give my consent to it. . . And *Amen* is indeed the word of the laity in the Church, expressing the function of the laity as the People of God, which freely and joyfully accepts the Divine offer, sanctions it with its consent. There is really no service, no liturgy without the *Amen* of those who have been ordained to serve God as community, as Church." [14]

Before we conclude this section on the theology of the layman in the Orthodox Church, let us mention just briefly a few other ways by which lay people share in the priesthood. When the priest blesses the congregation saying, "Peace be with you," the congregation participates by returning the blessing saying, "And with your spirit." The lay person is allowed to baptize and carry Communion to the sick in cases of emergency. In Russia today where the priest cannot take the Sacrament to the dying without governmental approval, the laity are smuggling the Sacrament into hospitals inside sandwiches. When the bishops of the Church decide on a matter of doctrine in an ecumenical council, their decision is ratified and approved by the conscience of the Church, the lay people. Mario Rinvolucri writes in his book "Anatomy of A Church," "In Orthodoxy the people are considered to be the ultimate *defensores fidei* (defenders of the faith). If they are not prepared for reunion by a gradual process of . . . enlightenment it will be reunion only on paper, at least as far as the Greek countryside is concerned." [15] This is how closely the Orthodox laity are called upon to share in the priesthood. In summary we may say that the priest is the coach and the lay people are the members of the team. To do the work of Christ, they must work together closely.

Clergymen are addressed as "Father" in the Orthodox Church since they are the ones through whom we receive our spiritual birth in Christ through baptism. Bishops are addressed as "Your Grace." They oversee the sacramental and educational life of Christians within a specific geographical area known as a diocese. The secular affairs of local parishes are governed by a parish council elected by the congregation. The title "Father" expresses the attitude of the faithful toward the role of the priest. He is a spiritual counselor who is there to serve, to lead, to guide, to counsel, to sanctify the Christian in his pilgrimage through this life to eternity.

SUMMARY

1. Every sacrament puts us in touch with Christ and applies to us the power of the Cross and Resurrection. They are ways by which we come into intimate personal contact with Jesus today.

2. Theologically speaking, a sacrament is a divine rite instituted by Christ or His apostles which through visible signs conveys to us the hidden grace of God.

3. If a sacrament happens whenever God's grace is mediated to us through matter, then there is no limit to the number of sacraments; the entire universe becomes a sacrament through which we see the presence of the invisible God.

4. Through the sacraments God shares His life with us, redeems us from sin and death, bestows on us the glory of immortality and makes the Kingdom of God accessible to us here and now.

[14] *"Clergy and Laity in the Orthodox Church"* p. 10 St. Vladimir's Seminary.
[15] *"Anatomy of a Church."* p. 34.

5. Participation in the sacraments must not be mechanical. We need to approach Jesus in the sacraments with a warm inner attitude of faith, love, obedience and deep penitence for our sins.

6. Through baptism Christ leads us through the Red Sea of sin and death to the glorious freedom of the children of God; He calls us His own sons and daughters, makes us heirs of His eternal kingdom, takes us in as members of His royal family, and makes us "partakers of divine nature." Baptism is our personal Easter through which we die with Christ to sin and rise with Him to the new life.

7. Confirmation or Chrismation, administered at baptism, is our personal Pentecost. Purified by baptism, we receive the manifold gifts of the Holy Spirit.

8. The Sacrament of Penance or Confession is a "new baptism" since it involves the forgiveness of all sins committed after baptism. It is the sacrament by which Christ comes to us today to liberate and heal rather than to judge. We need to remember that there are two kinds of confession in the Orthodox Church: private confession by prayer (to be practiced daily) and sacramental confession before the priest (to be practiced at least yearly and as often as one commits a serious sin).

9. The Sacrament of the Eucharist (Holy Communion) is the sacrament by which Christ unites Himself with us today. He comes to transubstantiate and change our lives into His beautiful life: "I live, not yet I, but Christ lives in me" (Gal. 2:20).

10. Through the Sacrament of Holy Matrimony Christ blesses the marriage of His children and cements it together with His special love and grace.

11. Through the Sacrament of Holy Unction Christ continues His ministry of healing through the prayers of the presbyters and the anointing of oil.

12. Christ continues to select apostles for His Church today; to authorize and empower them for this ministry through the Sacrament of Holy Orders (Ordination).

What We Believe About the Bible

When Martin Heidegger, the German philosopher, was asked some time ago whether he was an atheist he replied, "No, because I do not deny the existence of God; I merely say that He is absent." Heidegger's remark describes how many people feel today. They do not deny that God exists. But they live with little sense of His presence. God is absent from their experience, from their lives.

The sense of God's absence is not new. Thousands of years ago the prophet Amos spoke of God hiding Himself. He warned:

> "Behold, the days are coming, says the Lord God, when I will send a famine on the land; not a famine of bread nor a thirst for water, but of hearing the words of the Lord. They shall wander from sea to sea, and from north to east; they shall run to and fro to seek the word of the Lord, but they shall not find it."

Job's famous struggle was basically a search for God who seemed reluctant to make a stage appearance for him. "O that I knew where I might find Him! That I might come even to His seat," he cried.

DOES GOD HIDE?

Does God hide? St. John Chrysostom answered this question once. How can He Who is the Light of the World possibly hide? Yet, he said, even though the sun shines and is everywhere present it is the easiest thing in the world for man to shut out the rays of the sun and create darkness. All he has to do is to close his eyelids and he is in complete darkness.

God is not absent. Rather it is man who does not want God around. It is man who is absent from God. There are several reasons for this. One is *apathy*. People have no time for God. They are too busy with other things. Henri Nouwen writes, "Our lives might be filled with many events — so many events that we often wonder how we can get it all done — but at the same time we might feel very unfulfilled, and wonder if anything is happening which is worth living for. Being filled yet unfulfilled, being busy yet bored, being involved yet lonely, these are the symptoms of the absurd life, the life in which we are no longer hearing the voice of the One Who created us and who keeps calling us to a new life in Him." [1] God is absent because there is little desire on the part of people to have Him present. Time and time again the Bible insists that only those who seek God find God. He doesn't come where He is not wanted. He forces no one. He stands at the door and knocks waiting for us to open.

Another reason man does not want God around is sin. Sin is not comfortable in the presence of God. This is why Adam fled God's presence after he had sinned. St. John expressed this well when he wrote, "For everyone who does evil

---

[1] *"Spiritual Direction."* Article in "Worship" p. 399, 1980.

hates the light, and does not come to the light, lest his deeds should be exposed'' (John 3:20).

But God's absence does not mean that God is not interested. He may be absent because man does not want Him around, but He is forever waiting to be found. There is an old story about a boy who was playing hide-and-seek with his friends. He was thrilled when it came his turn to hide. But while he was hiding, the other boys lost interest and went off. The boy was heart-broken. His grandfather found him sobbing and said, ''Don't weep because your friends didn't come to find you. Perhaps you can learn from this disappointment that God too is waiting to be found and men have gone off in search of other things.''

If God is absent from many people today, it is because of our apathy, our pride, our sin, our moral indifference. But God is still waiting—in the quietness, in the shadow—waiting to be found. Not just waiting but actively seeking us in so many ways as the shepherd seeks the lost sheep. As the Hound of Heaven He never gives up His search for man.

Scribbled on the wall of a cellar in Cologne, Germany, during the violence and despair of World War II was this profound confession of faith:

> ''I believe in the sun, even when it is not shining;
> I believe in love, even when I feel it not;
> I believe in God, even when He is silent.''

But God is not silent unless we want Him to be. When God seems silent, it is because He has already spoken and there is nothing else to add. Of old He spoke through the prophets. In these last days He has spoken supremely in the person of His Son Jesus Christ. He continues to speak to each of us today.

How?

IF ONLY I COULD HEAR HIM

There are people who say, ''If I had the opportunity to hear God speak in person, I would run on my bare feet to the ends of the earth to hear Him.'' But God is present here and now and He is speaking to each of us personally. We do not have to travel to the ends of the earth to hear Him. He speaks to us all the time in and through His Word, the Holy Bible. What is the Bible but the Word of God speaking to us every Sunday in the liturgy and every day at home. It is God's Word just as surely as if God Himself were speaking to us in person.

St. Chrysostom writes, ''As when God became man in Bethlehem the eternal Word became flesh, so in the Bible the glory of God veils itself in the fleshly garment of human thought and human language.'' God is speaking!

Whenever I pick up the Bible to read, I need to say to myself, ''God is now speaking to me.'' He speaks not in thunder and lightning as He spoke to Moses on Mt. Sinai. He speaks to us as Jesus spoke to His disciples in the Sermon on the Mount. He sat down with them on a lovely hilltop and spoke to them personally the words of life.

As Dr. Pius Parsch wrote, ''The Bible is the living, actual word of God—to me and to you. When you are reading the Bible, you are not just reading something which God spoke (to others) in the dim and distant past. God is speaking to you *now*. Bible reading is a conversation with God; we are actually in contact with Him, and how greatly we ought to prize that fact! When you say your prayers you are *speaking to* God; when you read the Bible God *is speaking to you*—not as a stern judge but as a loving Father." [2] We must ever remember that more than a lawgiver God is lifegiver. That life comes to us through word and sacrament.

God speaks! Do we listen? Do we read? Every day every daily newspaper in the country has a horoscope. Millions look to astrology through the horoscope for daily guidance. Avidly, they study the position of the stars seeking to find in them the answers to their problems. All along, the Word of God is present in every home, in every hotel room. Yet, if it remains a closed book, is it a wonder that for many people today God is so absent that they turn to the stars for guidance.

God doesn't have to be absent. In fact, He doesn't want to be absent—not He who took the name EMMANUEL: *God with us*. Do you remember what it was that helped American P.O.W.'s survive those terrible years in North Vietnamese prisons? It was the Bible. They exchanged Scripture verses—secretly whispering them to one another, writing them on toilet paper, and tapping them out in Morse code. The Bible filled them with the assurance of God's presence, and they were able to survive a confinement that otherwise might have destroyed them mentally, physically, and spiritually.

When under brutal mental torture, they found that the only way that could prevent a breakdown was by feeding their minds on God's promises which they had hidden in their minds and hearts.

Jesus said in John 15:22, "If I had not come and spoken to them, they would not have sin; but now they have no excuse for their sin." God has come in Christ. He has spoken to us. He has given us His word. He holds us repsonsible for that word even if we have not read it, for He has placed it in our hands.

WHAT IS THE BIBLE

A person tells of being on a cruise. After being at sea for many days, he had still not met the captain. But one day as he was walking on the deck, he suddenly heard on the intercom, "This is your captain speaking."

His mind turned immediately to another ship that we are all riding on, the ship we call Planet Earth. We are spinning through space at an incredible rate of speed, orbiting through the universe. But we, too, have a Captain. And whenever we pick up His Book, the Holy Bible, and read, we are hearing the voice of the Master of this universe saying to us, "This is your Captain speaking." When we accept His words by faith and live by them, miracles begin to happen. Life changes. It is transformed. The Epistle to the Hebrews describes God's word as, ". . . living and active, sharper than any two-edged sword, piercing to the division of soul and spirit . . . and discerning the thoughts and intentions of the heart" (Hebrews 4:11-12). St. Basil compares the words of the gospel to "arrows sharpened by the power of the Holy Spirit falling in the hearts of those who were at some time enemies of the king, drawing them to a love of truth, drawing them to the Lord, so that they who were enemies to God are reconciled to Him. . ." St.

---

[2] *"Learning to Read the Bible,"* Liturgical Press. Collegeville, MN.

Augustine's life was completely transformed when he heard the Captain's voice saying through a child, "Take and read!" Opening to Romans 12:12-14, he read words that completely reversed the direction of his life.

A BLUEPRINT FOR LIFE

The Bible is God saying, "This is your Captain speaking." It is also a blueprint for life. An architect said to his client one day, "These are the plans for a large public building. They are the finest plans ever drawn in this office." Then he opened a desk drawer and took out a copy of the New Testament. "We draw plans for buildings," he continued, "but this little book does something more important. It draws the plan of a good and happy life. You may have read it before, I know, but read it again. You will find God's blueprint for a beautiful life."

A LOVE LETTER

In addition to being the Captain's voice and a blueprint for your life, the Bible is a personal love letter from God to you. A great Christian scholar said once, "I just cannot read the Gospel story without knowing that I am being sought out in love . . . and being offered life's highest prize." [3]

A young boy, eager to communicate with just anyone outside the walls of his orphanage, wrote the following words on a slip of paper: "To anyone who finds this, I love you." The wind blew the paper out beyond the walls to the world. In like manner, the Bible is God's love letter to you and me. Its message is: "To anyone who reads this, I love you" Signed: "J. C."

The Bible is more than a love letter, it is a love letter that contains a proposal for marriage from God to you. He wishes to enter into the most intimate possible relationship of love with you. He delivers the proposal to you through the Bible. He expects a response. It is the most important response you will ever make. Will you say "Yes" or "No" to your Creator, your Savior, your God? Your eternal destiny depends on that response.

When Elizabeth Barrett became the wife of Robert Browning, her parents disowned her because they disapproved of the marriage. The daughter, however, wrote almost every week, telling them that she loved them and longed for a reconciliation. After 10 years she received a huge box in the mail that contained all the letters she had sent. Not one had been opened! Although these "love letters" have become an invaluable part of classical English literature, it's really pathetic to think that they were never read by Elizabeth Barrett's parents. Had they looked at just one, the broken relationship with their daughter might have been healed.

The Bible is the box containing all of God's love letters to us. They express His earnest longing for reconciliation, fellowship and union with us. They were *not* written to remain unopened. So take, open, read and discover God!

There are many ways of saying "I love you." We can say it in poetry. We can say it in stone. We can say it in music. God said it on the Cross. He delivers the message — the Good News — to us in the Bible. As someone so aptly said, "God has written His heart out on paper."

---

[3] *"A Reasoned Faith"* by John Baillie. New York. Charles Scribner's Sons, 1963.

The Bible has also been described as a Father's letter to His children who are living away from home in a distant land. Imagine how children living in a far distant land would treasure such a letter from their father; how much they would be comforted, consoled and strengthened by the father's words.

As often as we open and read the Holy Scriptures we are united with Christ. Dr. Pius Parsch writes:

> ". . . like His holy Mother (we) bear the word of God within us. Think how carefully Mary wrapped her divine Child in swaddling clothes and laid Him in a manger. Think how tenderly she nursed her Babe and looked after Him. We must do the same with every word of Scripture, as though it were the divine Child Himself. It is with a mother's care and love that we must read the sacred Scriptures." [4]

The liturgy itself is nothing but a recapitulation, a true and living making present again of the events of the Bible. To participate fully in the liturgy is to immerse oneself in the Holy Scriptures. The hymns, the architecture, the icons, the prayers, the readings all serve to convey to us the living message of the Bible.

The Bible is the cradle in which we find Christ today. It is a mirror in which we see ourselves as we are, fallen in sin; and as we can become by the power of God's grace: children of God, heirs of His everlasting kingdom, partakers of divine nature.

"Where did I come from? Why am I here? What is my future beyond this life?" It is to these fundamental questions that the Bible addresses itself. It speaks as no other book can to the heart and needs of man. It speaks with authority. "The grass withers, the flower fades; but the word of God abides forever" (Isaiah).

The central actor of the Bible is not Eve, the first sinner; nor David, the adulterer; nor Solomon, the polygamist; nor Judas, the betrayer; nor Pilate, the crucifier; nor Peter, the denier; nor Paul, the persecutor turned preacher. The center of the Bible is Jesus. Just as in England almost every road from the smallest village is designed to lead to the heart of London, so in the Bible every verse leads directly or indirectly to Jesus, the Son of God, the Savior of the world. The Apostle John writes, "These things are written that you may believe that Jesus is the Christ, the Son of God, and that believing you may have life in his name" (John 20:31).

A MINIATURE LIBRARY

The Bible is a miniature library containing all sorts of writing. It contains poetry, prayers, hymns, love songs, riddles, fables, allegories, historical narration, folklore, biographies, prophecies, letters, etc. Each biblical author used the type of literature, or literary form, that best suited his purpose. Each literary form must be interpreted properly if the author is to be understood.

For example, a visitor to earth from another planet might read a newspaper and consider everything in it equally true — news columns, ads, comics, letters to the editor, etc. — whereas we know that each style of writing must be interpreted

---

[4] *"Learning to Read the Bible"* The Liturgical Press. Collegeville, Minnesota.

differently. When, for example, the 114th Psalm says, "The mountains skipped like rams, the hills like lambs," one has to be foolish to take that literally.

NOT A BOOK OF SCIENCE

The Bible is not a book of science. Its purpose is not to convey historical or scientific facts. God has other ways of letting us in on some of the secrets of the universe, i.e., geology, biology, astronomy, etc. Behind every science the faithful Christian sees God at work in the world. The biblical writers thought the world was flat, but that was before God used Copernicus and the space age to show us that the world is round.

The purpose of the Bible is to teach not science but theology, to reveal God and His will to us. The whirling planets don't tell us that God loves us. It is in the Bible that we find the promise and the record of His love. "God spoke to our fathers by the prophets; but in these last days He has spoken to us by a Son" (Hebrews 1). The Bible is inerrant (without error) when it speaks to us of God, of His will for us, and the way of salvation. It is not inerrant when it speaks of geology or biology. Its purpose is to tell us *who* created the world (theology) not *how* the world was created (geology).

Archimandrite Sophrony tells the story of a professor of astronomy who asked a priest among his students:

"What do your Scriptures say about cosmic space and its myriad stars?"

Instead of giving a direct answer the priest in turn posed a question:

"Tell me, Professor," he said, "do you think science will invent still more powerful telescopes to see even farther into space?"

"Of course, progress is possible and science will always be perfecting apparatus for exploring outer space," replied the astronomer.

"There is hope, then, that one day you will have telescopes that can show all there is in the cosmos, down to the last detail?"

"That would be impossible — the cosmos is infinite," replied the scientist.

"So there is a limit to science?"

"Yes, in a sense there is."

"Well, Professor," said the priest, "where your science comes to a full stop, ours begins, and that is what Scriptures are all about." [5]

CONTINUITY OF THOUGHT

Even though many human authors writing independently of each other over a period of many centuries were involved in the writing of the many books of the Bible, the divine Author, the Holy Spirit, is the same. Under His guidance the books of Holy Scripture do not contradict each other but supplement and explain each other.

For example, in Genesis, the first book of the Bible, we see the creation of the earth. In Revelation, the last book of the Bible, we are offered a preview of the transfiguration of the earth.

[5] *"His Life is Mine"* Archimandrite Sophrony. Translated by Rosemary Edmonds. St. Vladimir's Seminary Press. Crestwood, New York.

In Genesis: Satan's first rebellion; in Revelation his last.

In Genesis: the entrance of sin; in Revelation the end of sin.

In Genesis: death enters; in Revelation death exits.

In Genesis: man loses dominion over creation; in Revelation man's dominion is regained.

One of the marvels of the Bible is that even though it was written by many human authors over a period of a thousand years, its divine author, the Holy Spirit, keeps developing and maintaining throughout the common themes just mentioned. Its continuity of thought makes it easier for us to understand.

BIBLICAL FUNDAMENTALISM

The Orthodox Church nourishes a great respect for the Bible as God's word. In fact, the Holy Fathers viewed the Bible as an icon full of grace. Yet the Orthodox Church does not believe that every word in the Bible was dictated by God verbatim and written down word for word by the person who wrote each book. Such an approach would accuse God of using men as tape recorders — a notion that both dishonors God and destroys man. Fr. Theodore Stylianopoulos, Professor of New Testament at Holy Cross School of Theology, asks us to look upon the Bible as a *record of truth* and not *truth itself*. He writes, ". . . there emerged in Orthodox tradition the position that the Bible is the *record* of truth, not the truth itself. . . According to the Church Fathers, the truth itself is God alone." Such an approach to the Bible according to Fr. Stylianopoulos leaves room for "other records of the experience of God, such as the writings of the Church Fathers, the liturgical forms and texts, and the decisions of the Ecumenical Councils. It rescues the Church from an exclusive focus on the Bible . . . and thus guards Orthodox life from the error of idolatrous veneration of the text of Scripture (bibliolatry)." [6] In other words, God kept on talking even after His Book had gone to press. This is what Sacred Tradition is all about. Even though the Orthodox Church distinguishes between record and truth, and esteems also other records of the life of the Holy Spirit in the Church, "the Bible still remains the primary record in the theological tradition and worship of the Church. . . The main source of patristic theology is Holy Scripture. . . No other treasure in the tradition of the Church equals the accessibility, value and authority of the Bible. . . The Orthodox Church does not have a fundamentalist but it does have a fundamental view of the sanctity and authority of the Bible." [7]

I share with you two illustrations that may help us understand the Eastern Orthodox view of the Bible as the word of God.

A person asked a friend, "Does your wife wear a diamond ring?"

"Yes, a very big diamond," was the reply.

"What does the rest of the ring look like?" he was asked.

"It's a simple gold band," was the reply.

"Jesus is the diamond in Christianity," the friend continued. "The Bible is simply the gold band whose sole purpose is to hold forth that diamond in all its sparkling brilliance."

---

[6] - [7] *"Bread for Life"* Theodore Stylianopoulos. Dept. of Religious Education. Greek Orthodox Archdiocese. Brookline, Massachusetts.

A second illustration that may help us understand the Orthodox view of sacred Scriptures is the following. Someone asked the famous theologian, Dr. Tillich, "What do you believe about the Bible?" He replied, "The Bible doesn't concern me at all. All I'm interested in is Christ."

"What do you mean?" he was asked. Dr. Tillich replied, "I'm interested in the Bible only because it is the ship which brings Christ to me. You're running around the ship looking for leaks. Christ will say to you when He comes, 'O man of little faith.' "

The Bible is the wedding band holding the Pearl of Great Price; the ship that brings Christ to us. We do not worship the band or the ship but Christ alone. He alone is *the* Way, *the* Truth, *the* Life. The Bible is treasured only as the instrument that leads us to Jesus "in whom are hid all treasures of wisdom and knowledge" (St. Paul).

The recurring theme of the fundamentalists on what the Bible *says* gives way to the Orthodox emphasis on what the Bible *means*. For the Bible does not stand by itself. It needs interpretation.

WHOSE INTERPRETATION?

The Bible needs to be interpreted properly. When Philip asked the Ethiopian who was reading Isaiah, "Do you understand what you are reading?" he answered, "How can I unless some one guides me?" (Acts 8:30-31). Who can help us understand God's word?

Since the Bible was written under the guidance of the Holy Spirit, it is the Holy Spirit abiding in the Church Who is the Proper Interpreter of the Bible. The Church, in other words, is the custodian, the caretaker, the interpreter of the Bible. It is the Holy Spirit abiding in the Church Who has guided, and continues to guide, the Church through the centuries to the proper interpretation of the Scriptures.

As the founding fathers of the United States established the Supreme Court as the authorized body to interpret the Constitution, so God established the Church as the Body of Christ to interpret the Scriptures authoritatively. Imagine what chaos we would have if everyone began interpreting the Constitution for himself! The Apostle Peter writes, "First of all you must understand this, that no prophecy of Scripture is a matter of one's own interpretation, because no prophecy came by the impulse of man, but men moved by the Holy Spirit spoke from God" (2 Peter 1:20,21).

As custodian of the Bible, it was the Church which established conclusively under the guidance of the Holy Spirit exactly which of the many books in circulation at the time were to be regarded as genuinely inspired by God. Thus it was the Church that determined the composition of the Bible and guarantees it to be God's authentic revelation. Tertullian argued that the Scriptures belonged to the Church. The heretics appeal to them was unlawful. They had no right to foreign property.

Orthodoxy teaches that complete infallibility in the interpretation of God's word has been granted not to individuals but to the entire Body of Christ, i.e., the Church, which is indwelt by the Spirit of Truth. Thus, when the early Apostles held a meeting (Acts 15), they announced their decision with the words, "It has seemed good to the Holy Spirit and to us. . .'' The successors of the Apostles, the bishops, have continued to hold such meetings, known as Ecumenical Councils. The articles of faith formulated at such Councils are authoritative and serve to elucidate and explain the true meaning of Scripture. St. Irenaeus insists that we read the Bible with the presbyters of the Church who are in possession of the apostolic doctrine.

SACRED TRADITION

Sacred Tradition plays an important role in the interpretation of Scripture. By Sacred Tradition we mean, ''the life of the Holy Spirit in the Church'' (Vladimir Lossky). The Holy Spirit has been abiding in the Church since Pentecost guiding it to all truth, i.e., to the proper interpretation of Scripture. The Orthodox Church does not ignore what the Spirit has taught in the past regarding Scripture. On the contrary, it treasures this revelation which comes to us through the Church Fathers and the Councils of the Church. Thus Scripture and Tradition belong together. Both came from the same source: the life of the Holy Spirit in the Church. Because of this, we believe that the Bible needs Sacred Tradition as the living interpreter of God's word, just as Sacred Tradition needs the Bible as its anchor and foundation.

Those who deny Sacred Tradition replace the entire 2000 year period of the life and work of the Holy Spirit in the Church with one person's interpretation of Scripture, whether that person be Mary Baker Eddy or Brigham Young. According to Brigham Young, by the way, Jesus was married to Mary and Martha. He was also married to Mary Magdalene. And it was His own wedding He was attending at Cana.[8] These are some of the strange and profane ''traditions'' we get when we deny the life of the Spirit in the Church through the centuries guiding it to the proper interpretation of the Word of God.

We read the Bible not as individuals but as members of God's Church. The whole Church reads it with us and we read it with the whole Church.

Fr. Kallistos Ware writes,

> ''. . . we do not read the Bible as isolated individuals, interpreting it solely by the light of our private understanding. . . We read it as members of the Church, in communion with all the other members throughout the ages. The final criterion for our interpretation of Scripture is the *mind of the Church*. And this means keeping constantly in view how the meaning of Scripture is explained and applied in Holy Tradition: that is to say, how the Bible is understood by the Fathers and the saints, and how it is used in liturgical worship.''[9]

THE BIBLE IN THE LITURGY

We read in the book, ''Orthodox Spirituality'':

''The word of God present in the holy and divinely inspired Scriptures remains the foundation of the whole of Orthodox spirituality. 'Sanctify them through

[8] *"The Chaos of Cults"* J. K. Van Bealen, p. 163. W. B. Eerdmans Publ. Co. Grand Rapids, Michigan. 1948.

[9] *"The Orthodox Way,"* Kallistos Ware. St. Vladimir Seminary Press. Crestwood, N.Y.

Thy truth: Thy word is truth' (John 17:17). In Orthodox churches the book of the Gospels always lies in the middle of the altar, and, while no mark of worship is paid to the reserved Eucharistic elements . . . each priest approaching the holy Table kisses the Gospel first. The Holy Scripture is the very substance of the dogmas and liturgies of the Orthodox Church and, through them, impregnates the piety of Orthodox souls. . ." [10]

It is interesting that while in non-Orthodox churches the Gospel book is usually kept on the lectern, in the Orthodox Church it is kept *enthroned* on the holy Table.

The very liturgy itself begins with the elevation of the Gospel book above the altar. The priest holds it aloft and makes the sign of the cross with it.

In the small entrance the Gospel book is carried out before the people and elevated again as the priest says, "Wisdom, let us attend." He is saying in effect "God is about to share His wisdom with us through this book, let us pay special attention." What is this but a new epiphany, a new theophany, a new appearance of God. Christ is about to come to us again in the liturgy to reveal Himself to us, to speak to us His words of everlasting life. This advent, this coming, is acted out by the priest to prepare God's people for His coming. The instrument through which His appearance is signaled is the elevation of the Gospel book.

In the Orthodox service of Matins the Gospel book is carried out to the people, that they may kiss the Resurrected Christ engraved on its cover. The Resurrected Christ has appeared to the worshippers through one of the eleven Gospel lessons describing His post-resurrection appearances, one of which is read every Sunday during Matins. The Biblical appearance of the Risen Christ through the Gospel reading is so real that the worshippers come forward to kiss the figure of the Resurrected Christ engraved on the cover of the Gospel book. The Risen Christ is truly present in their midst through His Word.

The Bible is above all a theophany — an extension of the theophany of Christ—"the Word (Who) became flesh and dwelt among us" (John 1:14). He continues to be present among us to speak to us through His word.

St. John Chrysostom urges Christians to read the Sunday Gospel lesson at home on Saturday evening and meditate on it. This is how they are to prepare themselves in advance for the reading of the Gospel in the Sunday liturgy. When the liturgy is over, they are not to leave but to *stay and discuss it.*

It is significant that in the Orthodox Church the two things that are especially necessary for life are kept on the Holy Table: food and light. The Sacred Body and Blood of our Lord for the nourishment of the soul and the Gospel book which is a lamp unto our feet and provides light for us as we journey through this world to our true home in heaven.

It is interesting that the historian Harnack who usually criticized the Orthodox Church, praised its emphasis on the Gospel. He wrote: "Jesus' words . . . take the first place in this Church, too, and the quiet mission which they pursue is not suppressed. . . They are read in private and in public, and no superstition avails to destroy their power.''

---

[10] *"Orthodox Spirituality"* by a Monk of the Orthodox Church. St. Vladimir's Seminary Press. Crestwood, NY.

RELATIVISM

Nothing has so shaken our security these days as the philosophy of relativism, the so-called "New Morality" — the theory that holds ultimate truth to be a mirage; the theory that no values are fixed, that each person decides existentially in each situation what is right and what is wrong. Against this spineless fluidity the Bible says, *"Thus saith the Lord."* God has spoken. He has given us goalposts. He has given us stars to steer by. He has given us principles and values and truths that are valid not for a few generations but forever. "Heaven and earth shall pass away but my words shall not pass away," saith the Lord. Jesus said, "I am the truth." Apart from Jesus the lie becomes the truth.

INFORMS, REFORMS, TRANSFORMS

"Most books *in*form, a few *re*form, the Bible alone *trans*forms" someone said. The truth is that the Bible does *all three*. It *in*forms us about Jesus the Son of God Whom to know is eternal life. It *re*forms us for in it we find the ideal and the standard by which we ought to live. It *trans*forms us because in it we are brought face to face with the grace and power of Christ by which all things are made new. We look to other books for information but we look to the Bible not only for information but also for reformation and transformation. It has all three.

In the great Russian spiritual classic "The Way of A Pilgrim" we read of a Russian officer whose career was almost completely destroyed by the passion of drink until he came into contact with the power of God's word in the Bible. It transformed his life.

Solzhenitsyn writes of a person he met in one of the Soviet concentration camps. He could not understand how in such a place there could be a person who remained serene, cheerful, brotherly. Solzhenitsyn observed that in the evenings, when this man lay down in his bunk, he would pull out of his pockets pieces of paper on which were scribbled verses from the Bible. These words had transformed this man from a broken, sour, bitter prisoner into a loving, kind, peaceful human being!

HE STEPS OUT OF THE BIBLE

"Jesus Christ seemed to come right out of the Bible," said one of the teenagers from downtown New York who had been a drug addict. He had been saved through the magnificent ministry of the Rev. David Wilkerson. "He (Jesus) became a living person who wanted to stand with me through my problems." The power of God for salvation — that is what the Gospel is. God's power steps out of the Bible right into your life and mine!

Archbishop Anthony Bloom testifies that his life was transformed by an incident that happened during his student days. "While I was reading the beginning of Mark's Gospel . . . I suddenly became aware that on the other side of my desk there was a presence. And the certainty was so strong that it was Christ standing there that it has never left me. This was the real turning point (in my life)." [11] Jesus stepped out of the Bible into Anthony Bloom's life and transformed it.

---

[11] *"Beginning to Pray"* by Anthony Bloom. Paulist Press. Ramsey, N.J.

"IT FINDS ME"

One of the finest tributes ever paid to the Bible was that of Coleridge, the poet. He said simply, "It finds me." It finds me in my wrongdoing and convicts me of sin. It finds me in my loneliness and brings to me the companionship of God. It finds me in my need and brings the divine answer to that need. Are we giving the word of God a chance to find us? How often do we open the door to God's presence?

WHAT SCRIPTURE SAYS ABOUT ITSELF

Let us examine briefly what some of the many authors God used to write Scripture say about it.

St. Paul writes,

"But as for you, continue in what you have learned and have firmly believed, knowing from whom you learned it and how from childhood you have been acquainted with the sacred writings which are able to instruct you for salvation through faith in Christ Jesus. All scripture is inspired by God and profitable for teaching, for reproof, for correction and for training in righteousness, that the man of God may be complete, equipped for every good work" (2 Tim. 3:14-17).

The Apostle John writes,

". . . these are written that you may believe that Jesus is the Christ, the Son of God, and that believing you may have life in His name" (John 20:31).

St. Paul writes,

"For whatever was written in former days was written for our instruction, that by steadfastness and by the encouragement of the scriptures we may have hope."

The two disciples who had been walking with the risen Christ on the Road to Emmaus did not know it was Jesus. They thought He was a stranger until the end when He revealed Himself to them in the breaking of the bread. Then, looking back on the experience they said, "Did not our hearts burn within us while He talked to us on the road, while He opened to us the Scriptures?" (Luke 24:32). If we walk with the risen Christ today and let Him open the Scriptures to us, our hearts and minds too will burn with new light, new understanding, new power, joy and hope.

WHAT THE CHURCH FATHERS SAY ABOUT SCRIPTURE

"Ignorance of the Scriptures is a precipice and a deep abyss" (Desert Fathers).

"Reading Scripture is a fortification of the spirit" (St. Isaac the Syrian).

"For those who have chosen to major in holiness, there is special training in the word" (St. Clement of Alexandria).

"As in Paradise, God walks in the Holy Scriptures, seeking man" (St. Ambrose of Milan).

"Studying the holy and sacred Gospel, I found in it many and different teachings which are all pearls, diamonds, treasures, riches, joy, gladness — eternal life" (St. Cosmas Aitolos).

"And I, humble Seraphim . . . go through the Gospel daily. On Monday I read St. Matthew, from beginning to end; on Tuesday, St. Mark; on Wednesday, St. Luke; on Thursday, St. John; the other days I divide between the Acts of the Apostles and the Epistles of the Apostles. And I do not for a single day neglect to read the daily Epistle and Gospel, and also the readings to the saints. Through this not only my soul, but even my body rejoices and is vivified, because I converse with the Lord. I hold in my mind His Life and Suffering, and day and night I glorify and give thanks to my Redeemer for all His mercies that are shed upon mankind and upon me, the unworthy one" (St. Seraphim of Sarov).

"Listen, those of you are living in the world (that is, not clergy or monks) and have a wife and children; how to you also St. Paul commits especially the readings of Scripture (when he says, 'Let the word of Christ dwell in you richly in all wisdom' Colossians 3:16); and that not to be done lightly, nor in any sort of way, but with much earnestness. Listen, I entreat you, all that are careful for the Christian life and procure books that will be medicines for the soul. If you will not get any others, get at least the New Testament, the Epistles, the Acts, the Gospels for your constant teachers. If grief befalls you, dive into them as into a chest of medicine, and take comfort from them in your troubles, be it loss, or death, or bereavement . . . or rather do not just dive into them, but take them wholly into yourself, keep them in your mind. For this is the cause of all evils: not knowing the Scriptures" *(Homily IX on Colossians by St. Chrysostom).*

"The old men used to say: God demands nothing from Christians except that they shall hearken to the Holy Scriptures, and carry into effect the things that are said in them" (Desert Fathers).

"From his first entry into the monastery a monk should devote all possible care and attention to the reading of the Holy Gospel. He should study the Gospel so closely that it is always present in his memory. At every moral decision he takes, for every act, for every thought, he should always have ready in his memory the teaching of the Gospel . . . keep on studying the Gospel until the end of your life. Never stop. Do not think that you know it enough, even if you know it all by heart' (Bishop Ignati Brianchaninov).

"Ignorance of the Scriptures is ignorance of Christ" (St. Jerome).

"He (Jesus) entered the womb (of Mary) through the ear (at the Annunciation)" (St. Effrem the Syrian).

We greatly admire the early Fathers in the Orthodox Church. We have great reverence and respect for them. They are a part of our great tradition. But we need to ask ourselves: what made the Church Fathers so great? Was it not the fact that they drank heavily from the well of Scripture? St. John Chrysostom used to read the epistles of Paul "twice every week, and often three or four times." For many years he held Bible classes two or three times a week to instruct his flock. If we lose ourselves one-hundredth as much in reading the Word, we will reach depths of knowledge and experience that we can reach in no other way. The Word of God must become for us the other "food" of which Jesus spoke, "I have food to eat of which you do not know" (John 3:32).

"CRAMMING FOR FINALS"

A person asked a boy one day, "Why does your Grandma read the Bible so much?" The boy replied, "I think she's cramming for finals."

There is a far better way than "cramming," for one never knows if one will live long enough to be able to "cram." The better way is to walk with Jesus every day, to let Him give us daily His guidance and strength.

One of the ways by which we walk with Him is by letting Him speak to us daily through His Word.

The Bible is God's book. Make a friend of it and it will make you a friend of God.

Some books are to be tasted; some swallowed; some chewed and digested. The Bible is a book that should be tasted, chewed, swallowed and digested. For it is the living, active, incisive, life-giving word of God. In Rev. 10:8-11 we are told to literally "eat" the word of God: "Go, take the little roll which lies open in the hand of the angel . . . Take it and eat it. . ."

When the gushing spring of water flows into the desert sand, the water is swallowed up but palm trees appear instead. The water is translated into trees and fruit. So in our lives the daily watering of our souls with God's word produces the fruit of patience, peace, love, self control, hope and joy. (Is. 55:10-11).

HOW TO READ THE BIBLE

Orthodox Christians have great respect for the Bible. We bind it in gold and keep it enthroned upon the holy table. We kiss it in veneration. We carry it in pompous processions. We burn incense before it. We lift it up before the congregation in the small entrance of the liturgy and proclaim it to be the wisdom of God. We honor the Bible in all these ways. But do we honor it in the most important way? Do we open it to read its treasures? Do we proclaim its glorious good news from the roof tops?

NO TIME OR NO LOVE?

Many persons complain that they have no time to read the word of God each day. But it is not really a question of *time* as it is of *love*. We always find time to do the things we like to do. For example, there was once a girl who just did not care to read a certain book. Later, however, she fell in love with the author of the book. All of a sudden her whole attitude changed. She read the book over and over again, very, very eagerly. When we fall in love with the author (Jesus) it will not be a chore to read His personal letter to us. It will be pure delight. It has been said that the two people who read the Bible most carefully are the atheist and the saint. The atheist because he hates; the saint because he loves.

Father Florovsky has written,

"No one profits from the Gospels unless he is first in love with Christ. For Christ is not a text but a living Person, and He abides in His body, the Church." [12]

The highest form of Bible reading comes to those who love Jesus so much that to read His word is sheer enjoyment. They savor the sweetness of being with Him through His word.

We must not expect God always to be giving us great insights when we read His word. Reading God's word is also a way of being with God, basking in His presence, practicing His presence. A father goes fishing with his child not just to catch fish but also just to be with his child.

OPEN IT!

The Bible is our door to God's kingdom. In America alone, more than eight million such "doors" were purchased in one year. But a door, unless it is opened, is just another part of the wall. We need to ask ourselves: how often do we open our door to the kingdom? How often do we open it to find God and to let God find us?

The Bible *is* the Word of God but it will not become the Word of God *for us* unless we take it off the shelf and make it part of our mind and heart.

A serious investor would not think of not reading the "Wall Street Journal" every day. Could it be that the children of this world are still wiser, as Jesus said, than the children of the kingdom?

READ EXPECTANTLY

When a rich member of a family died, all the relatives were called together by the lawyer for the reading of the will. As it was being read, each person listened intently, expectantly, eagerly, waiting to hear his/her name mentioned. One older person, who had difficulty hearing, brought along an old hearing horn and placed it in his ear so that he might not miss a single word.

This is a picture of how expectantly we should be listening when God speaks. Everything He says is directed personally to us. We stand to inherit a kingdom. Everything He promises has our name on it.

READ IT PERSONALLY

Dr. Paul Tournier writes, ". . . it is above all through the Bible, the book of the Word revealed and incarnate, that God speaks, and personal contact with Him is established. And when it is established, Bible-reading is no longer an irksome effort to solve an enigma. . . It becomes a personal dialogue which . . . touches us personally." We become truly human to the degree that we allow God to speak to us.

---

[12] *Bible, Church, Tradition . . ."* Nordland Publishing Company. Belmont, Mass.

"Whenever you read the Gospel," says St. Tikhon of Zodansk, "Christ Himself is speaking to you. And while you read, you are praying and talking with Him."

Whenever St. John of the Ladder heard the Scriptures read in church, he literally trembled in awe as if Christ Himself were speaking directly to him.

READ IT PRAYERFULLY

Just before reading the Gospel in the Divine Liturgy the priest offers a prayer which reads:

> "Merciful Master, shine in our hearts the pure light of your knowledge and open the eyes of our mind to perceive the message of your Gospel teachings."

Every Orthodox Christian should offer a similar prayer before reading God's word. It is only with the guidance of the Holy Spirit that we can come to understand God's words.

Fr. Peter Chamberas, a New Testament scholar, wrote, "the place where the study of the Bible takes place should be before the holy icons, with the vigil light glowing and the fragrant incense burning. . . Every effort must be made to make our study of the Bible a liturgical experience, a true communion with our Lord and His Holy Spirit." [13]

TAKE A PROMISE WITH YOU

Never put the Bible away with memorizing at least one verse each day. Take it with you. Make it the controlling thought of the day. Return to it. Cling to it. Live with it all day. Chew on it as a cow chews her cud. Fall asleep with it at night. It is possible to carry the Bible around in your heart. "Let the word of Christ *dwell in you* richly" (Col. 3:16). We can keep our minds well stocked with beautiful thoughts from God's word. They can become our daily companions, bringing us strength, comfort and inspiration when we need it. Those divine promises will come to our assistance when we need them. They will serve as life preservers when we find ourselves adrift and shipwrecked on the sea of life. St. Jerome advised that a passage of Scripture be learned by heart each day, and two or three times a night one should rise to go over the Scriptures which one had memorized. [14]

"But Mary kept all these things, pondering them in her heart" (Luke 2:19). She feasted her mind and heart on the marvelous promises of God. "Thy word have I hid in my heart, that I might not sin against thee" (Psalm 119:11). The Psalmist stored God's word in his heart where in a moment of need it brought him strength.

We must not just *read* the Bible; we must *possess* it. There is something indestructible about these treasures of the mind. Nothing can take them away; no wind, no weather, no storm can destroy them. When life puts us to the test, we

---

[13] *"Studying the Bible In Church,"* Fr. Peter Chamberas. Article in the Orthodox Observer, January 14, 1981.

[14] Letter 22:37, CSEL 54:201

remember their sweep, their rise, their power. They challenge, they warn, they encourage, they inspire, they hold our hearts fast. Palladius says of Pachomius' monks: "They all learn the holy Scriptures by heart." [15]

In Pachomian monasticism the law was abundantly clear: "There shall be absolutely no one in the monastery who . . . does not at least know (by heart) the New Testament and the psalter."

A special task of novices, according to St. Basil, is the study of Scripture. Cassian speaks of the repetition of memorized texts so that the mind is formed in the image of Christ. Caesarius, in his statutes for nuns, spoke of one sister reading aloud, while the others work so that "they do not cease meditating the word of God and prayer of the heart." We see from these ancient practices how important Scripture reading was — and is — for spiritual growth.

In order to *possess* the Bible, we must not gallop through it. We should read slowly and look around. What do motorists see of wayside flowers when they go speeding along? We must let the word of Christ *dwell* in us richly, says St. Paul. We must never leave a passage of God's word until it has left its mark on us.

"Man does not live by bread alone but by every word that proceeds from the mouth of God," said Jesus. We are what we eat. We are what we feed our minds on. We are what we fix our hearts on. The human mind is like a computer. We get out of it only what we feed into it. If we feed garbage into it, we will get garbage out of it. If we feed the word of God into it, we will get the word of God out of it.

The Bible has been called "God's pharmacy." Within its covers may be found prescriptions to meet every need in life from loneliness to depression to forgiveness. For the Bible is not merely a history of the past, or an object of study, but "the power of God unto salvation for everyone who has faith" (Romans 1:16).

FROM HEARING TO APPLICATION

Fr. Elchaninov writes:

"In our understanding of the Word of God one may distinguish the following stages: hearing, understanding, the acceptance in the heart of what we hear and, finally, its application to our life. Examine yourself — at which of these stages are you at present? Do you always go even so far as to listen to God's word? Do you often read it? Hearing or reading it, do you take the trouble to penetrate its meaning, in order to understand it? Does it reach your conscience, your heart? Does it stir them? If so, has it yielded fruit, does it move you to action, breaking up the apathy of our normal, self-contented life? Examine yourself — and slowly, persistently, begin to ascend these steps." [16]

St. Mark the Monk wrote, "He who is humble in his thoughts and engaged in spiritual work, when he reads the Holy Scriptures will apply everything to himself and not to someone else." God's word is addressed not to everyone in general but personally and directly to us. What we read must be applied to ourselves. God is holding up a mirror before us to enable us to see what we are and what we can become by His grace.

---

[15] Lausiac History 32:12

[16] *"Diary of A Russian Priest"* by Alexander Elchaninov. Faber and Faber, Ltd. London.

If you think the Bible is hard to understand, says John Chrysostom, just remember that parts of it were written by simple fishermen. Do not be discouraged. The Bible was not written by philosophers for intellectuals. Simple peasants understood Jesus and followed Him!

A theological student came to a professor one day, greatly concerned that he could not grasp the meaning of certain verses in the Bible. The noted preacher replied kindly but firmly, "Young man, allow me to give you this word of advice. Give the Lord credit for knowing things you do not understand!"

There are indeed parts of the Bible that are difficult to understand but there are so many more that we *do* understand. Let us choose to concentrate on these. And the more we read, the more we shall understand. The Bible explains the Bible. One passage explains another, with the result that in a year or two we shall find ourselves quite at home in Scripture.

Mark Twain said once, "Most people are bothered by the passages of Scripture they do not understand, but I have always noticed that the passages that bother me are those I do understand."

When asked about those difficult passages in the Bible another person said, "I treat them like bones. I find plenty of meat in the Bible; when I come across a bone I cannot handle, I just lay it aside."

The Bible may be obscure at times but it is not unintelligible. John Ciardi of "The Saturday Review" said once, "Obscurity is what happens when a writer undertakes a theme for which the reader is not sufficiently prepared." What the writer says is intelligible and meaningful to the prepared mind, but not to the unprepared mind. In that sense, the message of the Bible is obscure to those who do not prepare themselves through prayer but not to those who live in the Church and receive its constant guidance in the proper understanding of God's word. Just as heaven is a *prepared* place for a prepared people so the Bible is a *prepared book* for a *prepared* people. "The unspiritual man does not receive the gifts of the Spirit of God, for they are folly to him, and he is not able to understand them because they are spiritually discerned" (I Cor. 2:14).

God will use some parts of the Bible more effectively than others. We cannot expect the long genealogies in Numbers to capture us as much as the 23rd Psalm or the Gospel of John. But in every one of the books of the Bible there will be something that will stir our mind and heart and send our spirit soaring in hope. We always urge those who have not read the Bible to begin by reading the four Gospels since they are the key to the understanding of the entire Bible. Since the Bible is supremely a book about Christ, it is important to begin with those sections which tell what He did and said when He was among us, i.e., the four Gospels.

We recommend a good translation of the Bible such as the RSV translation with the Apocrypha, i.e., "The Oxford Annotated Bible with the Apocrypha" by Oxford University Press. The ten so-called Deuterocanonical books of the Old Testament are included in the Orthodox canon of the Bible. According to Orthodox teaching, they may be read for personal edification but are not authoritative for doctrine. They are preserved in the Orthodox Bible because they were included in the Septuagint (the Greek translation of the Old Testament) which was in use at the time of Jesus. Roman Catholics accept only seven of these Deuterocanonical books, Protestants none. Thus there are 39 books in the Protestant Old Testament, 49 in the Orthodox and 46 in the Roman Catholic. All three accept the same 27 books of the New Testament.

THE HEARTBEAT OF GOD

A large hospital in New York City made a very simple but unusual discovery. They were having a problem in the nursery. The crying of some little ones disturbed other little ones. What could they do to give these newborn babies a sense of security and peace?

They tried soft music but it didn't work. Then someone suggested that the heartbeat of a mother be recorded and played over the sound system. It was like a miracle. The little ones who were restless grew still and went peacefully to sleep. The mother's heartbeat was a familiar sound to them. They had listened to it even before they were born. It was the sound of security and love.

What we have coming to us from the Bible is the sound of the heartbeat of God. Amid all the disturbing noises of this world, it is the only sound that can bring us the peace of God's presence and love. For, it is the sound — the voice — of the Creator's love.

The key phrase in the *Apophthegmata* (Sayings of the Desert Fathers) is "Speak a word, Father." This recurs again and again. The "word" that was sought was not a theological explanation, nor was it "counselling"; it was a word which would give life to the disciple if it were received.

When a monk came to Basil of Caesarea once and said, "Speak a word, Father," Basil replied, "Thou shalt love the Lord thy God with all thy heart," and the monk went away at once. Twenty years later he came back and said, "Father, I have struggled to keep your word; now speak another word to me"; and St. Basil said, "Thou shalt love thy neighbor as thyself." The monk then returned to his cell to keep that also.

How beautiful it is for us to come to our Abba, our Father in heaven, each day and to say to Him as we pick up the Bible, "Speak a word, Father, for your servant is listening." He will speak that word to us. And it will be a word that will give life!

WHAT HE TELLS US

In the Bible God is telling us:

"I created you; I created the universe. I know all about you — what your thoughts are going to be even before you think them. I love you and am concerned about you. And I'm going to let you in on a secret. 'To you it has been given to know the secrets of the kingdom of God' (Luke 8:10). I'm going to let you in on the nature of the universe I created. I'm going to let you in on the secret of who you are and why you were created. And I'm going to let you in on the kind of relationships that work between husbands and wives, between parents and children, and between you and Me, how you can begin to grow toward your rightful destiny — becoming the person I created you to be; becoming partakers of My nature."

Truly the Bible is the unique book of God's self-revelation. It possesses sacramental power, transmitting God's grace, truth and power to the faithful reader. It can bring each one of us to a personal encounter with the living God. For the Word of God becomes the living, incisive, powerful Word through the power of the Holy Spirit.

GOD'S DIALOGUE WITH HIS PEOPLE

The Bible is not God's *monologue* but rather God's *dialogue* with His people. Fr. George Florovsky brought this out beautifully when he wrote:

> "We hear in the Bible not only the voice of God, but also the voice of man answering Him — in words of prayer, thanksgiving and adoration, awe and love, sorrow and contrition, exultation, hope or despair. There are, as it were, two partners in the Covenant, God, and man, and both belong together, in the mystery of the true divine-human encounter, which is described and recorded in the story of the Covenant. Human response is integrated into the mystery of the Word of God. It is not a divine monologue, it is rather a dialogue, and both are speaking, God and man. But prayers and invocations of the worshipping psalmist are nevertheless 'the Word of God.' God wants, and expects, and demands this answer and response of man. It is for this that he reveals himself to man and speaks to him. He is, as it were, waiting for man to converse with him. He establishes his Covenant with the sons of men. Yet, all this intimacy does not compromise divine sovereignty and transcendence. God is 'dwelling in light unapproachable' (I Tim. 6:16). This light, however, 'lighteth every man that cometh into the world' (John 1:9). This constitutes the mystery, or the 'paradox' of the revelation." [17]

Thus God's word demands a response from each one of us: the response of obedience to His holy will, the response of an ongoing personal dialogue with Him through prayer.

SUMMARY

1. God is not an absent God or a God who hides. He has revealed Himself and is forever waiting to be found.

2. He waits to reveal Himself to us through His written word in the Bible which is like a blueprint for life, a cradle in which we find Christ, a love letter from God to us containing a proposal for marriage with an R.S.V.P.

3. The purpose of the Scriptures is stated in John 20:31, "These things are written that you may believe that Jesus is the Christ, the Son of God, and that believing you may have life in His name."

---

[17] *"Bible, Church, Tradition: An Eastern Orthodox View,"* Georges Florovsky, Nordland Publishing Company, Belmont, MA 1972.

4. The purpose of the Bible is to teach not science but spiritual truths about God and man. Since the Bible is a library of books containing many literary forms, i.e., poetry, parables, historical narration etc., it must not always be interpreted literally.

5. Although the Orthodox Church views the Bible as an icon full of grace, it does not venerate the text of Scripture in an idolatrous way as if every word of the Bible were dictated verbatim by God.

6. The Church is the divinely inspired Interpreter of the Bible. The Holy Spirit has been abiding in the Church since Pentecost guiding it to all truth.

7. As illustrated in the Small Entrance of the liturgy, the Bible is a theophany — an appearance of Christ in our midst today—as He continues to speak to us through His Word.

8. The Bible gives us the eternally valid truth of God. It informs, reforms, and transforms those who accept it with faith.

9. As a door to God's kingdom, the Bible is to be read lovingly, expectantly, personally, prayerfully, faithfully, allowing the word of Christ to dwell in us richly. It is a prepared book for a prepared people.

10. The Bible is not God's monologue but His dialogue with us. Included in the Bible is the vitally important response of man to God's offer of salvation.

What We Believe About Icons

It is impossible to visit Italy, Greece, Germany, Yugoslavia, Romania, Russia, Bulgaria, the Middle East without becoming acquainted with a form of religious art called *the icon*. Used extensively in churches and homes in these countries, it has now become quite popular in the West where such art is being used for decorative purposes. Eastern Christians consider this a blasphemous distortion of the original intent of the icon. Not a few tourists today pay expensively for what they believe to be 16th or 17th century icons but which unfortunately turn out to be antiqued lithographs beautifully decoupaged.

The word *icon* comes from the Greek word *"Eikon"* which means *image*. A famous German camera Zeis Ikon uses this word as a trade name. St. Paul speaks of Christ as the *Icon of God;* that is what the phrase is in Greek. Christ is the Icon of God, and the whole New Testament is written on the basis that if you want to know what the Eternal God is like, you look at Jesus and see.

In the West religious art was placed on the windows of a church or cathedral. In the East the windows were left quite plain and the walls were covered with religious art.

The purpose of icons is three-fold: 1. to create reverence in worship; 2. to instruct those who are unable to read; 3. to serve as an existential link between the worshipper and God.

WHY ICONS?

The Hebrew had as his form of icon the written word. He objected vehemently to any kind of picture, never realizing that a combination of letters conveying an idea was just as much an icon as any other form of portrayal. In dealing with other people, i.e., Greeks, Egyptians, Latins, the Church was faced with the need of expressing to them the idea of Christ embodied. He had already been embodied in the written word and in song. Now He had to be embodied in picture in order to appeal to the pope of the senses: the eyes.

THE ICONOCLASTS

The Church calendar sets aside the first Sunday of Lent as the Sunday of Orthodoxy. It marks the day on which the use of icons was reinstated after a period of opposition. It commemorates the triumph of Orthodoxy against the iconoclasts whose purpose it was to remove forcibly all icons from churches and destroy them as instruments of idolatry.

Since the icon is one of the most distinctive features of Orthodoxy, we shall consider briefly what it signifies, why it is used, its practical value as well as its doctrinal significance.

First, let us consider the charge of idolatry. Orthodox Christians do not *worship* icons; they merely *reverence* or *venerate* them as symbols. Leontius of Neapolis wrote in the seventh century:

"We do not make obeisance to the nature of wood, but we revere and make obeisance to Him who was crucified on the Cross. . . . When the two beams of the Cross are joined together I adore the figure because of Christ who on the cross was crucified, but if the beams are separated, I throw them away and burn them." [1]

GOD: INVISIBLE OR VISIBLE?

The iconoclasts (those who sought to remove all images from churches) held that God cannot be painted because He is eternal and invisible. "No man has seen God at any time" (John 1:18). But the Orthodox insisted that God can be painted because He became man. In the Old Testament any image of God would be a "graven image," an idol, because no image of God could exist. Nobody had ever seen God. But this changed the moment God became man in Christ. Because of this it is now lawful to make a picture of Him. Those who were denying the icon of Christ were denying the truth that He had become man. In other words, they were denying the very basis of our salvation: God become man in Christ. Thus, what we really commemorate on the first Sunday of Lent in the Orthodox Church is not a controversy about religious art, but about the Incarnation of Christ and the salvation of man.

St. John of Damascus expressed this well when he said, "Of old, God was never depicted. Now, however, when God is seen, clothed in flesh and conversing with man, I make an image of God, of the God whom I can see. I do not worship matter. I worship the God of matter who became matter for my sake . . . to work out my salvation through matter."

It would be theologically accurate to say that God Himself was the first icon maker by visibly reproducing Himself in the likeness of His Son. The iconoclast controversy was not simply a controversy over religious art, but over the entire meaning and implication of the incarnation. God took a material body, thereby proving that matter can be redeemed. "The Word made flesh has deified the flesh," said John of Damascus. The materials employed in the icons are but another expression of Eastern Christianity's appreciation of the material world. This has much to say to us today in the area of ecology: that matter is sacred and should not be abused or contaminated.

The Protestant Reformation of the 16th century was negative to icons. For Luther they were permissible as illustrations. Calvin could accept nothing more than historical scenes with more than one person depicted, so that it would not make the faithful stumble into idolatry.

Puritans in England and America took a dim view of religious art. They despised and prohibited all religious paintings. In a way they were probably right. Most "religious art" is offensive because it makes is hard to believe that the only begotten Son of God became man. The picture of the Christ as a bearded lady, sometimes with a bleeding valentine heart showing through a transparent chest, if taken seriously, denies that he was made man. Such pictures give the idea that he became a phantom, neither male nor female.

---

[1] Migne, Patrologia Graeca.

Eric Newton writes,

"But from the moment when God sent his only begotten Son to dwell on earth, born of a mortal woman, to preach, to perform miracles, to suffer death at the hands of the Jews, and to be resurrected, the situation for the artist changed, for the new religion contained within itself the fact of the invisible made visible, the Deity made human, the supernatural made physically manifest. At last there was no reason to forbid imagery, for if God Himself became incarnate there could be no possibility of the artist's image of Him leading to idolatry." [2]

WHAT IS AN ICON?

The tendency among some of the early Christians was *not* to use a realistic image of Jesus. Instead they used abstract signs — letters that would stand for Jesus, such as Chi-Rho, the first two letters of the Greek word for Christ, or IHS, the first letters for the name Jesus in Greek. They also used figures as the fish, which was a secret sign for Christ, or a sheep, standing for the lamb of God.

The Trullan Synod, held in Constantinople in 692 A.D., stated that it was wrong for the church to depict Christ in signs and symbols any longer. The Synod specifically decreed that it would be wrong to portray Christ as a sheep (lamb of God). If He really became man, the Synod said, then He must be portrayed as a human being — not as an animal or as a symbol.

The church fathers felt that the divine nature of Christ should be brought out in the images as well as His human nature. They said, in the same directive, that images of Him should not be "too carnal." The Seventh Ecumenical Council stated that the Church, even though she may depict the Lord through art in His human form, must not separate in the representation Christ's flesh from His divinity. Christ had to be represented in Orthodox art as God-Man. As such, it would be outright impious to represent Christ according to the natural beauty of some ordinary human model. This was not true in the West where "good-looking" and visionary young men became actual models for paintings of Christ. These humanly "beautiful" Christs of Western art were unacceptable to the Eastern Christians in view of the fact that they expressed the idea of only the human nature of our Lord. So, Orthodox art was faced with the special task of finding some iconographic type which would lead the spectator directly to the thought that in the represented person "the whole fullness of the divinity dwells bodily" (St. Paul). Moreover, Theodore Studites said, "If we say that Christ is the power of God and the wisdom of God, by the same manner His representation must be said to be the power and the wisdom of God."

For this reason, Orthodox art created for Christ an *idealized* type unlike any purely human model, with supranatural characteristics such as large eyes, nose and hands. Thus the Orthodox iconographer attempts to express the supra-natural, supra-rational and supra-conceptual elements of our Lord through hyperbole, exaggeration, excess, and even deformation of natural reality.

Thus, while the West has traditionally emphasized the human nature of Christ through the use of statues and human models of Jesus, the East has placed more

---

[2] *"2000 Years of Christian Art,"* Eric Newton and Wm. Neil, P. 18, Harper and Row. Used by permission.

emphasis on the divine nature of Jesus through the icon that lends itself very effectively to the expression of the divine, transfigured state of Jesus through the use of stylization.

THREE WAYS OF PORTRAYAL

There are three possible ways of "portraying" someone: the photograph, the portrait and the icon. The *photograph* records the features as they are. A successful *portrait* reproduces a person's features in a way that is true to life and recognizable; but at the same time it brings out his character and gives expression to his inner nature. An *icon* is not a photograph but more like a portrait. Yet it is more even than a portrait. It aims at giving a true likeness of the person, and at the same time it attempts to bring out in a person what he or she has become through the power of the Holy Spirit. An icon then is more than a photograph, more even than a portrait. Iconography portrays what happens to people after God touches them. They become new persons. By omitting everything irrelevant to the spiritual figure, the figure becomes stylized, spiritualized, not unrealistic but supra-realistic.[3] The icon is thus set aside from all other forms of pictorial art. It offers an external expression of the transfigured state of man, of a body so filled with the Holy Spirit, so trained in good, that it has become like the spiritual body which we shall receive at the Second Coming of Christ.

There are some who believe that abstractionism, the reduction of a figure to its purest essence, originated with the iconographers.

Icons have been called prayers, hymns, sermons in form and color. They are the visual Gospel. In reality, the Eastern Church has two Gospels: the verbal and the visual to appeal to the whole man. As St. Basil said, "What the word transmits through the ear, that painting silently shows through the image, and by these two means, mutually accompanying one another . . . we receive knowledge of one and the same thing." One has but to enter an Orthodox Church to see unfolded before him on the walls all the mysteries of the Christian religion. "If a pagan asks you to show him your faith," said John of Damascus, "take him into church and place him before the icons."

Through the icon the Orthodox Church appeals to the eye which, as we have said, is the pope of the senses. We remember much more easily what we see than what we hear. The Old Testament prophets, for example, often used the method of dramatic and symbolic action. Men might refuse to listen, but they could hardly fail to see. Jeremiah, for example, forewarned the people of the slavery that was to fall upon them by making yokes and wearing them on his neck. The current practice in Communist countries of hanging pictures of their leaders everywhere was borrowed by the Russian Marxists from the use of icons in the Russian Orthodox Church. The pictures are, in effect, icons of the new gods intended to stimulate a kind of worship and absolute obedience.

EXISTENTIAL ENCOUNTER

The icon is more even than a means of instruction. It is in effect a sacrament. For, an icon is not fully an icon until it has been blessed by the priest in church.

---

[3] I am indebted for this comparison of photograph, portrait and icon to Rudolf Muller's article, *"The Theological Significance of a Critical Attitude in Hagiography,"* that appeared in *"The Ecumenical Review"* some years ago.

Then it becomes a link between the human and the divine. It provides an existential encounter between men and God. It becomes the place of an appearance of Christ, provided one stands before it with the right disposition of heart and mind. It becomes a place of prayer. An icon participates in the event it depicts and is almost a re-creation of that event existentially for the believer. As S. Bulgakov said, ''By the blessing of the icon of Christ, a mystical meeting of the faithful and Christ is made possible.'' Many icons are regarded as ''wonder-working.'' These are considered to be the icons par excellence.

Standing in an Orthodox Church whose walls and ceiling are covered with icons of Christ and the saints, the worshipper does not feel alone. He experiences the communion of saints. He experiences a fellowship with Christ and the saints. He is made to feel that he is a member of the family of God. Cecil Stewart describes this well when he writes,

''The pictures seem to be arranged in a way which instills a feeling of direct relationship between the viewer and the pictures . . . each personality is represented facing one, so that one stands, as it were, within the congregation of saints. Byzantine art, in fact, puts one in the picture. . . . He (the viewer) observes and is observed.''

EGYPTIAN ART INFLUENCE

One of the forerunners of the icon is the Egyptian funeral portrait. It was the desire on the part of the deceased not to be forgotten that led the Egyptians to paint a picture of the deceased person's face on the mummy. The distinguishing feature of the Egyptian funeral portrait was the large eyes, wide-open and staring at the one who beholds them, as if to say, ''Here I am. You may think I'm gone and forgotten, but as I look at you with these eyes, I dare you to forget me.''

The early Christian icons followed the same pattern. The saints whom they represented had huge eyes that looked straight into the eyes of their beholders, as if to say, ''Here I am. I may seem dead to you, but I am very much alive in the presence of God.''

This is one of the principles that were incorporated into icon painting. The sensory organs (eyes, nose, ears) are not rendered according to true anatomy because each of them has been changed by divine Grace and has ceased to be the usual sensory organ of biological man. The eyes are painted large and animated to express physical intensity. Having been opened to God, they have seen great things. ''Mine eyes have seen Thy salvation.'' The ears are painted large as a symbolic projection of the ears of the soul that have heard and still hear the good news of Christ. The nose also is often larger than its natural length and thin to denote that it is not meant to smell the things of this world but the fragrance of Christ and the Holy Spirit. The mouth, on the other hand, is shaped small to express that the represented saint ''takes no thought of his life, what he shall eat and what he shall drink,'' but seeks first the kingdom of God and His righteousness.

THE HALO

Western religious art has relied on the crown of light or halo to denote the ''holiness'' of the represented person. Usually this was so because the sacred person is so worldly in appearance that the halo is required to signify that a saint is being represented. In the icon, however, one does not depend on the halo alone to understand that the represented person is a saint. Holiness is indicated by the entire form and style of the icon. This is why the halo is missing from some of the older icons as well as in the wall-paintings of the catacombs where Christ and the martyrs are represented without halos.

PRACTICAL USE OF ICONS

A Japanese girl in an American college was invited to spend the Christmas holidays with a classmate. Afterwards she was asked how she enjoyed the holidays. "Very well," she replied, "but I missed God in the home. I have seen you worship God in your church. In my country we have a god-shelf so we can worship our gods in our homes. Do not Americans worship their God in their homes?"

It has been traditional for Orthodox homes to have such a "God-shelf" in the form of an icon with a votive light burning before it. This serves as a reminder of God's presence in the home and as a center for family prayer. In old Russia, for example, every house—from the great winter palace of the Czar to the thatched hut of the peasant—had an icon of Christ or the Virgin Mother. At that time no Russian home was a home until it was consecrated by the icon.

Helene Iswolsky writes in her book "Christ in Russia,"

"In the old days . . . a Russian entering his home or visiting a friend would first of all bow low before the icons and make the sign of the cross before greeting his family or host. The icons symbolized God's presence; they were a constant reminder of the supernatural life, and appealed to morality and conscience. It is difficult to lie, to cheat, to be brutal in front of an icon. The communists in Russia did all they could to tear away the icons from men's homes, to deprive them of the image of their God, and to stifle the conscience of the people."

In fact, if the Church in Russia has survived under Communism these past many years despite lack of any facilities for instructing children in the Christian faith either at school or at church, it is due (humanly speaking) to the Christian family. Throughout Orthodox Christendom the family has been regarded as a "house church" with its own "altar" where prayers are offered before the icons.

The icon was never intended to hang on a wall as an aesthetic object. If it is used as an attractive piece of decoration, it ceases to function as an icon. For an icon can only exist within the particular framework of belief and worship to which it belongs. Divorced from this framework, it loses its functions as an icon.

In a fragment of a "Life of St. John Chrysostom" preserved in a work by St. John of Damascus (675-749), we are told that Chrysostom had an icon of the Apostle Paul before himself as he studied Paul's epistles. When he looked up from the text, the icon seemed to come to life and speak to him.

Icons in the home consecrate the profane; they transform a neutral dwelling-place into a "domestic church" and the life of the faithful into an unceasing liturgy.

Jesus said, "When you pray, go into your room" (Matthew 6:6). Archbishop Paul of Finland adds, "But even so we are not alone. The icon in the corner of the room where we pray is a window into the kingdom of God and a bond with its members."

One of the Patriarchs of the Russian Church said: "If in hospitals, which treat the diseases of the body, everything is arranged to make the surroundings conducive to the patient's return to health, what great care must be taken to order everything in a spiritual hospital, a church of God." We can apply this also to the Christian home which should include reminders of God's strengthening and healing presence.

ICON PAINTERS

It has been said that love is the great interpreter. It is the conductor of an orchestra who is in love with the music of a composer who can best interpret and express it. A young artist once brought a picture of Jesus which he had painted to a great painter for his verdict. The artist studied it for quite some time and finally said, "You don't love Him, or you would paint Him better."

This great truth is practiced among Orthodox icon painters who are usually monks. Such iconographers are not considered to be religious artists but rather as persons who have a religious vocation. They are missionaries preaching visual theology. The icon, like the Word, is a revelation, not a decoration or illustration. It is theology in color. More important than being a good artist is the fact that the icon painter be a sincere Christian who prepares himself for his work through fasting, prayer, Confession, Communion and has the feeling that he is but an instrument through whom the Holy Spirit expresses Himself. It is important to know Jesus better if one is to paint Him better. In the West, the theologian has instructed and even limited the artist, whereas in the East the iconographer is a charismatic who contemplates the liturgical mysteries and instructs the theologian.

GOD'S BEST ICON

Since we are talking about icons we would be remiss if we neglected to say that by far the best icon of God is man who was made in God's own image. This is the reason the Orthodox priest during the liturgy turns and censes the congregation after having censed the icons. Each person in the congregation is a living icon of God. Through censing we pay respect to the image of God in man which resides in all persons regardless of the color of skin or class. To pay respect to the icons in Church and to show disrespect to the living icons of God — our fellow humans — is hypocrisy of the worst sort. It is interesting to note here that in the Abyssinian Chruch Jesus and Mary are pictured as black people. All people — regardless of color — are living images or icons of God.

A Sunday school teacher once said to her first-grade class, "You know how you feel when you draw a picture. You want everybody to see it and admire it because you made it. That's how Jesus feels about you. You're the picture He draws."

A little boy asked, "Is *everybody* Jesus' picture?"

"That's right," said the teacher.

"Even Annie?"

"Yes."

Suddenly a scrap of brown paper fluttered into the teacher's wastebasket. "I was going to put flypaper in Annie's milk," he said sadly, "only Jesus drew her so I better not."

That little boy captured a great truth. The most precious icon of God is man and woman. As we treat each living icon, so we treat God.

ICONS EXPRESS OUR GOAL IN LIFE

Our goal in life according to Orthodox theology is THEOSIS. Simply put, this means that we are to become like God. This starts in baptism when the restored image is given to us. Our purpose is to proceed from the restored *image* of God to the *likeness of God*. The *likeness of God* is not given to us; we have to strive for it always by God's grace. The restored image is the gift we receive from God at baptism. But *likeness* to God is the task of personal holiness that we have to achieve as a fruit of our own spiritual life through God's grace. St. Seraphim of Sarov said: "The purpose of the Christian life is the acquiring of the Holy Spirit." To acquire the Holy Spirit is to acquire the likeness of God. There can be no likeness of God within us without the Holy Spirit.

This is what the icon shows us. Through the icon we represent Him, Who through His incarnation restored God's image in man. Or we represent the saints who through their constant openness to the Holy Spirit have acquired the true likeness of God and have become living icons. Our purpose as Orthodox Christians therefore, is to develop the gift we receive in baptism: *to proceed from image to likeness* by God's grace and thus become *living* icons of Christ in the world today.

A STUDY OF INDIVIDUAL ICONS

ICON OF NATIVITY

One of the most famous icons is that of the Nativity. Its symbolism is that of the Creator of the Universe entering history as a newborn babe. The little

helpless figure in swaddling clothes represents the complete submission of Christ to the physical conditions governing the human race. Yet he remains Lord of Creation. The angels sing praises. The Magi and the shepherds bring their gifts. The sky salutes Him with a star. The earth provides Him with a cave. The animals watch Him in silent wonder and we humans offer Him one of us, the Virgin Mother.

The lower scenes underline the scandal of the Incarnation. The right-hand scene shows the washing of the infant by the midwife and her assistant. It tells that Christ was born like any other child. The scene on the left portrays Joseph, who, having observed the washing of the infant, is once again assailed by doubts as to the virginity of his spouse. He is tempted by the devil, who suggests that if the infant were truly divine He would not have been born in the human way. The Mother Mary is in the center, and from her reclining position looks at Joseph as if trying to overcome his doubts and temptations.[4]

ICON OF CRUCIFIXION (Daphni or Osios Loukas)

Crucifixion paintings of Western art present a tragic drama of a man undergoing the ultimate agony of suffering. They depict the opened mouth of the Crucified-One in its final death spasm. They encircle the head with an excessively large crown whose sharp thorns pierce the forehead, dripping clots of blood. With the picture of the horror of the human corpse, they seek the creation of "sympathy" in the spectator.

How different the icon of the crucifixion! As Photios Kontoglou writes, "Here there is nothing from the world of corruption. The forms and colors do not impart the frigid breath of death, but the sweet hope of immortality. Christ is depicted as standing on the Cross, not hanging on it. His body is of flesh, but flesh of another nature, flesh whose nature has been changed through the grace of the Holy Spirit. The expression on His face is full of heavenly tranquillity; the affliction which has befallen Him is full of gentleness and forgiveness, exempt from agonized contractions on the face. It is the suffering redeemer, He Who has undone the pangs of death, Who has granted the peace of the life to come. This crucified body is not that of just anyone, but is the very body of the God-Man Himself. . . . It radiates the hope of the Resurrection. The Lord does not hang on the Cross like some miserable tatter, but it is He, rather, who appears to be supporting the Cross. His hands are not cramped, being nailed to the Wood; rather He spreads them out serenely in the attitude of supplication. . . . I repeat: the forms and colors of the liturgical icon do not express the brute horror of death, but have the nobility and gentleness of eternal life. It is illuminated by the light of hope in Christ. It is full of the grace of the Paraclete."

In some icons of the crucifixion the sun and the moon are placed in such a manner as to make it appear that the outstretched arms of the Savior are supporting them.

ICON OF CHRIST PANTOCRATOR

The typical Byzantine icon of Christ is that of the Pantocrator, the Lord Omnipotent. It is the image of the glorified Christ regnant on his heavenly throne.

---

[4] Nicolas Zernov, "*Eastern Christendom,*" G. P. Putnam's Sons. New York. The icons used were done by Fr. John Matusiak. Used by permission.

We are not even sure that it is not an image of the eternal God rather than that of Christ. But, as the Son is the image of the Father, so through the face of the Son we see the Father as well. Thus, the Pantocrator is really the icon of both Father and Son: the Godhead in all His glory and majesty. It is in reality an icon of the almighty and transcendent God.[5]

In the catacombs Christ was depicted as the Good Shepherd who tended His flock and won their allegiance. In an age where the Huns, the Vandals, and the Mohammedan infidels threatened the very fabric of the newly established Church, the Christians needed an emphasis on the Almighty God Who sat enthroned as Emperor, Monarch, Ruler, surrounded by His heavenly court of saints and angels and dominated His flock. It is somewhat of the emphasis we find in the hymn:

> "This is my Father's world:
> Though the wrong seems oft' so strong,
> He is the ruler yet."

It may be noted that the term "Pantocrator" and the idea behind it appear in the book of Revelation. Thus in 1:8 it is said, "I am the Alpha and the Omega, saith the Lord Who is, and Who was, and Who is to come, the Pantocrator" (Almighty). The use of the multicolored band around Him is based on Rev. 4:3 where the iris or rainbow is said to surround the throne of God.

Normally, the icon of Christ Pantocrator is the most remote of all the conventional poses, Christ distant with the presence of the law. Yet in Serbia we find an icon of the Pantocrator with dancing eyes. His face is sharp, his mouth tiny with the effort of suppressing a grin, his fingers thin and dancing, too, where they hold the book. The book is closed; but He knows what is inside: the glee of goodness, the good news of God's love.

ICON OF THE THEOTOKOS

In Orthodox hymnology the Theotokos is reverently said to be "surrounded with divine grace, shining with holiness, beautiful among women, who amazed the archangel with the brilliance of purity." As such no human model could possibly be found for her. Thus, as for Christ, an idealized type was created for her to express the above-mentioned qualities. This is in contrast to many Western painters who used sensuously beautiful women as models for Mary.

As one studies an icon of the Theotokos, one sees how the expression of the soul is concentrated on the face. The interest of the onlooker is withdrawn

---

[5] "*Russian Religious Mind*," Fedotov. A Harper Torch book.

from the body and focused on the face and especially the eyes. Here are expressed the virtues of meekness, humility, purity, spiritual love and wisdom.

The icon of the Virgin with Child is an image of the Incarnation. If one looks attentively at the icon, one will see that the Mother of God holding the child never looks at the child. She looks neither at the viewer nor into the distance but her open eyes look deep inside her. She is contemplating the mystery of the God who became man in her. Her tenderness is expressed by the shyness of her hands. She holds the Child without hugging him. She holds the Child as one would hold something sacred. All the tenderness, all the human love is expressed by the Child not the Mother. She remains the Mother of God and she treats the Child, not as the baby Jesus, but as the Incarnate Son of God. He in turn expresses to her all the love and tenderness of man and God to a person who is both His mother and His creature.

THE ICON OF THE DORMITION

Another famous icon is that of the Dormition or the Falling Asleep of the Blessed Virgin. Here is represented the Virgin's body asleep in the Lord. Behind her stands Jesus holding in His arms, right up against His breast, a tiny infant which is the Blessed Virgin's soul — newly born to eternal life. In front of the Virgin's body, in some icons, there is a strange little pagan character who tries to upset our Lady's bier, and an angel comes to smite him. The point involved here is the argument, decided at the Council of Ephesus, about the Theotokos, and the attempt at that time to upset the Church's faith that she was indeed the mother of God (Theotokos) and not just the mother of the man Jesus (Christotokos). All this is shown by this one little, silly figure trying to upset the bier on which the Virgin's body rests.

SUMMARY

1. The icon is theology in color. It acknowledges the Incarnation: God become man in Jesus. To deny the icon is to deny this very basis of our salvation.

2. The icon attempts to portray the two natures of Jesus: human and divine — not just the human. Icons of the saints portray also the transfigured state of the saint who has been sanctified by the Trinity.

3. An icon is more like a portrait than a photograph in that it portrays what happens to people after God touches them. Filled with the Holy Spirit, the physical body is transformed and becomes like the spiritual body which we shall receive at the Second Coming of Jesus.

4. The icon, blessed by the priest, becomes like a sacrament. It participates in the event it depicts and becomes, as it were, a making present again of that event existentially for the believer.

5. The icon is the distinguishing feature of every true Orthodox home. It transforms each home into a "church" where God abides and where prayers are offered daily.

6. Icon painters (iconographers) have traditionally been monks who prepared themselves for the painting of each icon through fasting, prayer and Holy Communion. It was believed that to paint Jesus better one must truly know Him better. Today, however, many iconographers are specially trained lay people.

7. The best icon of God is men and women who are made in God's own image. This is why the Orthodox priest during the liturgy turns and censes the living icons of God in the congregation (the worshippers) after having censed the icons on the icon screen and walls.

8. The whole Bible is about this image (icon) of God in man: how the image was marred by sin and how Jesus came to restore the image of God in each one of us. Through the icon we represent Him who through His incarnation restored God's image in us. Or, we represent the saints who through their constant openness to the Holy Spirit have acquired the true likeness of God and have become living icons. Our purpose as Orthodox Christians is to develop the gift we received in baptism: to proceed from image of God to likeness of God and thus become living icons of Christ in the world today.

What We Believe
About Prayers for The Dead

A psychiatrist recently listed five of the most upsetting experiences people can have. They were as follows: death of a child, death of a spouse, a jail sentence, death of a relative, an unfaithful spouse. Three of the five were related to death.

Some time ago an intriguing story appeared in one of our magazines. It was the story of a man on his way home from the office on a rainy Friday evening to face a cluster of minor problems involving the various members of his family. As he made his way home through mid-Manhattan, he happened to see a man who had just been run down by a car, lying dead in the middle of the street. This was only his second or third contact with death and it really shocked him. The conscious realization that he too was going to die one day hit him like a sledge hammer. It made a difference when he got home that night. The problems that he thought were so great, were not as big as he imagined. The thought of death had given him a new perspective.

REFUSING TO FACE REALITY

One of the striking characteristics of our time is the absurd lengths to which we go to keep death out of sight and out of mind. Dr. John Brantner, a University of Minnesota clinical psychologist, said recently that American society "deals very badly with death and the dying. . . . As a society we fear death and through our fear we foster it," he said. Studies have shown that dying patients want very much to talk about death. It helps them accept it and relieves anxiety, but few people are comfortable about bringing up the subject.

Tolstoy, in his masterful tale "The Death of Ivan Ilyitch," describes the conspiracy of silence that we maintain in the presence of the dying. "Ivan Ilyitch's chief torment was a lie — the lie somehow accepted by everyone that he was only sick, but not dying, and that he needed only to be calm."

Simone de Beauvoir, in "A Very Easy Death," writes of her mother dying of cancer, "At the time the truth was crushing her, and when she needed to escape it by talking, we were condemning her to silence, we forced her to say nothing about the anxieties and to suppress her doubts, she felt both guilty and misunderstood."

In earlier days, along with the other basic facts of life like birth, marriage, bearing children, and raising a family, death was openly accepted as a fact of life. The burial ground surrounding the church stood in the very center of the community. The body was not viewed in a funeral parlor; it was brought right into the living room of one's home. One could not evade the fact of death. One had to accept it and learn to live with it.

THE CAUSE OF MORBIDITY

Please do not misunderstand. The intention is not to be morbid. It is quite the opposite. If there is anything morbid about death, it arises out of the refusal to face it and take it into account. Our Orthodox Christian faith is not morbid when it takes death frankly and openly into account. Our Church calendar provides many occasions when we are asked to face up to the fact of death. Easter is one such occasion. Sunday is another. Every Sunday is a "little Easter" celebrating Christ's victory over death. On our Church calendar every year, there are special Memorial Saturdays or "Saturdays of the Souls" which provide another opportunity for us to face up to death. On these Saturdays the Divine Liturgy is celebrated and special prayers are offered for our deceased loved ones. We pray for the dead especially on Saturdays since it was on the Sabbath day that Christ lay dead in the tomb, "resting from all His works and trampling down death by death." Thus, in the New Testament, Saturday becomes the proper day for remembering the dead and offering prayers for them.

There are two questions often asked about the practice of praying for the dead that we have in the Orthodox Church: 1. WHY do we pray for the dead? 2. WHAT can we expect of these prayers?

WHY DO WE PRAY FOR THE DEAD?

Christianity is a religion of love. Praying for the dead is an expression of love. We ask God to remember our departed because we love them. Love relationships survive death and even transcend it. There is an inner need for a relationship with a loved one to continue to be expressed even after a loved one has died. Often *even more so* after a loved one has died since physical communication is no longer possible. The Church encourages us to express our love for our departed brethren through memorial services and prayers.

The anniversary of the death of a loved one is very painful. The Church helps us cope with this pain by encouraging us to have memorial prayers offered in Church for departed loved ones on the anniversaries of their deaths, i.e., forty days after the death, six months, a year, etc. This gives us the opportunity to *do* something for our loved one. It helps express and resolve our grief.

Death may take loved ones out of sight but it does not take them out of mind, or out of heart. We continue to love them and think of them as we believe they continue to love us and think of us. How can a mother forget a child who has passed over to the life beyond? The same love which led her to pray for that child when he lived will guide her to pray for him now. For in Christ all are living.

The same love makes her wish to communicate with him. Yet, all communication must take place in Christ and through Christ. No other communication with the dead is possible or lawful for the Christian. God is God of the living. Our dear ones live in Him. Only through Him is it possible for us to communicate with them. Every liturgy in the Orthodox Church contains prayers for the dead such as the following: "Be mindful of all those who slumber in the hope of a resurrection to everlasting life. Give them rest, O God, where the light of Thy countenance shineth." The ancient Eucharistic prayers of both East and the West intercede for the dead as well as for the living.

Just as we pray for the deceased, so we believe they continue to love us, remember us, and pray for us now that they are closer to God. We cannot forget the example of the rich man in Hades asking Abraham to send Lazarus to warn his brothers lest they, too, go to that place of torment. Though he had left this life, he did not cease to be concerned for his brothers still on earth.

The Orthodox Church prays for the dead to express her faith that all who have fallen asleep in the Lord, live in the Lord; their lives are hidden with Christ in God (Col. 3:3). Whether on earth or in heaven, the Church is a single family, one Body in Christ. Death changes the location but it cannot sever the bond of love. "God is not the God of the dead, but of the living" (Matt. 22:32). He is "the God of Abraham, the God of Isaac, and the God of Jacob" (Ex. 3:6). He is the God of persons who, though dead physically, are very much alive in His presence.

WHAT CAN WE EXPECT
OF OUR PRAYERS FOR THE DEAD?

Since a person's eternal destiny is determined immediately after death (though one must wait for the General Judgement to receive the full measure of one's reward), we must not expect our prayers to snatch an unbeliever from Hades to Paradise. It is our present life that determines our eternal destiny. Now is the time to repent and accept God's grace. Death puts an end to that state and commits each person to his special judgement. This is why the Lord said that work must be done "while it is day" because "the night cometh when no man can work." "Day" means the present life, "when it is still possible to believe," writes St. Chrysostom, while "night" is the condition after death.

What happens beyond the grave belongs entirely to God. He has told us as much as we need to know; the rest is covered with a veil of mystery which man's curiosity is incapable of piercing. The faithful have committed themselves to God for the duration of their earthly lives. Now, it is well and good for them to commit their departed loved ones to the mercy of God through prayer, for they have the assurance that God in the riches of His mercy has ways to help them beyond our knowing.

FOCUS ON OURSELVES

Whether our prayers for our departed loved ones bring any benefit to them is a question we must leave to the mercy of God. But of one thing we are certain: such prayers do benefit those who pray for the departed. They remind us that we too are going to die; they strengthen faith in the life beyond; they nourish reverence toward those who have died; they help build hope in divine mercy; they develop brotherly love among those who survive. They make us more cautious and diligent in getting ready for that ultimate journey which will unite us with our departed loved ones and usher us into the presence of God. They remind us that now is the time for moral development and improvement, for faith, repentance and love; now is the time to strive for the crown of righteousness which the Lord, the righteous Judge, will award to those "who have fought the good fight, finished the race and kept the faith." In other words, the Lord never told us that after we die, somebody else's prayers will get us into heaven — no matter how many memorial prayers they offer in our behalf. Salvation is a personal matter between each person and his Lord to be achieved in this life.

LOVE NEVER FORGETS

Dr. Paul Tillich believed that the anxiety of having to die is the anxiety that one will be forgotten both now and in eternity. Burial means a removal from the face of the earth. This is what men cannot endure. Memorial markers will not keep us from being forgotten. One day they will crumble to dust. The only thing that can keep us from being forgotten is our faith that God knew us before we were born and will remember us for all eternity.

In a lesser but still very real way, memorial prayers offered by loved ones serve to relieve the anxiety of being forgotten.

The first child of Dr. Martineau, an eminent minister, died in infancy and was buried in the French cemetery of Dublin. Before they left Ireland for Liverpool, the father and mother paid a farewell visit to the grave of their first-born son. The years went by. Mrs. Martineau died. At the age of 87, Dr. Martineau was a lonely old man. But when he was at the tercentenary of Dublin University, he stole away from the brilliant public function to stand once more by the tiny grave that held the dust of his first-born child. No other living soul recalled that little one's smile or remembered where the child was sleeping. But the father knew and the little buried hands held his heart. A father's heart never forgets. Love always remembers. That is why the Orthodox Church has always encouraged us to hold special memorial prayers and services for the departed.

A MEANINGFUL CUSTOM

It is customary among Orthodox Christians from Greece to bring a tray of boiled wheat kernels to church for the memorial service. The wheat kernels express belief in everlasting life. Jesus said, "Unless a grain of wheat falls into the earth and dies, it remains alone, but if it dies, it bears much fruit" (John 12:24). Just as new life rises from the buried kernel of wheat, so we believe the one buried will rise one day to a new life with God. The wheat kernels are covered with sugar to express the bliss of eternal life with God in heaven.

FOCUS ON CHRIST

When Orthodox Christians pray for loved ones, they focus not only on the departed, but especially on Christ who "by his death trampled upon death and to those in the tombs bestowed life eternal."

Memorial prayer services which affirm the reality of physical death and also the reality of resurrection into life eternal play a vital role in the healing of grief.

On Memorial Saturdays the Church prays universally for all the departed. However, a special litany is included to pray personally for departed loved ones whose names are submitted to the priest by parishioners.

One of the great theologians of the Orthodox Church, Prof. Christos Androutsos, stated that memorial prayers should be offered only for those who have repented and not sinned deeply. It is not proper—he said—that they be offered for the impenitent sinner. Since, however, the exact moral state of those departing is unknown, in practice they are offered for all. [1]

---

[1] "The Great Hereafter," by Christos Androutsos, Library of Idealism. Cleveland, OH.

In summary, we pray for the dead:

1. Because they are still living in God's kingdom. Our love for them still needs to be expressed. The bond of love does not cease. Through memorial services and prayers, love continues to be expressed.

2. Such prayers benefit those who offer them, strengthening their faith in eternal life.

3. Although we do not believe that someone else's prayers, offered after we die, will get us into heaven, we continue to pray for the deceased beseeching God's mercy in their behalf. Orthodox prayers for the dead invoke God's "mercy" to bestow "comfort" and "forgiveness" upon the deceased. The Anglican-Orthodox Dialogue held at Llandaff on July 18, 1980 agreed on the following statement regarding prayers for the departed: "After death and before the general resurrection the souls of those who have fallen asleep in the faith are assisted by the prayers of the Church, through the crucified and risen Christ—through Him alone and nothing else." [2]

4. Memorial prayers help us focus on the Risen Christ Who is the Resurrection and the Life.

---

[2] *"Sobornost"* 1981, vol. 3 number 1. St. Basil's House, London.

What We Believe About Prayer

IMPORTANCE OF PRAYER

The great importance of prayer can be seen in the life of Jesus. Every major decision in His life was preceded by prayer. It preceded His baptism: ". . . when Jesus . . . was praying, the heaven was opened, and the Holy Spirit descended upon Him in bodily form, as a dove, and a voice came from heaven, 'Thou art my beloved Son; with Thee I am well pleased' " (Luke 3:21-22).

He prayed all night before choosing His apostles: "In these days He went out into the hills to pray; and all night He continued in prayer to God. And when it was day, He called His disciples, and chose from them twelve. . ." (Luke 6:12,13).

He prayed before His transfiguration: ". . . He took with Him Peter and John and James, and went up on the mountain to pray. And as He was praying, the appearance of His countenance was altered, and His raiment became dazzling white" (Luke 9:28-29).

He prayed in the early morning: "A great while before day, He rose and went out to a lonely place, and there He prayed" (Mark 1:35). Jesus prayed while others were sleeping. Jesus healed when others were helpless. Can the two be unrelated?

He prayed before His Passion: "Then Jesus went with them to a place called Gethsemane, and He said to His disciples, 'Sit here while I go yonder and pray'. . . And going a little farther He fell on His face and prayed, 'My Father, if it be possible let this cup pass from me; nevertheless, not as I will, but as Thou wilt' " (Matthew 26:36-40). Note that Jesus *"fell on His face"* and prayed, displaying utter humility before the Father. He was persevering, praying the same prayer three times. When He did not get His own will, He yielded to God's will because He trusted; He believed that God knows when to give, how to give and what to give and whether to withhold.

THE PENDULUM OF GREATNESS

Arnold Toynbee said once, "There is a pendulum of greatness. Its movements are two: withdrawal and return." We see the pendulum in action in the life of Jesus. He withdraws into God's presence through prayer, then returns strengthened and renewed to do God's will.

Prayer can be an escape from life but it was never intended to be so. It is meant to be a powerhouse and a guidance center as it was for Jesus.

In the words of Staretz Silouan:

"Sometimes the Holy Spirit draws a man so completely to Himself that he forgets all created things and gives himself entirely to contemplation of God. But when the soul remembers the world again, filled with the love of God, she feels compassion for all and prays for the whole world. In thus praying, the soul may again forget the world, only to return once more to her prayer for all mankind." [1]

---

[1] *"The Undistorted Image"* by Archimandrite Sofrony, translated by Rosemary Edmonds. The Faith Press. London. 1958.

The two great movements of the soul have always been withdrawal and return. Withdrawal into God's presence through prayer for strength and vision and return to the world to serve God and His people. Without prayer the quality of our service deteriorates. Without prayer we forget the world; with prayer we remember. Prayer is the dynamic for involvement.

Let me share with you these words of Henri Nouwen:

"In the morning, long before dawn, he got up and left the house, and went off to a lonely place and prayed there.' In the middle of sentences loaded with action—healing suffering people, casting out devils, responding to impatient disciples, traveling from town to town and preaching from synagogue to synagogue—we find these quiet words: 'In the morning, long before dawn, he got up and left the house, and went off to a lonely place and prayed there.' In the center of breathless activities we hear a restful breathing. Surrounded by hours of moving we find a movement of quiet stillness. In the heart of much involvement there are words of withdrawal. In the midst of action there is contemplation. And after much togetherness there is solitude. The more I read this nearly silent sentence locked in between the loud words of action, the more I have the sense that the secret of Jesus' ministry is hidden in that lonely place where he went to pray, early in the morning, long before dawn." [2]

GOD'S PROMISES

Some favorite Scriptural promises concerning prayer are:

"Call to me and I will answer you, and will show you great and hidden things which you have not known" (Jer. 33:3).

"Before they call I will answer, while they are yet speaking I will hear" (Is. 65:24).

"In nothing be anxious but in everything through prayer and supplication with thanksgiving let your requests be made known to God and the peace of God which passes all understanding will keep your mind, and your hearts in Christ Jesus."

Jesus was convinced that God always heard Him in prayer. After he resurrected Lazarus from the dead, He prayed:

"Father, I thank You that You have heard Me. I know that You always hear Me . . ." (John 11:41).

"Ask, and it will be given you; seek and you will find; knock and it will be opened to you. For every one who asks receives, and he who seeks finds, and to him who knocks it will be opened. Or what man of you, if his son asks him for bread will give him a stone? Or if he asks for a fish, will give him a serpent? If you then, who are evil, know how to give good gifts to your children, how much more will your Father who is in heaven give good things to those who ask Him!" (Matt. 7:7-11).

If you ask Him for bread will He give you a stone? If you ask Him for fish, will He give you a serpent? Never!

---

[2] "Out of Solitude." Nouwen, Ave Maria Press. Notre Dame, Indiana.

As someone so well said, "Man finds it hard to get what he wants because he does not want the best; God finds it hard to give because He would give the best, and man will not take it."

I share with you a personal testimony on prayer written by A. Levitin who spent many years suffering for the Christian faith in Soviet prisons. He writes under his pen-name, A. Krasnov. These are his words:

"The greatest miracle of all is prayer. I have only to turn my thoughts to God and I suddenly feel a strength which bursts into me from somewhere, bursts into my soul, into my entire being. What is it? Psychotherapy? No, it is not psychotherapy. For where would I, an insignificant old man who is tired of life, get this strength which renews me and saves me, lifting me above the earth? It comes from without, and there is no force on earth that can even understand it.

"I am not a mystic by nature, nor am I characterized by susceptibility to supernatural phenomena or special experiences. I am susceptible only to that which is accessible to every man; prayer. Since I grew up in the Orthodox Church and was raised by it, my prayer pours forth in Orthodox forms (I do not, of course, deny any other forms).

"The basis of my whole spiritual life is the Orthodox liturgy. Therefore, while in prison I attended the liturgy every day in my imagination. At 8 a.m. I would begin walking around my cell, repeating to myself the words of the liturgy. At that moment I felt myself inseparably linked with the whole Christian world. Therefore during my Great Litany I always prayed for the Pope, for the Ecumenical Patriarch and for our own Patriarch Alexi. Reaching the central point of the liturgy, I would say to myself the eucharistic canon—and then the words of the transubstantiation, standing before the face of the Lord, sensing almost physically His wounded and bleeding body. I would begin praying in my own words, and I would remember all those near to me, those in prison and those who were free, those who were alive and those who had died. And my memory would keep suggesting more and more names . . . the numerous priestly servants whom I had known from childhood, and my own numerous teachers.

"The prison walls moved apart and the whole universe became my residence, visible and invisible, the universe for which that wounded, pierced body offered itself as a sacrifice. Then the Lord's Prayer sounded in my heart especially insistently, as did the prayer before the communion; "I believe Lord and confess." All day after the liturgy I felt an unusual élan of spirit, a clarity and spiritual purity. Not only my prayer, but much more, the prayers of many faithful Christians helped me. I felt it continually, it worked from a distance, lifting me up as though on wings, giving me living water and the bread of life, peace of soul, rest and love."

WHAT IS PRAYER

Prayer is "to stand with the mind in the heart before God, and to go on standing before Him unceasingly day and night, until the end of life" (Theophan).

Prayer is the test of everything . . . the source of everything . . . the driving force of everything . . . the director of everything (Theophan).

Prayer is the raising of the mind and heart to God in praise and thanksgiving to Him and in supplication for the good things that we need, both spiritual and physical (Theophan).

Prayer is to stand before God with the mind, mentally to gaze unswervingly at Him, and to converse with Him in reverent fear and hope (St. Dimitri of Rostov).

Prayer . . . uplifts and unites human beings with God (St. Gregory Palamas).

Prayer is our personal communication system with our home base.

Prayer is a booster cable from our depleted lives to the ever dependable power of God which never fails to start us up again.

Prayer is the response of the soul to the love of God.

Prayer is taking our burdens to God, knowing He will help us carry them and renew us for the journey.

Prayer is the prelude to peace, the prologue to power, the preface to purpose, and the pathway to perfection (W.A. Ward).

Prayer is listening to God.

Prayer is opening the door of the heart to receive the Holy Spirit.

Prayer is a gift from God to us.

Prayer is the treasure buried within.

Prayer is tuning in to God's eternal, unchanging love.

Prayer is heaven in the heart . . . the kingdom of God within you.

Prayer is creating an openness where God can give Himself to us.

Prayer is Jacob's ladder by which we ascend to God and God descends to us.

Prayer is placing the human predicament, however confused it may be, in the hands and care of God, with confidence He knows how best to untangle the complication and bring calm.

Prayer is best felt in the heart when I trust God enough to bring Him into the depths of my life and into the deeply personal hurts of my life.

Prayer is not bargaining with God, trying to convince Him to change. It is, rather, our asking Him to change us so we can see His ways and His plans more clearly.

Prayer is the heart's moment to bathe itself in the beauty of God's love and the cleansing of God's care.

Prayer is sorting out life's options and choosing the best with God's help and counsel.

Prayer is the destruction of fear (Fr. John of Kronstadt).

Prayer is holding all people in our hearts through love (Fr. John of Kronstadt).

Prayer is the descent of heaven into the soul (Fr. John of Kronstadt).

Prayer is the abiding of the most Holy Trinity in the soul in accordance with the words of Jesus, "We will come to him, and make our home in him" (Fr. John of Kronstadt).

Prayer is to be with God (Origen).

Prayer is an ascent of the spirit to God (Evagrios Ponticus).

Prayer is a continual intercourse of the spirit with God (Evagrios Ponticus).

The soul came forth from God and to God it may ever ascend through prayer (Fr. John of Kronstadt).

Prayer is remembering to call home because you are a child of God.

The pulse of prayer is praise. The heart of prayer is gratitude. The voice of prayer is obedience. The arm of prayer is service (W. A. Ward).

Prayer is a matter of love. The more one loves, the more one prays.

Prayer is remembering why we serve. If we forget to pray in order to have more time for service we shall soon forget the meaning of service.

Prayer is helplessness that asks Jesus to come in and take over (O. Hallesby).

Prayer is giving my worries to God and receiving His peace in return (Phil. 4:6-7). What an exchange!

Prayer is learning to love others as unselfishly as Christ loves me, which includes bearing their burdens and praying for them as persistently and fervently as I pray for myself.

Prayer is coming to know God as I open myself to Him.

Prayer is standing at attention before God.

Prayer is a dialogue between two persons who love each other.

Prayer is heart-to-heart talk with Jesus.

Prayer is spiritual breathing.

Prayer is slipping into God's presence.

The man who has learned to pray is no longer alone in the universe; he is living in his Father's house.

Prayer is a means of grace, a sacrament.

Prayer is the "hot line" between God and us—a line always open for communication.

Prayer is light in darkness and hope in despair. A former American P.O.W. from North Vietnam said, "Apart from prayer there was nothing—absolutely nothing—that gave me hope. Without my contact with God through prayer all was darkness—absolute darkness."

Prayer is a state of continual gratitude (Fr. John of Kronstadt).

Prayer is the slender nerve that moves the mighty hand of God.

Prayer changes others, changes our circumstances because it changes us.

"The essence of the state of prayer is simply 'to be there', to hear the presence of another person, Christ, and also our fellow man in whom Christ challenges me. . . The perfect prayer seeks the presence of Christ and recognizes Him in every human being" (Evdokimov).

Prayer is raising my eyes to God lest I begin to think that I am the highest point in the universe.

Prayer is friendly conversation with God—sharing our thoughts, feelings, needs and appreciation. It is making earnest, sincere requests to God, for yourself and others.

Prayer is hemming the day in with God, thus making it less likely to unravel.

Prayer is what Abraham said, "May I presume to speak to the Lord, dust and ashes that I am?" (Gen. 18:27). Yes! You may!

Prayer is coming to God with great faith and great expectations:

> "Thou art coming to a King,
>   Great petitions with thee bring;
>   For His grace and power are such
>   None can ever ask too much."

God does not exist to answer our prayers, but by our prayers we come to discern the mind of God.

Prayer is the blank canvas before the Painter. (Dr. Alexis Carrel).

Prayer is the empty cup standing before God asking to be filled.

Prayer is God's action in us through the Holy Spirit.

Prayer at its best is a grateful day opener, a beautiful day brightener, and a joyful day closer.

Prayer is not saying to God, "Please do with me what I want," but "Please do with me what You want."

Prayer is to bring to light the Divine Presence within us, to remove the obstacles of sin so that the grace of Baptism may become fully active in the heart. Thus prayer is to become what we already are, to gain what we already possess, to come face to face with the One Who dwells even now within our innermost self.

There are four answers to prayer: "No." "Yes." "Wait." "I never thought you'd ask."

Prayer is asking that we may receive. Even the royal and divine Son of God had to ask in prayer. A person said to a politician once, "I voted for you even though you did not ask me." The politician replied, "But you're such a close friend I didn't think I had to ask." Whereupon the voter replied, "Yes, but it's *nice* to be asked." "*Ask* and you shall receive," said Jesus.

Most modern industries now schedule morning and afternoon coffee breaks when a worker can pause for a moment and refresh himself. Efficiency experts have determined that a person will be more productive if he is given a break from his work.

Our spiritual life is similar to this in many ways. We need "prayer breaks" throughout the day—special and scheduled times to spend with God in prayer. Such "prayer breaks" become in reality "power breaks" for us, making us more poised and productive Christians in the world.

WE CAN PRAY

We cannot always be near
Our friends to help,
To share with them in time of need
And sweet communion find
In their blest fellowship—
    But we can pray.

We cannot always speak
The winning word
To one who needs to find the way.

Our minds oft fail, our spirits lag,
Or doors are closed to our approach,
    But we can pray.

Prayer can multiply our work
Our presence, our range of good,
Leap o'er miles, go through doors,
Bind us close to those we love
And bless all those who need our help—
    So let us pray!

DESCEND WITH THE MIND
INTO THE HEART

Theophan the Recluse defines prayer as "standing before God with the mind in the heart." What do these words mean?

Fr. Kallistos Ware explains,

"So long as the ascetic prays with the mind in the head, he will still be working solely with the resources of the human intellect, and on this level he will never attain to an immediate and personal encounter with God. By the use of his brain, he will at best know *about* God, but he will not *know* God. For there can be no direct knowledge of God without an exceedingly great love, and such love must come, not from the brain alone, but from the whole man—that is, from the heart. It is necessary, then, for the ascetic to descend from the head into the heart. He is not required to abandon his intellectual powers—the reason, too, is a gift of God—but he is called to descend *with the mind* into his heart." [3]

A HEAD AND HEART FAITH

The head seeks God but it is the heart that finds Him. "For man believes *in his heart* and so is justified . . ." writes St. Paul (Romans 10:10). When the head descends into the heart, the "head" faith becomes a "heart" faith. It becomes not just a "head" faith or just a "heart" faith but a "head-in-the-heart" faith. Just as love, charity and the other important virtues cannot exist only in the mind but are primarily of the heart, so it is with our faith and trust in God. We are not to let Jesus remain in the mind and give Him only a cold intellectual allegiance. He must descend into the heart where we shall be able to feel His presence and yield our will to Him.

To return again to Theophan the Recluse:

"You must pray not only with words but with the mind, and not only with the mind but with the heart, so that the mind understands and sees clearly what is said in words, and the heart feels what the mind is thinking. All these combined together constitute real prayer, and if any of them are absent, your prayer is either not perfect, or it is not prayer at all."

St. John Chrysostom says that God hears our prayers more loudly when we are praying with the mind in the heart.

---

[3] *"The Art of Prayer"* compiled by Igumen Chariton. Faber and Faber Ltd. London.

A UNION OF MIND AND HEART

The over-intellectual scholars in Constantinople criticized St. Gregory Palamas and his way of prayer. Faith to them was only a matter of the mind not of the heart. For Gregory Palamas it was both. And the Church supported his view.

"You must descend with your mind into your heart," Theophan insists. "At present your thoughts of God are in your head. And God himself is, as it were, outside you, and so your prayer and other spiritual exercises remain exterior. Whilst you are still in your head, thoughts will . . . always be whirling about like snow in winter, or clouds of mosquitoes in the summer. . . All our inner disorder is due to the dislocation of our powers, the mind and the heart each going its own way. The mind must come to an initial concord with the heart, growing eventually into a union of the mind with the heart."

WE THINK WE PRAY

Father John of Kronstadt talks about people who "call prayer that which is not prayer at all: for instance, a man goes to church, stands there for a time, looks at the icons or at other people, and says that he has prayed to God; or else he stands before an icon at home, bows his head, says some words he has learned by heart, without understanding, and without feeling, and says that he has prayed— although with his thoughts and his heart he has not prayed at all, but was elsewhere, with other people and other things, and not with God."

He goes on to say, "Thus he who does not pray with his heart does not pray at all, because only his body prays, and the body without the mind is nothing more than dust."

Theofan writes,

"Descend from the head into the heart. Then you will see all thoughts clearly, as they move before the eye of your sharp-sighted mind. But until you descend into the heart, do not expect to have due discrimination of thoughts. . .

". . . the union of the mind with the heart is the union of the spiritual thoughts of the mind with the spiritual feelings of the heart. . .

"Do not be lazy about descending. In the heart is life, and you must live there. Do not think that this is something to be attempted only by the perfect. No. It is for everyone who has begun to seek the Lord."

THE JOURNEY WITHIN

By descending with the mind into the heart through prayer the Church is calling on us to make what Dag Hammarskjold called "the longest journey, the journey inward" to the center of our being which is nothing other than the Presence of God within.

The secret of sanctity and of happiness is open to all. If for five minutes a day we can quiet our imagination, close our eyes to the things of our senses, enter within our soul which is the temple of the Holy Spirit, and there commune with our Lord, life will flow happily, serene and consoled even in the midst of pain.

When you are on an ocean-going vessel you are not meant to remain indefinitely in any harbor, no matter how attractive it might be. You are to sail the seas of life. Your visits to any harbor should have only one purpose—to make you a more seaworthy vessel. The purpose of prayer is just that: not to keep us anchored in safe harbors but to enable us to sail the seas of life no matter what the weather.

Dive into prayer often. Let the words not remain only on your lips. Let them go from your lips to your mind to your heart. Let your heart be without words but never your words without heart. As you so pray, the strengthening presence of Jesus will be with you. The healing love of Jesus will be poured upon you. The resurrecting power of Jesus will flow through you to touch, bless and heal your mind, soul and body.

"Executives are hard to see
Their costly time I may not waste;
I make appointments nervously
And talk to them in haste.
But any time of night or day,
In places suitable or odd,
I seek and get without delay
An interview with God."

(Authur Unknown)

+ + + + + + + + + +

"Come now, little man! Flee for a
while from your tasks, hide yourself
for a little space from the turmoil of
your thoughts. Come, cast aside your
burdensome cares, and put aside
your laborious pursuits. For a little
while give your time to God, and
rest in Him for a little while. Enter
into the inner chamber of your mind,
shut out all things save God and
whatever may aid you in seeking
God; and having barred the door of
your chamber, seek Him."

—Anselm of Canterbury

THE FRUIT OF PRAYER

St. Isaac the Syrian said once, ''Capture the mother (prayer) and you shall have the daughters.''

The daughters of prayer are many.

A recent study at Harvard revealed that people who pray regularly suffer less from high blood pressure. One of the daughters of prayer is less pressure, more inner peace, because there is more trust in God.

Dr. Alexis Carrel, a famous doctor and Nobel Prize winner, said:

''Prayer is a force as real as terrestrial gravity. As a physician, I have seen men, after all other therapy has failed, lifted out of disease and melancholy by the serene effort of prayer. It is the only power in the world that seems to overcome the so-called 'laws of nature'; the occasions on which prayer has dramatically done this have been termed 'miracles.' But a constant quieter miracle takes place hourly in the hearts of men and women who have discovered that prayer supplies them with a steady flow of sustaining power in their daily lives.'' So here is another one of the beautiful daughters of prayer in addition to inner peace: healing power.

THE HOLY SPIRIT

The third daughter of prayer is the Holy Spirit.

''Spiritual life comes entirely from His most Holy Spirit'' (Theophan). And the Holy Spirit comes through prayer. ''And when they had prayed, the place in which they were gathered together was shaken; and they were all filled with the Holy Spirit and spoke the word of God boldly'' (Acts 4:31).

It was when they were gathered together in prayer that they were filled with the Holy Spirit. On Pentecost the Holy Spirit descended on the Apostles as they were praying. Prayer was the key that unlocked the door to the Holy Spirit. ''Prayer is always possible for everyone, rich and poor, noble and simple, strong and weak, healthy and suffering, righteous and sinful. *Great is the power of prayer; most of all does it bring the Spirit of God and easiest of all is it to exercise''* (St. Seraphim).

UNION WITH GOD

Another daughter of prayer is union with God. Prayer unites us with God. It brings us into His very presence. There is no other virtue as important as prayer. None of the other virtues unites us with God. They only try to make us fit to be united with God. Prayer—and prayer alone—unites man with God. When Jesus said, ''I am the vine, you are the branches, without me you can do nothing,'' He was talking about union with Him. What is it that keeps the branches attached to the vine? It is prayer.

To be with God is an end in itself. It is not a means to an end. To pray is to be with God. Thus prayer is not a means but the end itself, the ultimate.

''The effect of prayer is union with God'' (St. Gregory of Nyssa). St. Nicodemos the Hagiorite writes concerning prayer and the union of God: ''There is no other virtue that is either higher or more necessary than sacred prayer, because all other virtues—I mean fasting, vigils, sleeping on the ground, ascesis, chastity, almsgiving, and all the rest—even though they are ways of imitating God, even though they cannot be taken away from us and constitute the immortal ornaments of the soul—do not unite man with God, but only render him fit to be united. *Sacred prayer, and it alone, unites. It alone joins God with man, and makes the two one spirit.''*

''Prayer . . . uplifts and unites human beings with God'' (St. Gregory Palamas).

LOVE

In addition to the Holy Spirit and union with God another one of the daughters of prayer is love. In fact, it is one of the most beautiful daughters of prayer.

Love comes from our union with God Who is Himself the only source of love. There can be no genuine love unless we are united with the Source of Love: God. And it is prayer that unites us with God. And this is why we tell young couples who are about to be married, that if they desire a strong and lasting love relationship in their marriage they must open the door of prayer every day and let God's love flow into their lives through prayer.

"Love comes from prayer" (St. Isaac the Syrian). St. Maximos the Confessor adds: "The person who truly loves God also prays incessantly; and whoever prays incessantly, that person genuinely loves God."

Here, then, are the daughters of prayer: inner peace, healing power, the Holy Spirit, union with God, and love. Capture the mother (prayer) and you shall indeed have all her beautiful daughters.

THE SACRAMENTS AND PRAYER

In his famous "Commentary on the Divine Liturgy," Nicolas Cabasilas emphasizes that all sacraments are accomplished through prayer. He mentions the consecration of Chrism, the prayers of ordination, of absolution, and of the anointing of the ill. "It is the tradition of the Fathers," he writes, "who received this teaching from the Apostles and from their successors, that the sacraments are rendered effective through prayer; all the sacraments, as I have said, and particularly the Holy Eucharist."

It is because of prayer that we have Holy Communion. It is the prayer of consecration—the Epiclesis—that changes the bread and the wine in the Eucharist and brings Jesus to us today. He comes to us through prayer!

THE IMPORTANCE OF PRAYER

Emphasizing the importance of prayer St. Gregory of Nyssa said, "It is necessary for us to persist in prayer which is like the leader in a circle of dancers which are the virtues. It joins the person who persists in prayer to God. . ." "The work of God is simple: it is prayer—children talking to their Father, without any subtleties." [4]

One of the greatest theologians of the Roman Catholic Church is without doubt Thomas Aquinas. One of the most prolific teachers and writers who ever lived, he searched all his life to know God. Few people have ever written more about God than he did. Shortly before he died he knelt before the Crucified Christ and prayed. He knew he was dying. He said that he had learned more about theology on his knees in those fifteen minutes than from all the theology that he had ever studied and written about in his many volumes. In fact, it is said that after that experience of God in prayer before his death he asked that all his books be burned. He had captured the mother—prayer. All else seemed far less important.

THEOLOGY AND PRAYER

Since Thomas Aquinas was a great theologian perhaps we need to listen at this point to what Evagrius Ponticus says about prayer and theology: "If you are a

---

[4] *"On the Invocation of the Name of Jesus"* by a Monk of the Eastern Church" p. 106.

theologian, you truly pray. If you truly pray, you are a theologian.'' According to the Eastern Church, doctrine is shaped by prayer and prayer by doctrine. The great Fathers of the Church theologized from their experience of God in prayer and in His scriptural word. The doctrine of the Church is not only expressed through prayer; it comes from prayer. St. Gregory Palamas came up with a doctrine of God that was shaped entirely by prayer. Not too many of our doctrines have been shaped by prayer as directly as the one by Palamas.

These, then, are the many beautiful daughters of prayer: inner peace, healing power, the Holy Spirit, union with God, love. They all come from prayer. And all of the sacraments and all of the theology of the Church flow from prayer. Its power is tremendous. It unites us with God and makes us truly God-like. It fills us with God's love and life. It is the ladder to heaven. We climb it to be with God. Mother of all virtues, it is easiest of all to practice.

Listen to the words of Blessed Augustine:

"God does not ask us to tell Him our needs that He may learn about them, but in order that we may be capable of receiving what He is prepared to give.''

Former Senator Hughes of Iowa was an alcoholic. His family left him. He lost all his money, his home, his friends, everything. In great desperation he decided one night to commit suicide. He took one last drink and went up to the bedroom to get the gun. Because he had seen other suicides with brains splattered all over the walls and floor, he was concerned that he not leave a mess. He wanted to make a clean job of it. So he got into the bathtub. Before pulling the trigger, he decided to pray for God to forgive him for what he had done to his family and friends. He had not prayed for years. While praying—he said—something happened to him. He suddenly came to his senses. He had a conversion experience right then and there in the bathtub. God spoke to him and the whole direction of his life changed. As a result he gave his life completely to Jesus and entered full-time Christian service leading others to the source of renewal and power: Christ.

The miracle began when Hughes opened the door slightly through prayer to let God come into his life to forgive him. He came not just to forgive him but to renew and change him completely.

God asks us to come to Him in prayer because he has tremendous resources that He is prepared to give us. So when we come to Him let us think big, pray big, expect big, because God is big—bigger than we can ever imagine.

"Call upon me and I will answer you and I will show great and mighty things that you know not of'' (Jer. 33:3).

THE KINGDOM OF GOD
WITHIN YOU

Theophan the Recluse states that the first stage of prayer is bodily prayer consisting of reading, standing, making prostrations, etc. After this comes the prayer of inner attention when the mind prays by centering its full attention on the words of the prayer. Then comes the prayer of the heart when the mind descends into the heart and the thoughts of the mind are combined with the feelings of the heart to produce the warm feeling of God's presence within. To find God we embark on a journey from without to within; from the outer to the inner man.

THE INNER CLOSET

Jesus said, "The Kingdom of God is within you." The Church Fathers siezed upon these words to remind us that God is to be found in the "inner closet" of the heart. Even though we may be unaware of it, the Spirit of God dwells within us from the moment of baptism. The whole purpose of the spiritual life is to rediscover the grace of baptism or the Holy Spirit within us. This is done through inner prayer as man descends into the heart with his mind and discovers there the kingdom of God.

ST. MAKARIOS OF EGYPT

St. Makarios of Egypt writes, "The heart is a small vessel, but all things are contained in it; God is there, the angels are there, and there also is life and kingdom, the heavenly cities and the treasures of grace."

"The kingdom of God is within you."

ST. DIMITRI OF ROSTOV

Commenting on these words, St. Dimitri of Rostov says, "Man needs to enclose himself in the inner closet of his heart more often than he need go to church: and collecting all his thoughts there, he must place his mind before God, praying to Him in secret with all warmth of spirit and with living faith."

The heart is the bridal chamber where we are to meet our Lord and Savior, the Bridegroom of our soul.

Where else but in our heart shall we find the Garden of Eden where Adam walked with God?

Man's heart is a chapel where continuous prayer can be offered to God. This is part of the image of God in us. This is why St. Paul calls us "temples of the Holy Spirit."

THE LORD'S RECEPTION ROOM

Theophan the Recluse says,

"You seek the Lord? Seek, but only within yourself. He is not far from anyone. The Lord is near all those who truly call on Him. Find a place in your heart and speak there with the Lord. It (the heart) is the Lord's reception room. Everyone who meets the Lord, meets Him there. He has fixed no other place for meeting souls."

"Strive to enter within your inner chamber and you will see the chamber of heaven. For the two are the same and one entrance leads to both" (Philokalia).

In Orthodox spirituality the monk is asked to become conscious of the actual presence of Jesus in the interior of his being without any images. The Presence is there fully and existentially through the Life of God received in the Sacraments.

Nicephoras says, "The kingdom of God is within us, and for a man who has seen it within, and having found it through true prayer . . . everything outside loses its attraction" (Philokalia).

Fr. John Meyendorff writes:

"Since the Incarnation, our bodies have become 'temples of the Holy Spirit within us' (I Cor. 6:19); it is there, within our own bodies, that we must seek the Spirit, within our bodies sanctified by the sacraments and engrafted by the eucharist into the Body of Christ. God is now to be found within. He is no longer exterior to us. Therefore, we find the light of Mount Tabor within ourselves." [5]

SIR ISAAC NEWTON

The brilliant scientist, Sir Isaac Newton, said that he could take his telescope and look millions and millions of miles into space. Then he added, "But when I lay it aside, go into my room, shut the door, and get down on my knees in earnest prayer, I see more of heaven and feel closer to the Lord than if I were assisted by all the telescopes on earth."

St. Isaac the Syrian wrote,

"Enter eagerly into the treasure-house (the heart) that lies within you, and so you will see the treasure-house of heaven. For the two are the same, and there is but one single entry to them both. The ladder that leads to the Kingdom is HIDDEN WITHIN YOU, AND IS FOUND IN YOUR SOUL. *DIVE INTO YOURSELF*, and in your soul you will discover the rungs by which you are to ascend."

In view of these thoughts the words of Ralph Waldo Emerson have special meaning:

> "What lies behind us and
> what lies before us are
> tiny matters compared to
> what lies within us."

"Greater is He who is within you than he who is in the world," says the Bible.

Who is within us? Listen to St. Paul in Col. 1:26,27, ". . . the mystery hidden for ages and generations but now made manifest . . . Christ in you, the hope of glory."

AUGUSTINE

"Where can we find Him?" asks Augustine. "Not on earth, for he is not here. And not in heaven, for we are not there. But in our own hearts we can find him. He ascended to heaven openly so that He could come back to us inwardly, and never leave us again."

ST. EPHRAIM

Listen to St. Ephraim the Syrian,

"The kingdom of God is within you. In so far as the Son of God dwells in you, the Kingdom of Heaven lies within you, also. Here within are the riches of heaven, if you desire them. Here, O sinner, is the Kingdom of God within you. Enter into yourself, seek more eagerly and you will find without great travail.

[5] *"St. Gregory Palamas and Orthodox Spirituality"* by John Meyendorff, p. 113. SVS Press. Crestwood, N.Y.

Outside you is death, and the door to death is sin. ENTER WITHIN YOURSELF AND REMAIN IN YOUR HEART, FOR THERE IS GOD.''

ST. MAKARIOS

St. Makarios of Egypt:

''Within the heart are unfathomable depths. There are reception rooms and bedchambers in it, doors and porches, and many offices and passages. In it is the workshop of righteousness and of wickedness. In it is death; in it is life. . . The heart is Christ's palace: there Christ the King comes to take His rest, with the angels and the spirits of the saints, and He dwells there, walking within it and placing His kingdom there.''

There is a beautiful story of a little girl who went to see the pediatrician for her first-grade physical exam. He took out his stethoscope to listen to her heartbeat. With all the seriousness of a six-year-old, she touched her chest and chided him, ''Don't mess around with that. Jesus lives in there!''

She was right. ''The kingdom of God is within you.''

''The Sayings of the Fathers'' tell of a young woman who had many lovers. One of the governors approached her and said, ''Promise me you will be good, and I will marry you.'' She promised this and he took her in marriage and brought her to his house. Her former lovers, seeking her again, said to one another, ''That lord has taken her with him to his house, so if we go to his house and he learns of it, he will condemn us. But let us go to the back, and whistle to her. Then, when she recognizes the sound of the whistle she will come down to us; as for us, we shall be protected.'' When she heard the whistle, the young woman stopped her ears, withdrew to the inner chamber, and shut the doors.

The young lady of this story is our soul. Her former lovers are the passions and sins. The Lord who married her is Christ. The inner chamber is the presence of God within the heart. Those who whistle are the demons. But the soul through prayer always takes refuge in the Lord Who is present within.

''The Kingdom of God'' said Jesus, ''is not above you or beneath you, or outside you, or beyond you, but—within you.''

When we pray we are not trying to make contact with a God Who is far away. We are not calling God down from the clouds. He is present within us through His Holy Spirit; we are simply calling ourselves to wake up to His presence.

THE JESUS PRAYER

The prayer in which the spiritual tradition of the Eastern Church finds its deepest expression is the Jesus Prayer consisting of the simple words: ''Lord Jesus Christ, Son of God, have mercy on me.''

In the book ''The Way of A Pilgrim'' a Russian peasant tells how he travelled from village to village, and monastery to monastery trying to find someone to teach him how to pray unceasingly (I Thess. 5:17). Finally he finds a monk who teaches him the Jesus Prayer by reading to him the following words of St. Symeon the New Theologian:

"Sit down alone and in silence. Lower your head, shut your eyes, breathe out gently and imagine yourself looking into your own heart. Carry your mind, i.e., your thoughts, from your head to your heart. As you breathe out say: 'Lord Jesus, have mercy on me.' Say it moving your lips gently, or say it in your mind. Try to put all other thoughts aside. Be calm, be patient and repeat the process very frequently" [6]

After following these instructions and reaching the point where he could repeat this prayer thousands of times a day, the pilgrim says:

"Under this guidance I spent the whole summer in ceaseless oral prayer to Jesus Christ, and I felt absolute peace in my soul. During sleep I often dreamed I was saying the Prayer. And during the day, if I happened to meet anyone, all men without exception were as dear to me as if they had been my nearest relations . . . I thought of nothing whatever but my Prayer, my mind tended to listen to it, and my heart began of itself to feel at times a certain warmth and pleasure" [7]

The Jesus Prayer transforms the pilgrim's relationship with the material creation about him, changing all things into icons or sacraments of God's presence. He writes:

"When I prayed with my heart, everything around me seemed delightful and marvellous. The trees, the grass, the birds, the earth, the air, the light seemed to be telling me that they existed for man's sake, that they witnessed to the love of God for man, that everything proved the love of God for man, that all things prayed to God and sang His praise. Thus it was that I came to understand what 'The Philokalia' calls 'the knowledge of the speech of all creatures' . . . I felt a burning love for Jesus Christ and for all God's creatures" [8]

The Jesus Prayer transfigured the pilgrim's relation not only with the material world but also with other people. He writes:

"Again I started off on my wanderings. But now I did not walk alone as before, filled with care. The Invocation of the Name of Jesus gladdened my way. Everybody was kind to me, it was as though everyone loved me. . . If anyone harms me I have only to think, 'How sweet is the Prayer of Jesus!' and the injury and the anger alike pass away and I forget it all." [9]

From these words we see that the Jesus Prayer is not world-denying but world-changing. It helps us see Christ in all men, and all men in Christ.

THREE BOOKS TO READ

Where does one go to learn how to master the Jesus Prayer? First, to the book "The Way of A Pilgrim." Then "The Way of A Pilgrim" itself sends us to another book "The Philokalia": "You will learn how to master it (the Jesus Prayer) by reading this book, which is called The 'Philokalia': it comprises the complete and minute knowledge of incessant inner prayer, as stated by twenty-five Holy Fathers. It is full of great wisdom and is so useful that it is regarded as the first and best guide by all those who seek the contemplative, spiritual life."

---

[6] *"The Way of A Pilgrim,"* translated by R. M. French, p. 10. London. S.P.C.K.
[7] Ibid. p. 16.
[8] *"The Way of A Pilgrim"* P. 31-2,41.
[9] Ibid. p. 17-18.

"The Philokalia" has been called by Fr. George Florovsky, "That famous encyclopedia of Eastern piety and asceticism which . . . is increasingly becoming the manual of guidance for all those who are eager to practice Orthodoxy in our time." [10]

Besides "The Way of A Pilgrim" and "The Philokalia" another book I wish to commend to your reading is "The Art of Prayer", an Orthodox anthology on the prayer of the heart. Compiled by Chariton of Valamo, it contains gems from the spiritual writings of 19th century Russian spiritual writers, especially of Theophan the Recluse. Let me share with you two brief gems from "The Art of Prayer" on the Jesus Prayer, both by Theophan the Recluse:

"I will remind you of only one thing: one must descend with the mind into the heart, and there stand before the face of the Lord, ever present, all seeing within you. The (Jesus) prayer takes a firm and steadfast hold, when a small fire begins to burn in the heart. Try not to quench this fire, and it will become established in such a way that the prayer repeats itself: and then you will have within you a small murmuring stream." [11]

Again by Theophan:

"One of the early Fathers said, 'When thieves approach a house in order to creep up to it and steal, and hear someone inside talking, they do not dare to climb in; in the same way, when our enemies try to steal into our soul and take possession of it they creep all around but fear to enter when they hear that . . . prayer welling out." [12]

The Jesus Prayer became the center of Orthodox spirituality because of its utmost simplicity and its emphasis on the Invocation of the Divine Name.

ITS SIMPLICITY

First, its simplicity. John Climacus writes:

"Let there be no studied eloquence in the words of your prayer. . . Do not launch into long discourses that fritter away your mind in efforts for eloquence. One word alone spoken by the Publican touched God's mercy; a single word full of faith saved the Good Thief. Many words in prayer often fill the mind with images and distract it, while often one single word draws it into recollection" (Step 28).

ITS GREATNESS

Secondly, the greatness of the Jesus Prayer is to be found not only in its simplicity but also in its constant invocation of the all-powerful Name of Jesus, our Lord and Savior. See for a moment what the Holy Scriptures say about the Name of Jesus:

"There is none other name under heaven given among men, whereby we must be saved" (Acts 10,12).

"Wherefore God also hath highly exalted Him, and given Him a Name which is above every name: that at the Name of Jesus every knee should bow, of things in heaven, and things on earth, and things under the earth" (Phil. 2:9-10).

[10] "Aspects of Church History" p. 21 Nordland Publ. Co. Belmont, MA

[11] "The Art of Prayer," Compiled by Chariton. p. 110. Faber and Faber Lt. London.

[12] Ibid. p.110

"Hitherto have ye asked nothing in my name . . . whatsoever ye shall ask the Father in my name, he will give it to you" (John 26:24,27).

"No man can say, Lord Jesus, except by the Holy Ghost" (I Cor. 12:3).

Based also on the prayer of the blind man, "Jesus, Thou Son of David, have mercy on me," and that of the Publican, "God, be merciful to me a sinner," we can see that in addition to its utter simplicity and invocation of the Name of Jesus, the Jesus Prayer is entirely scriptural. If the Jesus Prayer is stronger than other prayers, it is so only by virtue of the all-powerful Name of Jesus.

NOT SUFFICIENT UNTO ITSELF

The Jesus Prayer is not sufficient unto itself. It hangs on the Church and the sacraments. As Fr. John Meyendorff has stated, "For the Christ Whom this prayer seeks in a man's own heart, the Divine Name that it invokes, can be found within his heart only in the measure in which he is ingrafted into the Body of the Church by baptism and the eucharist. The Prayer of Jesus, as the Fathers understood it, never replaces the redemptive grace of the sacraments but rather is its fullest realization." [13]

The surest way to union with God," writes Bishop Justin, "next to Communion of His flesh and blood, is the inner Jesus Prayer." Prayer is anchored in the Eucharist and nourished by it. It is not a substitute for the Eucharist but an added enrichment.

THE JESUS PRAYER AND OUR SALVATION

St. Nicodemos the Hagiorite writes on the function of the Jesus Prayer in our salvation:

"Because, brethren, we have fallen into sins after baptism and consequently have buried the grace of the Holy Spirit which was given to us at our Baptism, it is necessary that we make every effort to recover that original grace which is found deeply buried underneath our passions, like an ember in the ashes. This ember of grace we must fan into a new flame in our hearts. In order to do that, we must remove the passions from our hearts as ashes from a fireplace, and replace them with the firewood of obedience in the life-giving commandments of the Lord. We can blow upon the spark with heartfelt repentance of the mind and with the repetition of this prayer: 'Lord Jesus Christ, Son and Word of God, have mercy on me.' When this prayer remains permanently in our heart, it cleanses us from the ashes of the passions, and finding the ember of grace within, it strikes up a wondrous and strange fire. This fire, on the one hand, burns away the temptation of evil thoughts, and on the other, it sweetens the whole inner person and enlightens the mind."

The division of prayer into three parts—of the body (lips), of the mind, and of the heart—applies also the the Jesus Prayer. It begins as a prayer of the lips and the tongue that is prayed orally. Gradually it becomes more inward and is prayed silently with the mind. It becomes "a small murmuring stream" within. Finally, it enters the heart and dominates the entire personality. Then we have received the

---

[13] "St. Gregory Palamas and Orthodox Spirituality" p. 172. SVS Press, Crestwood, N.Y.

gift of unceasing prayer. The Jesus Prayer continues uninterrupted within us even when we are engaged in other activities. To use the expression of Theophan, "The hands at work, the mind and heart with God."

"Some godly thoughts come nearer the heart than others," says Theophan. "Should this be so, after you have finished your prayers, continue to dwell on such a thought and remain feeding on it. This is the way to unceasing prayer." [14]

". . . every Christian should be united with the Lord in his heart, and the best way to achieve such a union is precisely the Jesus Prayer" said Bishop Justins. [15]

And so we pray:

"Lord Jesus Christ, Son of God, have mercy on me a sinner."

SUMMARY

1. The importance of prayer is to be seen in the life of Jesus where almost every great event was preceded by prayer, i.e., the Baptism, the Transfiguration, the call of the Disciples, etc.

2. The two great movements in the life of Jesus were: the *withdrawal* into God's presence for prayer and the *return* into the world strengthened to do God's will.

3. Our whole life can become a prayer, a hymn of adoration to God.

4. Prayer is the abiding of the Most Holy Trinity in the soul in accordance with the words of Jesus, "We will come to him and make our home in him."

5. Prayer is not merely speaking to God with the mind (knowing about God). It is descending with the mind into the heart where we can love God, feel His presence and yield our will to Him.

6. The fruit of prayer is inner peace, healing power, the Holy Spirit, union with God and love. All the sacraments and all the theology of the Church flow from prayer. In the words of St. Isaac the Syrian, "Capture the mother (prayer) and you will have the daughters." The daughters are many.

7. The whole purpose of the spiritual life is to descend with the mind into the heart through inner prayer and to discover there the kingdom of God (the grace of baptism and the Holy Spirit). The heart is the Lord's reception room. Meet Him there. "The kingdom of God is within you," said Jesus.

8. One of the most famous prayers of the Orthodox Church is the Jesus Prayer: "Lord Jesus, Son of God, have mercy on me, a sinner." As this prayer takes hold in the heart, one begins to pray without ceasing. A small fire begins to burn in the heart for the Lord.

---

[14] *"The Art of Prayer"* P. 80.
[15] Ibid. p. 88.

In View Of All This, What Therefore Is Expected Of Us?

The final chapter of this book must deal with the question: in view of all that God has done for us (as we have seen in the preceding chapters), what therefore is required of us?

In the letter to the Romans, Paul writes eleven long, difficult "theological" chapters, explaining to the Romans what Christian faith is, who Jesus Christ is, what He has done for us and so on. Straight theology! Then what? Chapter 12 begins, "I appeal to you *therefore* brethren," and Paul gives a long list of specific things Christians are to do—things like:

> Let love be genuine.
> Hate what is evil.
> Hold fast to what is good.
> Love one another with brotherly affection.
> Bless those who persecute you.
> Live in harmony with one another.
> Repay no one evil for evil.

In other words, Paul is saying, *because* God has done all these things for you, *therefore* this is the way you must act.

The same thing happens in the letter to the Ephesians. The first three chapters expound the work of Christ upon the Cross. And the fourth chapter begins,

"I *therefore,* a prisoner of the Lord, beg you to lead a life worthy of the calling to which you have been called, with all lowliness and meekness, with patience, forebearing one another in love, eager to maintain the unity of the Spirit in the bond of peace" (Eph. 4:1-3).

Because this is what God in Christ has done for you, says Paul, *therefore* this is the way you must live.

In Philippians Paul tells us that Christ, who was in the form of God, emptied Himself, took the form of a servant and became obedient unto death, even death on a cross (Phil. 2:3-8). Because God in Christ did all this for us: humbling Himself, becoming a servant for us, dying the death of a slave in our behalf, *therefore* we are to humble ourselves and become servants to our fellow men, serving one another in love.

Whatever we do as Christians, we do *not* to buy the love of God, *not* to purchase our way into heaven with our good works, *not* to pride ourselves on being better than the next man. Whatever we do as Christians, we do as *a grateful response to what God has done for us in Christ.*

Because God has forgiven us, *therefore* we are obligated to forgive those who have hurt us. "You wicked servant! I forgave you all that debt . . . should not you have mercy on your fellow servant, as I had mercy on you?"

Because God humbled Himself and became a slave for us on the cross, *therefore* we must be first in our willingness to serve. "If I then your Lord and Teacher, have washed your feet, you also ought to wash one another's feet" (John 13:14). Every Christian is engaged in *diakonia,* servanthood for Christ in the world, serving Christ in the least of His brethren.

Because God comforts us, *therefore* we must comfort others. As St. Paul writes, "Blessed be . . . God . . . who comforts us in all our affliction so that *we* may be able to comfort those who are in any affliction, with the comfort with which we ourselves are comforted by God" (2 Cor. 1:3-5). The comfort that comes to us from God must pass through us to others. Let us examine a few more of the "therefore's" that are expected of every Orthodox Christian.

OBEDIENCE

Keeping the commandments is not a slave morality that is imposed upon us by God. Before God gave the ten commandments He said to His people: "I am the Lord your God, who brought you out of the land of Egypt, out of the house of bondage." It is only after this statement that God proceeds to give the ten commandments. Because God has redeemed His people from slavery, *therefore,* their grateful response will be to obey His commandments. The Israelites first experienced God's redemptive love in the exodus from Egypt; then they were called to return that love through obedience. We obey because we love. Our obedience is always a *grateful response* to God's grace and love.

LOVE

So it is with the commandment to love. Jesus said, "A new commandment I give to you, that you love one another even as I have loved you, that you also love one another. By this all men will know that you are my disciples, if you have love for one another" (John 13:34-35). The commandment to love is based on what God has already done for us in Christ: He loved us even unto death on the cross. Our love is to be a *grateful response* to His love for us. "In this is love, not that we loved God but that He loved us and sent His Son to be the expiation for our sins. Beloved, if God loved us, we also ought to love one another. . . We love, because He first loved us" (I John 4:10-11,19). Before we can confess the Nicene Creed in the liturgy, we are called upon to "love one another." Love must precede even our confession of faith.

DOXOLOGY

Another grateful response to what God has done for us in Christ is doxology and praise. In fact, the dominant theme of our Orthodox Christian faith is doxology. The Sunday liturgy in the Orthodox Church is preceeded by the singing of the great Doxology. This sets the tone for the entire liturgy which is one of complete *eucharistia:* gratitude and praise. "Glory be to the Father and to the Son and to the Holy Spirit. . ." "Blessed be the Kingdom of the Father and of the Son and of the Holy Spirit. . ." This is the major theme of Orthodox worship as it was the dominant motif of the early Christians. What do we find in the New Testament?

Tribulation, demons, suffering, crucifixion—yet always with a doxology because Christ has taken the worst of man and overcome it. "In the world you have tribulation," said Jesus, "but be of good cheer, I have overcome the world." Not crucifixion but resurrection has the last word! Not death but life! What can our response to this victory be but one of constant doxology and praise.

OUR WITNESS FOR CHRIST IN THE WORLD

Another one of the great responses to God's love is to share Christ with others, to confess Him before men. "So every one who acknowledges me before men, I will also acknowledge before my Father who is in heaven; but whoever denies me before men, I also will deny before my Father who is in heaven" (Matt. 10:32-33).

Today we confess Christ before men publicly every time we recite the Nicene Creed in the liturgy. Our job is to keep confessing Him in the "liturgy after the liturgy" when we return to our places in the world. This is not a difficult task. Look at the blind man who was healed by Jesus. He confessed Christ among men simply by stating what Jesus did for him: ". . . one thing I know, that though I was blind, now I see" (John 9:25). For example, you fall into a conversation with a neighbor, co-worker, or stranger. They, not you, bring up a problem or concern. As they talk, you remember how God helped you with one of your own problems. If you share your experience, you may fumble with words or even blush. You may come away certain that you have made a grievous mistake by sharing. But the outcome of your sharing is not up to you. It is the Lord's job to take your witness, however grand, or simple or weak, and use it to get to the heart of the one hearing you; to get him to connect to the Source of Power that will help him also, as it helped you. Who can tell what it might mean to others if we quietly testified what the Lord did for us in time of weakness or sorrow?

CONFESSING CHRIST STRENGTHENS FAITH

We are greatly strengthened when we make a public confession of faith in Jesus. Our faith is tremendously fortified by such an act. Try it! Say to a member of your family, "You know, one of the most precious persons in my life is the Lord Jesus. I simply cannot tell you what He has meant to me in my life—how He leads me, and guides me, and enriches my life every day." Just a simple confession, but how greatly it strenthens your faith when you say it with your lips. You will actually feel your faith growing stronger within you. Or take another example: you meet someone who does not come to church and you confess Christ by saying, "You know, I simply cannot tell you how much guidance and strength I receive in church every Sunday. Why, I can hardly wait for Sunday morning to come along. Mind if I pick you up next Sunday and we worship together?" Not only will your faith grow stronger when you confess Jesus this way, but you have His word for it that He will not forget it: one day He will "acknowledge" you before His Father in heaven.

John Berryman wrote a poem in which he recalls how boldly the martyrs of the early Church confessed their faith in Christ. He looks at his own life and thinks of the many things that can happen to him before the end comes. He prays that no matter what happens his lips may be ready to confess his Lord: "Cancer, senility, mania, I pray I may be ready with my witness."

THE STEWARDSHIP OF TIME, TALENTS AND POSSESSIONS

Another response to God for His gracious love is the stewardship of our time, talents and possessions. We are called to use our God-given talents to serve God and glorify Him.

The word *steward* is derived from the Greek word *oikonomos,* which means manager. Every Christian is a manager of the time, talents, and possessions God has loaned to him. He is responsible to God for the use of these gifts and will be called on by God one day to give an account of how he used them.

Much needs to be said about the importance of stewardship since the entire work of the Church as the Body of Christ in the world today depends on it. Our monetary gifts to the Church are translated into deeds of love. Consider what our gifts to the Church can do. They give legs to a word like love and send it off on urgent errands of mercy. They bring hope, health, sanity and salvation to people in the spirit of Christ. They put clothing on the naked, food in the stomachs of the starving. They preach God's words. They administer the sacraments. They educate young people in the faith. They gather workmen to build schools, hospitals, colleges, seminaries, churches. They bring new life to the handicapped.

TWO PLATES—NOT ONE

Someone said one Sunday during the offering, "Here we go again! There's always a plate." The person was right in one way and wrong in another. There is not one plate—but two! One is man's: the offering plate that is passed to us every Sunday. The other is God's. And that is the paten, the plate that carries the Precious Body of our Lord during the liturgy.

God gives *first.* He gives us our body, mind, life, health, talents. On the paten—the plate of God's mercy—He gives us Himself as the Bread of Life, the manna from heaven. He gives forgiveness, strength, courage. He gives victory over sin and death. He gives eternal life. "In Him we have redemption through His blood, the forgiveness of our trespasses, according to the riches of his grace which He lavished upon us" (Eph. 1:7-8). God gives! That is the meaning of the first plate—the paten.

THE SECOND PLATE

The second plate which is passed to us every Sunday is the offering plate. It represents our response to the first plate. We are invited to give in gratitude for God's generosity, for His limitless forgiveness and mercy. The emptiness of the offering plate represents the aching needs of the world—spiritual hunger, physical hunger, etc., which we are called to help remedy through our sharing. It represents the great spiritual hunger that exists in the world—the God-shaped vacuum in every heart—that only Christ can fill.

We give, but He gives first. However much we give, it will never be more than just a fraction of what we receive.

"There's always a plate." Indeed there is. Not one but two. First God's, then man's.

A woman traveling through Europe sent this cable to her husband: "Found a bracelet. Price: $75,000. May I buy it?" He promptly wired back, "No, price too high." But the operator missed the comma, and the reply read, "No price too high." So the woman bought the bracelet. Later the husband sued the cable company.

When it comes to our giving to God, there is no minimum and no maximum. No price is too high for Him Who is the Pearl of Great Price.

How should we give to God? Following are some guidelines.

GIVE PROPORTIONATELY

The trouble with most of church giving is that it is out of proportion to what we have, to what we earn. The important thing in Christian giving is not "how much" we give, but "how much in comparison to our ability." A gift does not need to be large in order to be significant. It is great or small in proportion to the amount of other things we possess. One of the great examples of Christian stewardship is the poor widow who came into the Temple one day and gave "all that she had." It wasn't very much, just a fraction of a cent, but it caused the treasury bell to ring and Christ to give her a commendation that keeps ringing down through the centuries: "Truly, I say to you, this poor widow has put in more than all of those who are contributing to the treasury. For they all contributed out of their abundance; but she out of her poverty has has put in everything she had, her whole living" (Mark 12:43,44).

GIVE LOVINGLY

Give proportionately as God has blessed you. And then give lovingly. True Christian giving begins with my personal commitment to Christ, and it proceeds from there. It says, "If you don't love God, don't give. God does not need the token support of those who do not really care." And conversely, Christian giving says, "If you do love God, let your giving be some indication of the measure of that love."

GIVE GENEROUSLY

Give proportionately, lovingly. Give generously. "He who sows sparingly will also reap sparingly." When it comes to giving to God and His work, if you must err, err on the side of generosity, as you would if your loved one were in need and presented a request. Err on the side of going beyond what is practical and try what is spiritual. "He who sows bountifully, will also reap bountifully," writes Paul in the epistle lesson. Give abundantly and you will receive abundantly.

GIVE WISELY

Give proportionately, lovingly, generously. Give wisely. Many of the ancient Greek coins have an owl on them. The owl was to remind people that they should be as wise as owls in the spending of money. How does a Christian spend money wisely? A wise Christian will sit down and make two columns. Column # 1 will be entitled, *"WHAT ARE WE LIVING FOR?"* And Column # 2 will be called *"WHAT ARE WE SPENDING FOR?"* We can never determine wisely what we shall spend for until we realize what we are living for. What we are living for will determine what we do with our possessions.

GIVE GLADLY

Give proportionately, lovingly, generously, wisely. Give gladly! "Everyone must give," St. Paul says, "as he has determined in his heart; not grudgingly, nor of necessity, for *God loves a cheerful giver*." Give from your heart—cheerfully.

An example of cheerful giving is Alvin Dark, a former manager of the San Francisco Giants. He wrote,

"Tithing . . . Giving the first tenth of my income back to God was just as unquestioned in our home as putting on my socks before my shoes. And a nickel out of every 50 cents was quite a lot when I got up every day before dawn to pedal around my paper route. But as the years went by and my income increased, I found out I could never win in this game of giving to God. He always outgave me. He gave to me physically, financially and in a dozen other ways. He led me into a satisfying career in baseball. Actually, if I belong to Him, He owns me and my income too, all of it. I have learned that tithing is just a symbol of my trust in Him."

GIVE HUMBLY

Give proportionately, lovingly, generously, wisely, gladly. And finally give humbly. Those who follow the Hindu religion must bring their thank offerings to the local priest in the following manner. They fall to their knees, close their eyes, and then place the offering in the open hand of the priest. When asked the reason for this they reply, "We close our eyes because we are ashamed to bring so little. We are ashamed because no matter how great our gift, it is tiny when compared to His love for us. So, as we present our gift, we fall to our knees in deep humility."

No matter how much we give to God, we ought to close our eyes and fall on our knees humbly because we bring so little when we think of how much He gave for us on the Cross and still gives.

BLESSED TO BLESS

Our response to God's gracious act of salvation, therefore, is a constant doxology of thanksgiving and praise. God said to Abraham, "I will bless thee . . . and thou shalt *be* a blessing" (Gen. 12:2). We are blessed to bless. We are forgiven to forgive. We are loved to love. We return that love through obedience. We are saved to help others find salvation. We are comforted to comfort. We are served to serve. Christ confesses us before His Father in heaven as his very own that we may confess Him among men in the world. He daily loads us with blessings that we may use them to glorify and serve Him proportionately, lovingly, generously, wisely, gladly and humbly.